undaunted

dark tales of courage witnessed
through the eyes of a homicide detective

DAVE SWEET
WITH SUSAN FOREST

undaunted

dark tales of courage witnessed
through the eyes of a homicide detective

DAVE SWEET
WITH SUSAN FOREST

STARK PUBLISHING

Copyright © 2024 Dave Sweet and Susan Forest
Original butterfly art © 2023 Coral Simpson
Cover design by Juan Padron
Edited by Brent Nichols, Jonas Saul

All rights reserved. No part of this publication may be reproduced, distributed, or transmitted in any form or by any means, including photocopying, recording, or other electronic or mechanical methods, without the prior written permission of the publisher, except in the case of brief quotations embodied in critical reviews and certain other noncommercial uses permitted by copyright law.

The opinions, views and philosophies reflected in this book are those of the author and may not represent those of the organization he works for. Every effort has been made to respect the privacy of citizens and the delicacy of the situations described in the book. Identifying descriptors, such as names, dates, and specific details, have in many cases been changed.

Stark Publishing
Waterloo, Ontario, Canada
starkpublishing.ca

First printing July 2024

Hardcover ISBN: 978-1-998331-07-9
Paperback ISBN: 978-1-998331-08-6
eBook ISBN: 978-1-998331-09-3

ATTENTION SCHOOLS, BUSINESSES AND BOOK CLUBS:

This book may be provided at quantity discounts for educational, business, or book club purchases. The authors are also available to speak to groups both virtually and in person.

For inquiries, please contact Stark Publishing: info@starkpublishing.ca

Dedicated to all the courageous souls whose stories have been told to inspire, empower and educate us all.

Contents

PROLOGUE 9
INTRODUCTION 12
CHAPTER 1 – BOOGEYMEN: UNDERSTANDING FEAR 21
    FEAR 23
    UNSHACKLING 29
CHAPTER 2 – FOR F'S SAKE: OUR RESPONSE TO FEAR 56
    TRAINING 65
    EMPOWERMENT 80
CHAPTER 3 – ETHOS: ETHICAL CHANGE 97
    CHAMPIONING 99
    INITIATIVE 109
    INTEGRITY 118
    PURPOSE 124
CHAPTER 4 – FRANK: SOCIAL COURAGE 128
    CHALLENGE 131
    HUMILITY 138
    SYNERGY 147
    LEADERSHIP 152
CHAPTER 5 – GALILEO: INTELLECTUAL COURAGE 157
    EXPERTISE 159
    SEEKING GROWTH 172
    REASONING 182
    INGENUITY 189
CHAPTER 6 – TRANSCENDENT: SPIRITUAL COUGAGE 193
    BELIEF 194
    ENVISIONING 203
    GRACE 214
    MINDFULNESS 218
CHAPTER 7 – APANIIWA: RESILIENCE 224

  Rebound 226
  Patience 236
  Stamina 249
  Adaptability 256

CHAPTER 8 — LION-HEARTED: PHYSICAL COURAGE 268

  Preparedness 270
  Decisiveness 278
  Selflessness 281
  Discipline 285

CHAPTER 9 — GHANDI: EMOTIONAL COURAGE 293

  Empathy 294
  Vulnerability 302
  Love 310

CHAPTER 10 — STRATA: DEVELOPING COURAGE 319

  Ethical Courage 320
  Social Courage 320
  Intellectual Courage 321
  Spiritual Courage 322
  Resilience 323
  Physical Courage 323
  Emotional Courage 324
  And Finally 325

APPENDICIES 327

  Solutions to Logic Challenges 327
  Our Take Aways 330
  30 Virtues of Uncommon People 333

ACKNOWLEDGMENTS 334

DAVE SWEET 337

SUSAN FOREST 338

A CALL FOR ACTION 339

THE UNCONVENTIONAL CLASSROOM 342

Prologue

On a bright Friday in January, near Fort St. John, B.C., my brother Ken was home nursing a cold with lemon tea. His high school biology classes were in the hands of a substitute teacher. Ken curled up with his binoculars in the bay window of the log cabin he'd built ten years previously. Two elk were pawing in the snow at the far edge of his lawn.

The elks' heads snapped up.

As one, they were gone, and a frantic rapping sounded on the door. Ken disentangled himself from his blanket and answered.

Disheveled and wearing only a T-shirt and jeans, his nearest neighbor, Sara, panted, her cheeks red with cold, eyes wild. "My house is on fire! The baby—"

Ken's breath caught. He threw his shoes on.

"—he's still in the house—"

Ken pointed to the phone. "Call 911."

He ran, laces flying, across the frozen, sugary snow of his front lawn and up the driveway where tire treads had flattened a narrow path. The icy air slapped his skin, and cold burned his lungs as he reached the top of the hill. He dashed through Sara's gate and up her drive to the old, rented bungalow. Smoke leaked from the closed windows, chimney, and eaves, forming a wisp of gray in the crystal blue air. The crackle of flame was audible behind the walls.

Ken dashed up the steps and rattled the front doorknob. Locked.

He plunged into the mounds of snow at the side of the house.

The windows were all shut and too high to reach with any hope of entry. He plowed through the heavy snow to the back, up the three steps to the door.

It opened.

Ken stepped into a wall of heat. He slammed the door, the better to strangle the fire.

"Braden!" he called. The child was only two.

The dim interior seethed with thick, choking smoke. He dropped to his knees, eyes watering, and crawled across the linoleum.

"Braden!"

The crackle of flames and the hoarse breath of the fire were his only response.

Fumes from the basement streamed from the vents below the cupboards to join the clouds just above his head. Chair legs. A few scattered toys. His eyes and throat burned.

There. A small, stockinged foot extended from behind the refrigerator.

Ken slid across the floor and pulled on the foot. A wail erupted from the crevice.

He reached in, found the small, wriggling body, and scooped the child into his arms.

"Mummy!" the boy screeched.

Coughing and cradling the child in one arm, Ken lowered his head and crawled to the door. He shoved it open with a shoulder and scrambled down the steps and away from the building. The oxygen from the opened door gave new life to the flames as Ken ran with the crying child. Sara, waiting in the snow, half-frozen and half-roasted by the conflagration, grabbed the terrified boy.

Courage.

A number of months later, Ken was given the Medal of

Bravery by Canada's Governor General, but when asked about the events of that day, he never said much about bravery or courage. He wasn't the kind to talk about emotions, though he did admit that some distant part of him was aware—very aware—of the danger of the situation. Perhaps, like many, he had a release of disquiet after the fact when he truly realized what he had done.

Some might say anyone would have done the same, though Sara (not her real name) didn't. For Ken, there was no choice.

Stories like this—like the stories of bomb experts, helicopter rescue pilots, or captains of sinking vessels—are often the examples that come to mind when we think of courage. But on reflection, it's clear there's a multitude of different kinds of courage, from the heroic to tiny acts of personal determination.

This is a book about courage. About what it means, about its role in our lives, and about how each of us, in our own daily situations, can lead courageous lives. Mostly, though, this is a book of stories, which we hope will inspire readers to consider more deeply the personal choices they make every day to make the world a better place—for themselves and for others.

—Susan Forest

Introduction

*If you don't want to get criticized, hide from the world.
Be nobody, stand for nothing. Never express yourself.
Keep your creativity hidden.
But realize that a life lived in fear and anonymity is no life at all. Progress and growth demand bravery. Have the courage to be disliked while staying kind.
Meet cruelty with grace and stand tall in who you are, no matter the noise.*

—Vex King

Within the policing organization where I worked, we recognized those who overcame adversity, faced paralyzing fear, or did something extraordinary for the people and community they served. These individuals saved lives, filled needs in places where needs needed filling, or demonstrated investigative excellence in the pursuit of truth and justice.

In my world, we refer to it as *earning your bricks*, an award reserved for those who exemplify exceptional acts. Normal people called upon to do extraordinary things demonstrate that strength, resilience, and valor do exist within all of us.

Undaunted is a book of "bricks," a tip of the hat to some of the most amazing people I have had the pleasure to know or learn about in my two-decade-long journey in law enforcement.

For centuries, courage has been celebrated, awarded, and

admired. It has been revered as one of the greatest attributes of character.

Most of us view courage as an exceptional brand of bravery, heroically overcoming something others would view as physically, politically, or personally dangerous. Throughout history, many courageous people have committed inspirational acts. People like the students who marched on Tiananmen Square, defying laws they thought unjust and standing up to communist tanks in support of something they considered "better;" like Viola Desmond who, as a black woman in 1946—eleven years before Rosa Parks—chose to sit in a whites-only section of a segregated movie theater in New Glasgow, Nova Scotia, despite demands to leave—an action that went on to help start the civil rights movement in Canada; and like Jane Goodall, who lived in solitude in the jungles of Africa, championing her passion for chimpanzee conservation.

From my early days as a patrol officer to my time as an undercover narcotics officer, to my last fourteen years in Homicide, and now as an author and public speaker, I have had a unique opportunity to witness inspiring acts of resiliency, perseverance, and courage from an eclectic group of uncommon people, some whom I have served and some whom I have served alongside. I believe these people exemplify that greatness is in all of us.

Those called to the professions of emergency medicine, search and rescue, and policing are often drawn by the desire to help. They enter such vocations with an understanding that lives may depend on their decisions and actions. They train their skills, reactions, and teamwork to be prepared for not only the expected but the exceptional circumstances that may require their help. One such case stands out in my mind:

One March a few years ago, multiple police units were

dispatched to reports of an armed suspect raising havoc in one community after he had committed a series of robberies and several attempted carjackings. The suspect, fleeing to a suburban neighborhood, first pounded on the glass door of a house where a nine-year-old girl was home alone. Then, spooked by the police response, he disappeared, possibly into one of the many unlocked sheds and detached garages in the area.

After an hour of scouring the vicinity with police dogs and a helicopter, officers reluctantly called off the search, scratching their heads in frustration. This left only one team behind—two officers—to finish up the paperwork and write reports from inside their police car parked on the street.

Then, in the distance, the silence of their weekday afternoon was disturbed by the sound of breaking glass.

Alerted now, the two looked at each other, then slipped from the patrol car.

They walked cautiously up the alley in the direction of the sound, listening and watching. It was a beautiful spring day, but after the dragnet, the area was deserted. Anyone who wasn't at work was staying indoors.

"I thought it came from over here," one officer said. They popped the gate to a bungalow's yard and took a few steps onto the path between the lawn and a detached garage, guns out, pointing down. A window in the garage was broken.

A bit of black smoke wafted out. "He's in there."

Then—a flash, like a camera—the crack of a gun blast—

The bullet hit the lead officer's armpit, bypassing the vest, like the wallop of a baseball bat, but needlepoint. *"I'm shot."*

Training and survival responses kicked in. The second officer thrust himself between his partner and the gunman, calling for reinforcements over his radio. They backed out of the yard, shooting at the window to keep the gunman down. The injured officer held the house with one hand, trying not to vomit.

Out of the yard and struggling to breathe, a feeling like the *worst flu ever* came over the critically injured officer. He collapsed onto the street in front of the house, falling into what he later described as the deepest, most peaceful sleep of a lifetime.

Pop-pops of gunfire pierced his consciousness. *Oh, yeah, I'm at work.* But there was no pain. No worries. *I'm going to stay awake this time.* Images of his wife and infant child washed him with overwhelming bliss and love.

"Stay awake."

Officers starting to arrive. A dodge truck in front of the residence. Cops running past.

"Come on. Stay awake."

"Stay awake, now!"

Then the paramedic was there, his competent hands cutting the uniform off, cleaning the wound, putting on chest seals. With relief, the officer found he could breathe again.

He was loaded into the back of the ambulance, and the vehicle screamed to the hospital, lights and siren flashing, the officer in critical, life-threatening condition.

But he knew at that moment he would survive; that the peaceful sleep he'd been woken from would not return; that the bandaging used to temporarily fix the wound was doing its job. In the hands of his colleagues, the officer relaxed with a firmly planted resolve to survive—and he did.

But the perpetrator was still inside the garage. Arriving officers took up containment points around the structure, which was now a dangerous and chaotic situation. Undeterred gunfire continued to ring out from the garage.

The smoke, which the first officers observed escaping the garage window, had transformed into a raging inferno sweeping through the garage. Still, gunfire thundered from inside. The officers prepared to face a person who, at any moment, would be driven from the heat of the flames.

He never left.

I am sure the irony of this situation was not lost on any of them. One incident, two desires. One, a desire to live; the other, a desire to die. For the man in the garage, the smoke choked out his last breath, and fire consumed his body. The building burned to the ground.

This event captures many of the characteristics and virtues that make up uncommon people:

Initiative. Well before a single shot was fired—though they no doubt felt slogged down by paperwork—the officers did not ignore the sound of glass breaking. While I'm sure some of us would have chosen to brush it off (after all, it was just a faint sound, and it could really have been anything), for the officers in this story, it was worth investigating. Disregarding it would go against their values and purpose—service. So, they took the *initiative* to do just that. They put away the distraction of their heavy workload to investigate something that could have easily turned out to be nothing.

Discipline and Preparedness. Diligent, studious, and well-trained, they put their schooling to use as they entered the backyard of the residence where the noise had come from. With a keen awareness of their surroundings, they were drawn to the broken window of the garage and had already and subconsciously mapped out an egress route in case that broken window masked a threat. When gunfire erupted and one of the officers was struck, their reactions were *disciplined* and exactly as *trained*. They did not run. They held their ground while calling for help; they put distance between themselves and the threat, providing timely information others would need as they responded.

Trust. Each officer *put trust in the other* to survive this encounter.

Selflessness. For the officer who was not struck, his willingness to lead his injured partner to safety demonstrated, on a grand scale, the *willingness to put himself into jeopardy in the face of extreme threat and risk*, something I will assert takes unimaginable courage to do.

This same level of valor was, ultimately, required of those other officers who returned to the area of the shooting. They responded, knowing there was an active shooter on scene, knowing he had already shot one of their colleagues and was demonstrating intent to shoot more. Yet they did. Multiple cars went to the scene, and despite the risks, officers were able to contain the threat to this one area of the neighborhood, warn neighbors, and evacuate them into their basements. Each again *relied on their teammates* to do this, and from these actions, no one else was hurt or killed, with the exception of the perpetrator.

Resiliency. The injured officer's decision to fight and live made right there on the roadway despite suffering such a catastrophic injury, was another form of courage. He *faced his suffering*, and struggled to follow paramedics' orders to stay awake. In fact, it was only weeks after this incident that this officer returned to work. His *resiliency* has never let this event hold him back or prevent him from continuing in his work. His gratitude to his partner and all who helped him has been unwavering and heartfelt.

Courage. One example in many forms.

But, as inspiring as this illustration is, there are other kinds of courage, too.

At a book signing several years ago (for my first book, *Skeletons in My Closet*) my then co-author Sarah Graham and I were collecting donations of jewelry and cash for a charitable organization supporting survivors of domestic abuse. We had been signing for about an hour when I caught a glimpse of a woman who appeared to have had better days. She seemed disheveled and a bit out of sorts.

"What is this charity all about?" she asked.

I explained the organization's goals and their commitment to supporting women in shelters who had survived domestic abuse through a Christmas jewelry drive.

She told us she was living on the street as a bottle picker and dumpster diver (her words) and found it difficult that people no longer talked to her or wanted anything to do with her, something she attributed to being in the place she was. She told how, only hours earlier, she had been turned away from a large retail store in the mall after inquiring about getting a few free samples of makeup to cover some bruises along her jawline.

"You see," she said, "a man broke my jaw a month ago."

As she spoke, she reached into her backpack and pulled out a small, worn change purse. A shimmer of gold-plated jewelry peeked out from inside the pouch, a stark contrast to the grime on her fingers and nails.

"Here," she said as she dropped her donation into the jewelry chest. "I found this in the garbage a few days ago, but I've earned enough money picking bottles that I have a home for the week and won't be needing it anymore. It can go to someone else who does."

Her gesture could not be refused. To do so would be to deny her dignity, even though its value probably equated to a small meal, which she in turn also refused when offered. This was something she wished to do, with no expectation of return to herself.

How is it that someone who had just been passed over by another still had the strength of spirit to give to someone else she felt was in need?

This, too, is courage.

Many stories, many examples, all describing the word we call "courage."

So, how do we define this concept?

I don't know.

Philosophers and linguists have discussed courage as a broad category that can be broken into component parts. Physical courage has been called the choice—and willingness—to confront agony, pain, danger, uncertainty, hardship, intimidation, even death or threat of death. Moral courage might be thought of as the ability to act rightly in the face of popular opposition, shame, scandal, discouragement, or personal loss. Fortitude is the mental or emotional strength that enables resilience in the face of adversity: courage for action and fortitude for suffering. Other thinkers have broken courage down into still smaller sub-components. Bravery, perseverance, honesty, and even zest might play into this concept. Social, intellectual, emotional, and spiritual courage could be considered. All of these are worthy

---

Circle of Courage

A synthesis of aboriginal beliefs and Western psychology, the Circle of Courage teaches that we all need four aspects to our lives:
- Everyone needs a sense of belonging.
- Everyone needs a sense of mastery, of competence or skill.
- Everyone needs to feel independent, in the context of interdependence.
- Everyone needs to have opportunities to be generous to others.

—Larry Brendtro, et al

concepts.

Ultimately, however, this book comes from our own personal reflections on courage—it should not serve as an academic study on the topic. *Undaunted* will instead focus on stories of courage and the virtues of uncommon people through our own personal lens of experience witnessing it.

All forms of courage, whether it's facing a physical confrontation, a social one, or even wrestling with one's inner moral, spiritual, and intellectual core beliefs, is a confrontation with one's own fear. *Undaunted* will finish with a look at how each of us can transform these concepts into our own everyday life. How each of us might, in some ways, join the ranks of the *uncommon people* featured throughout.

Matthew McConaughey once said, "We all have two wolves in us, a good one and a bad one, and they both want to eat. We just have to feed the good one more than the bad one."

I believe courage is exactly this: our response to the valiant fight between the good and bad thoughts that exist in all of us. Without our own resiliency—without our small, daily acts of courage—we might find that self-doubt, negativity, and the not-so-helpful opinions of others would triumph, affecting both individuals and society.

Why the butterflies? The butterflies are an important symbol used throughout this book to represent the insights and reflections we hope our readers will take away at the end of each section. They highlight the key messages we have tried to convey through the people whose stories we've been privileged to tell.

For me, stories of courage signal hope. The best way to inspire courage is through stories about courage. It is for this reason we have written this book.

Happy reading.

—Dave Sweet

Chapter 1–Boogeymen: Understanding Fear

"Can a man still be brave if he's afraid?"
"That is the only time a man can be brave," his father told him.
— George R.R. Martin, *A Song of Ice and Fire*

More than once in my career, I have stood over the work of a coward—someone who has allowed fear to undermine their morality—as I watched his victim's body cool and stiffen. At such times I have wondered how someone could so purposefully harm their wife or child, peacefully asleep in their beds. This act, to take the life of someone close, demonstrates what most of us could never understand—selfishness and cowardliness.

Cowardice—courage's shadow—born of fear.

So this is where our book starts: fear.

Without understanding fear and its underpinnings, it is difficult to truly appreciate courage when it is displayed in all its forms.

Over my career, I have come to discover that some of the most notorious people I had a hand in convicting of murder were people I would have paid no attention to if I had brushed shoulders with them in a grocery store instead of a police station.

Take one man who came to Canada from the Philippines to work as a nanny. His unassuming look comforted the family. Dark-rimmed glasses framed his baby face, and his body type would suggest he spent more time in front of the television or computer than in a gym. Then, one day, in an episode of rage, he stabbed the woman and one of the children he had cared for, killing both while the rest of the family was away at work and school.

Movies and television reinforce what we are told about what bad people look like. Images like the night stalker Richard Ramirez or the infamous cult killer Charles Manson are two examples; so is the heavily tattooed gang member who denotes his affiliations through markings that go over the face and neck, masking any innocence that person may still have. Some people think bad people act like the fictional MTV characters Beavis and Butt-Head, heavy metal punks who act and talk like they are always stoned.

We all learned as kids that "bad guys" or dangerous people drove white panel vans advertising "free candy" on the side. Hopefully as we got older, we became wiser and more aware: the real wolves in sheep's clothing come in other shapes and sizes. They do not only live in the darkest of alleys; they are found online and in any community, rich or poor.

The real-life couple, Karla Homolka and Paul Bernardo looked—if pictures told the complete story—more like Barbie and Ken than infamously sadistic serial killers who terrorized Scarborough and St. Catherine's Ontario in the late '80s and early '90s. Schmoozy John Wayne Gacy ran in elite circles during the week and played clown on the weekends. The charismatic and intelligent serial killer Ted Bundy was complimented by the judge during his trial (in which he represented himself) as being a "bright legal mind."

Can we really know what dangerous people look like?

Of course not. Yet, we expect victims should be able to do so.

We expect police should, and probation and parole officers should, and even judges.

Certainly, once we learn what a person is capable of, they *begin* to look creepy to most of us, but that vibe only bubbles to the surface after their dastardly deeds are discovered.

This is why it's important to take the time to check facts. Gut and intuition—a "funny feeling"—are important guideposts. But when these are based only on the way a person carries him or herself or how they look, they aren't foolproof.

Fear is often a perception – not a reality

Fear

The American Psychological Association defines fear as a rational reaction to a potentially dangerous event or object. Its function is to keep us safe: keep us from touching a hot stove or walking into traffic. Or, in the case of undercover police officers, keep them hypervigilant regarding their surroundings and the people in them. When we are startled, fear gives us the adrenaline-fueled energy to fight or run. Fear has been a part of the evolved brain since fish appeared in Earth's early oceans, and it is still with us because it has helped us survive.

But fear can also prevent us from trying new things. Take fire. Fear of fire is rational because of a fire's destructive potential when it is unconstrained. This is where common sense and respect for dangerous things come in. But when we have skill and respect for fire's dangers, fire brings us warm homes, cooked foods, candlelight dinners, and backyard sing-alongs around a fire pit. When one is restricted by fear, there are a lot of life-enriching experiences, as well as survival and convenience measures, that are off the table. This is what fear does: it restrains us; it tricks us into playing it safe when, in fact, risk and exploration are necessary to life.

Fear is profoundly interconnected with courage. Sometimes, it is seen as courage's antithesis; fearlessness is equated to bravery. Yet it is also true that a person who acts to help or save another in the absence of fear might not consider their act brave at all: as Ned Stark, in the quote opening this chapter, points out, it takes immense courage to *face* fear and overcome it. So, the relationship is not a simple one of opposites.

Susan would point out that one of the few times in her years as an elementary school principal that she has had to deal with a student bringing a weapon to school, the cause was fear. A student who had been teased and bullied thought his only recourse was to defend himself by coming to school with a knife. The child may have lacked the social courage to stand up to the bullies, but

> **The relationship between fear and courage is not a simple one of opposites.**

his experience told him he had good reason to fear the unforgiving group. Unfortunately, he'd also lost faith in the adults in his life to help him negotiate his problems.

Fear can be one of our most dangerous emotions: fear of losing a spouse who has fallen out of love with us, fear of empty store shelves in a pandemic or war zone, fear of losing privilege when traditionally under-represented classes gain status. Some politicians have used fear to gain votes or to dehumanize others to justify war, slavery, or economic subjugation. It is much easier to shoot or enslave someone if our fear of them causes us to not recognize them as human.

> Excesses or deficiencies in either fear or confidence can distort courage:
>
> - High fear / low confidence is cowardice
> - Low fear / high confidence is foolhardiness
> - High fear / high confidence is courage.
> - Low fear / low confidence is hopelessness or fatalism.
>
> —Daniel Putman

Fear and courage are deeply intertwined. Identifying an act as either "fearful" or "courageous" relies on three factors:

- The danger of the situation
- The worthiness of the cause
- The perception of one's ability

There is a close connection between fear and confidence. Knowing one's skills and abilities and being able to determine when to fight fear or when to flee it gives us confidence. And, a part of this decision-making depends on how important the cause may be that one is called upon to fight for or defend. Neither rigid control of fear nor a denial of fear is helpful: the ideal is to judge a situation and allow reason to guide us toward a goal we deem worthwhile.

Without an appropriate balance between fear and confidence when facing a threat, one cannot have the courage to overcome it.

A Three-Headed Monster

I believe fear is a three-headed monster. Each head represents a facet of fear that needs to be overcome if we are to understand ourselves and live fuller lives – beginning with the first of the three heads – Most of our fears are learned.

The Origin of Fear

Where does fear originate? Some fear is inborn, but most is learned, either through trauma or through our socialization as we grow up. Fear can also be reinforced through the story we tell ourselves about our identity: "I am afraid of ___."

Newborn babies have two innate fears: loud noises and a fear of falling. This means our other fears are learned through the experiences that have shaped us on our journey through life.

Thinking back to my days raising my own babies, I certainly remember seeing these startle responses in both of my children. Their arms would fly up if they were lowered too quickly, or their fists clench up and shake before a cry formed on their face if something was dropped noisily on a floor.

Some inborn fears (such as fear of heights), may be common to all mammals and may have developed early in our evolutionary history. Others, such as the fear of snakes, may be common to all primates, and still others, such as fear of mice and insects, may be unique to humans and developed when mice and insects became important carriers of infectious diseases in early settlements.

In my career, I have never lived with more daily fear and anxiety than during my time working undercover in the Drug Unit.

No doubt somewhere in my childhood—perhaps through "just say no to drugs" campaigns and parental lectures on the subject—I learned that drugs were bad, drug dealers were evil, and illicit substances went hand in hand with violence. Such sentiments were further

> Nadia Kounang, in "What is The Science Behind Fear?" researched innate fears in babies. Her study evaluated depth perception among six- to fourteen-month-old infants and animals by using Plexiglas hung over a high ledge. In most cases neither the children nor the animals made the decision to step onto the glass, suggesting that the fear of falling is a fear ingrained in most of us from a very young age.
>
> Regarding loud noises, Neuroscientist Seth Norrholm at Emory University stated that loud sounds stimulate an acoustic startle reflex that causes most people to react with a fight or flight type response.

reinforced as I grew older and turned on the evening news to hear "police believe this crime was drug motivated" or after marveling at the before-and-after photographs of people who had physically declined through addiction—the faces of methamphetamine users, for example. These entrenching beliefs raised my anxiety, particularly in my first year of undercover work, each time I went out to meet a new, unsuspecting drug trafficker.

Looking back on those days now, I chuckle when I think about how many times I went to meet someone new, assuming by the sound of their gruff voice on the phone that they were going to be 6'5" and 300 pounds—only to learn they were some 120-pound kid from the suburbs driving Mom and Dad's Range Rover.

Because of my early learning, the fears I had about the drug subculture before working in it colored my initial understanding of the overall drug world. It turns out not all drug dealers are scary. Not all "druggies" are dangerous. Not all violent crimes are drug-related. In fact, in my city, the number one motivation for murder (five-year average) is not drugs but a heat-of-the-moment confrontation: unplanned, unscripted homicides that happen literally in the blink of an eye. The second motivation for murder is a poor indictment of our community: domestic homicides. Over a five-year average, these out-paced both drug and gang-motivated murders.

Reminiscing, I believe my fear was likely not innate or born of trauma but more likely nurtured in response to social expectations about the drug subculture and reinforced through self-perception. Of course, in the case of an individual who fears something different, it is impossible to say what has precipitated their fear: all four could be contributing factors.

Regardless of cause, though, people who wish to move forward can consider the words of Will Smith: "Fear is not real. It is the product of thoughts you create. *Danger* is real. But fear is a choice."

Manage danger—unshackle yourself from fear.

Unshackling

Moving past and unshackling ourselves from our learned fears may start with a small feat, as was the case for a very dear friend of mine. Born into a home where mental illness and substance abuse afflicted both of her parents, at the age of five, she vividly remembered the last time she heard the words "I love you" from the lips of her mother. At the age of eight, she recalled a moment in time when she thought, "I must only endure this life for ten more years."

Through her young, chaotic childhood, her family never stayed settled for any length of time, and she was shuttled around from place to place, town to town, knowing any friends she had would be difficult to see again, and new ones would be only in her life for a short period of time. Her situation was the result of choices by her parents, who, through their own illnesses, could not see the anxiety and chaos that filled their daughter's heart.

At sixteen, she did what she had dreamed of at eight. She left her family two years earlier than she had planned. Moving from her rural roots, she came to the city and, armed with a dream, settled into a one-bedroom apartment and enrolled in college. Self-conscious around other people, she struggled with the feeling that everyone was looking at her, judging her, and sizing her up.

One day, coming home from school, she walked in to find her apartment had been broken into. And then a week later, broken into again. Shattered, she moved, left school, and fell into a state of reclusion, fearful of leaving the sanctity of her new space, fearful of venturing into the world.

Then, one day, she took that first small step to break her

fear—she unlatched the door, headed to a nearby coffee shop, and ordered herself a coffee—one cream, two sugars. With the aromas of roasting coffee beans surrounding her, she sat quietly, reading a paper and soaking in the comforting ambiance. Feeling proud of what she had just accomplished, a smile came over her face.

She had done it. She had begun her path of healing from the sadness of her past: a past that had socialized her to feel vulnerable, afraid, and unsure of the world and people around her and from the trauma of having her sanctum violated. Facing the fear that had developed through both mechanisms, she went on from that day to beat her paralyzing fear, one small step at a time.

Now an outgoing, vibrant, and successful jewelry designer, she delivered this story to a room full of people whose hearts swelled upon hearing her message: regardless of the origins of your fears, choose to be brave enough to take one small step, unlatch the door, and face the greatness of the world around you.

Notice, however, one key point to this story: she began with a small step. The girl in this story did what I think we all know we must do to move past our personal demons, and that is: face them head on while maintaining an emotionally safe environment. But—as many of us can relate—this isn't always easy to do. A decision to engage in personal change requires us to become uncomfortable.

Of course, there is much more to developing courage than a simple "buck up and move on" determination. It is counterproductive to merely step into a fearful situation and re-traumatize oneself. In many cases, particularly those involving phobias, Post-Traumatic Stress Disorder, or those frightening situations where a stalker continues to be a true threat, simply willing yourself not to be afraid is not an option, and one should seek the support of a trained professional.

Yet, for appropriate situations and for those who are able, this is one step.

There are many large and small steps on the journey to heal, and for some, healing may not involve overcoming the event, so much as it is learning to live with it.

Fear can influence us through power and control

This is the second head of the monster.

In some circles, the adage, "snitches get stitches," is a pervasive belief, and the bolded exclamation point tattooed onto the monster's second head. This credo hampers too many homicide investigations today.

One example from my work dates back to nearly a decade ago. One night, a young marijuana trafficker was abducted by a group of men, likely seeking to profit by extorting him. When the young man refused to pay, the aggressors bound him and lit him on fire in the back of his car. They left him to burn to death, but he didn't—not immediately, anyway.

After the fire had incinerated his clothing and the bindings that kept him restrained, the victim was able to escape the burning car and run a short distance for help while still engulfed in flames. Neighbors who heard his screams came to his rescue and extinguished the fire, but not before he had been burned over ninety percent of his body. When the first responding officers and medics arrived, the victim was still conscious and able to provide his name and date of birth. However, when asked what had happened and who had done this to him, the victim said nothing more. Twenty-four hours later, the victim died from his injuries, and we were starting at square one to try to identify the culprits. His case remains unsolved to this day.

Fear has a persuasive ability to influence us.

A witness's or victim's fear of reprisal is likely due to a belief they will become the next victim if they speak up, something we have all learned through watching television and movies. However, is this fear realistic? Not from my experience.

After being involved in the investigation of almost three hundred murders, I can truthfully say I am unaware of a single case in my city where a witness to a murder has ever been killed after giving statements to the police or court. With that said, there have been a few cases where a criminal has preemptively struck out at a person who has information *before* they ever had a chance to go to the police.

In one instance, a young man who'd been exploited for almost a year as cannon fodder and muscle for a band of thugs discovered his criminal associates had just committed a heinous murder. Investigating officers believed the gang decided this young man's drug addiction was too serious a liability, and as a result, he could not be trusted to keep the group's secret intact. To protect themselves, he was executed. A quote I once read on the back of an old biker's shirt—belonging to a fellow I had been chummy with in my undercover days—encapsulates the act: "Three can keep a secret if two are dead."

This case and others like it have led me to believe that a witness may be safer talking to the cops than not.

The other option, of course, is to get out of a criminal life before the gang decides you are the group's weak link or the target in the next police investigation. That is exactly what this next person decided to do. Bucking the trend and speaking out against his criminal associates, he became a key witness for police grappling with a major gang war between two rival factions back in the mid-2000s.

First, a bit of context:

During that time, shootings had become too frequent in our city and could occur anywhere: noodle houses, malls, or out front of residences in the suburbs. I remember this time vividly, as at that point in my career, I was working in our drug unit as an undercover operative, and we were often asked to infiltrate the inner circles of gangs. It's no surprise that the root of all this violence centered on the lucrative drug scene.

I also remember how nonchalant gun violence was becoming. In one case, a gang member had gone into a restaurant with his prospective love interest. As the pair sat at a table eating noodles, rivals moved in to assassinate him. The gunman entered the restaurant. In a blink, he shot and killed both in front of a restaurant of shocked patrons.

This open display of gun violence demonstrated almost weekly that not one area of the city was safer than another.

Another situation that put the unsuspecting public at risk, including a number of Christmas shoppers, occurred when automatic weapons fired round after round from a moving vehicle circling an intended target in a mall parking lot. The victim was hit but survived after his associates loaded him into a vehicle and dropped him at the front doors of a nearby emergency department.

At the height of the violence, a well-known case involved three shooters who entered a noodle house hunting for rivals inside. Likely tipped off that members of the opposing group were at the restaurant, the soon-to-be assassins drove into the restaurant's parking lot. Three gangsters exited the vehicle and entered the premises. Gunfire erupted, and one patron, unconnected with the gangs, attempted to flee. He was shot and killed, his life taken wantonly along with the two gang associates inside.

This violence—the randomness of it in open public places—was obviously a major concern for the police and, likely, for the gangsters involved, as well. Killing had become easy for both groups, and because of this, the ties binding members of each group grew even stronger.

Given this context, here is the story:

A lay-it-on-the-line investigator who "could sell ice to a penguin" understood the only way we were going to get a hold on the problem was if we could find someone inside one or both of the groups to become cooperative with the police. He took it upon himself to find that person. The informant he found turned out to be a central figure in all the violence. In part for his own self-preservation and in part for a desire to make changes in his life, he did the unthinkable and turned on his gang to become a police witness. Multiple homicides were cleared with charges, and a half dozen people went to jail, ultimately dismantling one of the two major groups behind much of the bloodshed.

After the trials were completed, the now-cooperative gangster, serving time for the five murders he committed, went on—from a jail cell—to participate in the creation of a video detailing his descent into gangs. His message, now played for youth across our city who attend the police interpretive center, is one of warning. In his delivery, he talks about how, in the beginning, he and his friends were only interested in making money through drug trafficking. But when the violence started between the two gangs competing for the same markets, he and his friends progressed from being "just" drug traffickers to kids who were now hunting rival gang members every day. He spoke about the recruitment process to bring new kids to the gang and the importance of those recruitment efforts. For him, the recruitment of new kids into the gang was a way to distance himself from the drug trafficking. He understood if the gang treated the new recruits well, better than their own families—buying them expensive clothes and so forth—their loyalty would know no bounds. They would eventually do whatever was asked of them, and they did it all.

Fortunately for the police, this man's loyalty did have boundaries. It was those boundaries that led him ultimately down a different path and demonstrated that even a person full of hate and evil might still possess a sliver of good waiting to be unshackled.

Fear. Fear is likely front and center in the minds of any person experiencing intimate partner violence. Facing that fear and acting—*when it is possible* and *by whom* it is possible—is what is courageous.

When I was just a young officer, I attended several murder scenes as a first responder. While there, I would be tasked with holding a security point, or continuity, around the perimeter of the scene. It was at one of these early scenes I heard a chilling story that emphasized the importance of never leaving threats unchecked. It was a demonstration of how instantaneously dangerous an abuser can become.

It was spring. A young gal had just separated from her boyfriend, with whom she shared a child. From the outset, the breakup was tumultuous. Through the rollercoaster of this drama, the girl met a new fellow, a nice guy with whom she fell in love. But the ex did not take this new love interest well. Additionally, he felt threatened by the new man's relationship with their young daughter. Days before the woman was murdered, an ominous message appeared, scrawled onto the doorway of her home. *Stay Away!* On the eve of her death, the ex recorded a threat on her answering machine: "I'm going all the way, all the way. You can laugh about it now ... but I promise you won't be laughing soon. I am the best there was, the best there is, the best there ever will be."

The following morning, she was dead. The ex slit her throat and left her to die on the back patio of her home.

The worst part? This terrible crime did not need to happen. It was wholly foreseeable. But the man's words and actions, days before she was slain, went unreported to the police.

Intimate partner violence crimes are layered with complexity. It is important to recognize that those within an abusive relationship may experience many emotions, from fear to hate, to love for the person they thought they married, to hope, to despair, to life-sucking hopelessness that bleeds away their capacity to act, or even to know they should act. As much as many of us—not only the police, but torn friends and family, and the victim herself—wish the world was black and white, and "just say no" or "just leave" was as simple as the phrases suggest, this simplicity does not describe the real world. Many who suffer need help to take those first few courageous steps—and this requires courage also on the part of the sympathetic onlooker who has been patiently waiting for the day they can help.

And once the abused person has taken those first steps, the journey is not over. There are many kinds of fear that can haunt a person for years.

Not unlike gangsters or people who abuse their partners, sex traffickers also use the constant threat of violent repercussions as one way to control the women enslaved to them. Young girls inexperienced in dealing with the charm of a silver-tongued devil are no match for the predator who lives off the back of a sex trade worker. To create vulnerability, pimps begin by wining, dining, and manipulating their prey into vulnerable positions and often introduce drugs or special gifts like free rent or new clothes to the targeted girl. As the "tab" grows, his talons sink deeper until one day, she is trapped and forced to sell her body for sex so she can pay back what she owes and/or maintain her blooming addiction.

Here is the story of one remarkable young woman who had the courage to unshackle herself from a life of enslavement.

Though she came from a loving family, when she was six years old, she was sexually abused by a family friend. She kept the incident from her parents because "they were such good people" but instead developed poor coping mechanisms to deal with her trauma.

By eleven, she was drinking and smoking and hanging out with people older than her and learned she could numb things with alcohol. Running with the wrong crowd, making poor decisions, and acting out to feel accepted, when she hit fifteen, she dropped out of high school.

"I started working full time to support myself—not that I had to leave my house, but my dad said, 'If you don't want to go to school, you've got to work. You have to pick one or the other.' I wanted to live my life, so I chose to live on my own. Still, I had their support if I needed it."

This young woman wasn't naïve about crime. She dated boyfriends who dealt drugs and had friends involved with the police or who had records or had been in jail. But she'd never been involved in illegal drugs or crime herself. "And I always maintained a full-time job in spite of my drinking."

However, she fell into debt. A *lot* of debt. "That's how the situation started. I didn't want help. I wasn't ready to get sober."

She was twenty-nine when she met the man who would lure her into the sex trade. "The crazy part of it was, *because* I'd always been around, say, 'interesting characters,' I felt I knew how to read people. But when I met *him*, I had no idea of the manipulation I was about to walk into."

They met at a nightclub and began to party, spending more and more time together. She knew he sold drugs, though he tried to hide it. "Like, he didn't think I knew what was happening. And I'd say, 'I know exactly what you're doing. I dated drug dealers before. I know your lingo.'"

At the time, she was working a full-time job plus a part-time job, and when he asked why, she told him about her debt. "And he's like, 'You've never looked at doing other stuff?' and I was like, 'Absolutely not. I wouldn't sell drugs. Why would I want to put myself at risk?'"

But one time at his house, while drinking, she blacked out, something that had never happened to her before. It was only later she realized she'd been drugged.

"I remember coming to, and it was very hard for me to wake up. But there was some guy on top of me, engaging in sexual activity. I fought him off and went into the other room where the guy I was dating was with some other people. He kept me there, held me there, talked to me, and started to slowly spin that *I'd* created this situation. That *I* did this. He said, 'You know, I want to be with you, and you do *this*? It's your fault, but I forgive you.' And he was so good at manipulating me, I believed I'd done something wrong." This incident and the manipulation that followed was the beginning of her nightmare, forced into the sex trade.

She didn't see any of the money. If she had money from a client, she had to bring it to him. "He'd say, 'You have two options. You can come here with the money, or I'm going to rob you. You decide how you want to do this.'" When she protested that she needed money to pay her debts, he'd tell her to wait and pay it later with more money. "He'd have me do in-calls in my apartment, and he'd say, 'I have to hold the money because it's too dangerous to keep money at your place.' If I started to push back on it, he'd get abusive, physically, mentally, and emotionally." It got to the point where she'd think, *why would I even fight with him about this?*

Over the two years she worked, and later, as the trial went forward, she found out other things that were "mind-blowing. For instance, his family owned a restaurant I'd been to many times. I'd walked by his mom, but I had no idea because he told me his mom was sick in Toronto with cancer. He used lies about his mother dying of cancer to keep me in line. Yeah, there were a lot of lies. Tons."

It was very well-ingrained in her never to call the police. "I believed if I ever did, he and his network would get to me. And for me, it was, *Why would I? Police would never help me.*"

Over time, she started to pull back and beg him to find somebody else, but he told her if she didn't want to work, she'd have to figure out how she was going to get money—a lot of money. "I didn't want to do it, so I started to take money from my line of credit to pay him. I withdrew, like, $5000. But my mom could see this line of credit, and so she asked, 'What are you doing? Who are you involved with?' So, I made up another lie, saying that I got myself involved with people to try to clear up my debt. I said, 'They're dangerous. I just need to pay them and hope they'll go away.' My parents swallowed it—as much as they didn't want to—and I asked them to trust me, stay out of it."

But he was pushing her to go to Toronto—he wanted her to leave in September—and she learned later that if she'd gone to Toronto with him, she'd never have come back. She tried to get out of this, telling him she wanted to go to alcohol treatment. "I told him I could be better because I wouldn't be drunk. I was trying to find excuses not to work." But it got to the point where he told her if she stopped working for him, he'd go to her family, saying, 'If you don't pay me, then your family will.' He knew where her parents lived, and if her family didn't give him money, he'd take it from them. And if something happened to her parents, "it would be on me, and I'd have to live with that."

However, his strategy backfired. "I'd given up on myself. I didn't care about myself anymore, but when he started to threaten my family—that's when everything changed."

She took him seriously. He had guns, and she'd seen them.

The night of the blowup, he was punching her in the head, and "I just knew, like, I was going to die. And how could I protect anyone else in my life if I'm dead? I couldn't risk that. I was terrified for *them*." She remembers running, getting into her car, hitting the gas, and calling 911. "That was the first time … that's weird, but … that was the first time I knew I needed to live. I was scared. It was huge."

It was April 5. "I'll always remember that because that's my sober date. That was the last day I ever took a drink. I never went back to that way of life."

When she met with police, they disabled her phone and all her social media so the pimp couldn't get to her. She had to call her mom from the police officer's phone and she just said she was with the police now. "They were elated. Mom just said,

'We knew it was him. We just couldn't say anything because we knew if we pushed you away, you'd leave, and we would never see you again.'"

Police moved her to a hotel that night. "I remember I could see a liquor store from my window. Everything in me was like, *I can't*, because the minute I walked out there to get alcohol, he was going to be in my head. I knew I'd be thinking, *What am I doing? I can fix this. Just tell him it was a mistake.* That was his manipulation. And I thought, *No. I'm here. I need to stay here, in this room. I'm not leaving.*"

The young woman's life had to change completely. Due to the level of violence he was displaying, and because the police could only hold him for so long—they'd arrested him on a domestic knowing that building a case was going to take months—she had to change cities. Her parents had her condo packed up and had movers there the next day, and she went to a substance abuse treatment program in another province. "My parents said, 'Don't come back. You don't need to be living here.'"

Police told her not to take money out of the bank, just in case the pimp could use it to get to her. He had access to her laptop and keys to her apartment. "I remember packing a bag, and the officer was like, 'Take your passport, take your credit cards, take what's important, and then we just have to go.' It was surreal. Everything was gone. I remember begging the police, 'I just want to get my cat. I don't care about my house. I don't care what they do to it, but I need to move my cat because they'll kill him.'"

However, the story was not over. She had to return to her home city seven months later for court. The police didn't want her to stay with her parents, so she had to stay in a hotel. She didn't want her parents to come to court. "He'd seen pictures of them but I didn't want him seeing them in person."

The day she was to testify, about twenty-five of his friends and family packed in the courtroom. The pimp was mouthing things to her, intimidating her from where he sat. "Yeah, it was hard. It was so many emotions. I hadn't seen him since I left. That was the one and only time I ever saw him again."

She was asked to point out people in the court, and she started to break down. "I remember saying to one of the officers, 'I'm not here to rat on other people. These guys have threatened me before.'" She needed a break, but the pimp's friends and family blocked the door.

At the preliminary hearing, the court found that all charges could go forward, but with delays, the trial didn't occur until over a year later. Then the pimp died a month before his trial.

"I remember the day the officer called me. She said, 'Are you sitting down?' and I said, 'No, do I need to?' and she said, 'Well, they found him dead.' It was ... oh, overwhelming. At first, I didn't believe it. I said, 'Please tell me. Like, someone has to go see this body. Are we sure?' Cause in my head, I'm going, 'Is his family trying to help him?' In their eyes—I saw this in court—what I was saying was a pure lie. *This was not their son. This was not true. I was making this all up.* They even employed him at their restaurant to prove he had work, and they wrote a fake letter saying he was employed because he was on conditions. So I just thought, 'Are you sure? He's really dead?' And she said, 'Yes, it's true.'" He had been found dead of an overdose at a party.

After he died, she was still wracked by anxiety and paranoia. But working with a therapist over the next two years, she came to realize his friends and cousins would not, in fact, pursue a vendetta against her. They had their own problems, their own gang and police problems, their own drug issues. It wasn't about her anymore. She had to do her own healing.

She'd built up all that courage to go to court. She even wrote a letter to the crown prosecutor, who was considering a plea deal, before he died—and that made her mad—to say *I'm going through with this.* She wanted her time in court. She wanted people to know, *He did this.*

"Yeah. I was mad. I was told by the police and by my family not to come back to my home city. I was born and raised there, and he wasn't. My parents had to have a protection order on their home because of him. That's not fair. And when I found out there were more victims, I just thought, 'You're *not* going to get away with this.'"

It was true. There were prior victims—victims who couldn't bring themselves to initiate court proceedings. She didn't want him to victimize any more young women like her.

One focus of her healing had to do with emotionally freeing herself from the nonrational thinking her relationship with this man had instilled in her. "One thing I've learned about manipulation is that he didn't even need to be with me physically. He was already in my head. Anything I did, it's like, that voice was there."

With his death, she had some closure, but it took her a couple of years to make that voice stop. "That's the one thing I think people don't understand when they say, 'Well, you could have just left at any time. Like, he didn't physically ...' Yes, there were times when I was physically held in rooms, but that didn't even matter because I'd been so manipulated by him that his voice was never out of my head."

She learned through her therapist to use the term "sex trafficking" rather than more abusive language because "I blamed myself. I believed I had created everything I went through. But, no. I was *not* a victim. I had a huge problem with that when I first left."

However, with time and support, she carved out a new life. She went back to school, taking a two-year college diploma in criminal justice, partly so she could understand how the criminal justice system worked and also because she wanted to go into policing and work with victims. She'd developed trust with the police. "I feel like you can talk to them because there's no judgment. They deal with this on a day-to-day basis."

Ultimately, though, she took up work for the government—police work would be too intense. "My mental health is good now, but if I went into policing, I'd be dealing with all this trauma again on the other side. For me, it was … my mental health meant more. I love what police do, and if there's anything I can do to educate or help people, I would. But for my own growth, I couldn't do police work."

If she was going to talk to somebody involved in sex trafficking, male or female, what advice would she give? "I'd tell them, 'You can get away. You can get help. It's going to be hard. It's going to be one of the hardest things you ever do, but when you look back at it, it will be the best.' You have that hold on you, and you may think you can't do it, or you're weak. But—looking back—I was strong enough to *endure* all that. I was strong enough to leave. That doesn't make me weak."

And more:

"It doesn't define you. What you went through … yeah, it's going to follow you in the sense that you'll always have those memories. But you can leave. You can change your life. Even if you don't have good parental support like I did, if you have just one person you trust. Yeah, I know—you don't *think* so, you really don't. You feel completely alone, and *that's what they use*. The guy keeping you there manipulates you into believing he is your everything, but he's not. Because he's the person who's hurting you."

Find that one person. A friend. An old schoolmate or teacher. Employer. Parent.

"Yeah, my parents. I think of what they've endured, and that gets me more than anything. I asked them, point blank, 'How, how did you do this? Showing that support with no judgment?' As much as they may have wanted to go there and say something, they never judged me, never shamed me. The shame's huge. I don't know if it's similar for females in domestic violence situations, but he always said to me, 'Nobody would ever want to be with you now. No one would ever want to marry you. Look what you're involved in. Do you think anyone would want to marry you? You have to stay with me. There's going to be no one for you.'

"And that's not true. Your past doesn't define you. It doesn't make you who you are. It's the shame but also the manipulation.

"My family never judged me. I could trust them. They believed me. When I was fifteen, the traumas earlier in my life came out, and my mom said, 'Why didn't you tell us?' and I said, 'I don't know. Like how would you have believed me? It was your best friend's son.' My mom said, 'Absolutely. You're our daughter. We'll do anything to support you.' I'll never be able to repay them.

"I know I am a stronger person now than I was. I had to change my life. And I did."

When a person can stand up to a bully or a gangster, leave an unhealthy relationship, or fight the demons of addiction, they are making a courageous choice to unshackle themselves from whatever has been holding them back.

A social worker who worked with sex trade workers once made this point to me. In her service to these women, she found it difficult for most of them to find the will to trust men again—a substantially different fear from the fear they had to overcome to leave behind an abusive life. There were many reasons for this, but an important one was that they had lost the ability to understand what healthy attributes looked like in a normal relationship. She asked me what I thought could help these women move past their learned fear of men.

I pondered her question. For me, it isn't words but actions that are the most reliable communication of intent. People can say whatever they like, whenever they like, but it is what they *do* that provides a glimpse into their hearts. A man can tell his partner a hundred times over that he loves her, all the while dragging her along the kitchen floor by her hair and beating on her. Such actions have nothing to do with love at all; they are all about violence and control. But if a man, without speaking a word, holds her hand when she is near; if he kisses her forehead just because; if he smiles when he looks her way or shares in the chores and functioning of the home, then this is a person whose heart one might be able to trust.

Made sense to me, anyway.

The question posed by the social worker really cuts to a central issue: when will it be safe for a woman who has survived abuse to place trust in a new relationship? For a woman to choose not to open herself up to be vulnerable again, not to trust in another at the risk she may be hurt, is understandable. She is working through the first head of the monster, overcoming a learned fear of abuse; working through the second head of the monster, stepping out from under a fear that controls them; and coming up against the third head of the monster. Fear can make us risk-averse.

> Unlearning what scares us liberates us.

Fear can make us risk-averse

A person who has experienced trauma may quite understandably be risk-averse and may, more than likely, need the support of professional help. But let's step back a bit to the lives of most of us. If you're not taking risks, you are performing like most human beings. But what else may you be doing? You could also be short-changing yourself and providing zero challenges in your life.

Think about how many times in a day, a week, or a year we find ourselves making a decision that allows us to play it safe, a decision based on fear. For

> Bestselling author, speaker & leadership authority, Margie Warrell, states, "Human beings are wired to overestimate risk and underestimate opportunity."

example, how many people stay in unhappy relationships out of fear of loneliness or fear of financial loss? Some stick with a job they hate out of fear that they will not find another one that is a better fit. Others don't want to report their suspicions of the scary drug dealer down the street out of fear of reprisal—until he starts selling drugs to their kid.

Risk aversion also creeps into the daily lives of police officers. A *Los Angeles Times* article in August 2019 written by Anita Chabria claims that police fear "suicide by cop" cases. So, in some instances, they've stopped responding to certain calls. In her article, she references the case of a sixty-three-year-old carpenter who took his own life by suspending himself from a chain hung around the rafters in his garage. Before he did, though, he texted his sister to say goodbye and gave her directions to call the police and have them come to his garage. Desperate, she did as directed and, according to the article, was "flabbergasted" when 911 operators informed her that police would not go to her brother's residence because of the fear that her brother's direction to have the police go there could be the brother's way of setting officers up for an ambush and potential suicide-by-cop scenario. Chabira writes: "Some small and midsize law enforcement agencies across the state have stopped responding to certain calls because of the potential dangers to both officers and the person attempting to end his or her life. They also present a financial liability from lawsuits—especially if the situation turns violent."

On the other hand, police speak about the counter-intuitive action of walking away [disengagement] as sometimes the best alternative. Police recognize that their mere presence can escalate events, making a police response not the best option, for instance, in a mental health crisis.

I appreciate that sometimes disengagement may be a plausible action to be taken, but I am not sure that doing nothing from the start is necessarily the best response, either. In the case described by Chabira, having the police not attend the residence and leaving the onus on the family to do so instead leaves a family open to unnecessarily experiencing severe trauma. In recent months and years, the call has come increasingly for mental health professionals to be available as first responders or as team members with police in such situations.

Risk-averse thinking has crept into Canadian law enforcement as well. Police pursuit policies nationally have changed, and in some cases, these changes have been for the better. For instance, pursuing a culprit for a minor offense is now a no-go, as rightfully it should be. There have been terrible tragedies as the result of police chasing a stolen vehicle for a minor traffic offence.

In other cases, the policy to disengage has resulted in tragedy. On one occasion, a mentally ill man baited officers called to a commercial premise to escort him from the privately owned property. When officers were unable to contain him through non-invasive means, the man in question got into a vehicle and drove onto a major thoroughfare. Police pursued but backed off and kept a distance as the subject made his way home and entered his residence before officers could catch up to him. The officers continued their policy of disengaging from the situation and left the man inside his basement.

Then, the family living upstairs returned home. Thumping, banging, and screaming prompted this family to call the police. The first unit responding exited from their car and made their way to the home, unaware an ambush was planned for them. The offender came out of nowhere, armed with a gun. The officers were left with no other option except to open fire on the young man, ending his life. Thankfully, the family upstairs was physically unharmed, though no doubt the scars from that night still torment them. One can only wonder, however: if the police had apprehended the man before his behavior escalated, would the result have been different today?

But perhaps the most significant threat to modern-day policing is a new phenomenon rooted in a call to defund police, and public and political apathy toward police officers and police organizations.

The *defund the police* movement began because of a public outcry against a number of injustices perpetrated by police,

> **Crime soars in Minneapolis as cops fear being unfairly targeted in woke viral videos: Traffic stops drop by 74% and problem area patrols by 76% in wake of George Floyd death and de-fund police movement**
> - In-depth analysis shows policing plunged in Minneapolis starting last June
> - Traffic stops dropped 74% and foot patrols plunged 69%
> - Cops were apparently reluctant to engage after furor over George Floyd's death
> - Some even slow down their response to calls in hopes suspects will leave first
> - But fewer stops meant fewer people being searched for drugs and guns
> - Residents say the city has become a 'gangster's paradise' for criminals
> - Murders in Minneapolis are on track to reach a 20-year high

mostly against people of color across North America, and has been felt by every officer as a result—even those who had nothing to do with such criminal actions. Despite the law enforcement community as a whole taking this hit, every person who lives in a community that is policed should know that there *will* be an officer available to them if and when they call.

Just as no arbitrary—or even organic—grouping of people is ever uniform in its attitudes, the same is true of the police. If the culture in some policing organizations defaults to the assumption that "all (name your group here) are lazy, or drunks, or lowlifes," similarly, there can be a perception among some people that "*all* police are brutal, racist, and uncaring." Both statements are equally untrue.

This book would not be complete, and this section of the book would be at fault, if we don't acknowledge harm done by people in positions of power and authority, and police in particular. Every profession has, at one time or another, been at fault, and as the voices of those affected have become amplified in today's world, mostly through social media, these abuses are coming more and more to light.

The "Me Too" movement has thrown a light on men, many in the entertainment industry (but other industries, too), who have used their positions of power to sexually assault—even rape—women, as well as to use sexual favors as the fee for advancement.

Doctors—particularly since the discovery of antibiotics—have been raised onto pedestals as miraculous life savers, resulting in a power dynamic with patients, many of whom have given over responsibility for their health care to them. In recent years, this power dynamic has been challenged more and more through malpractice lawsuits.

Teachers are another group that have been brought to task for past aggressions against students. Just as *not* every employer or doctor has abused their privilege, so too most people can remember—and will credit—many amazing teachers in their lives. But those who have belittled or unfairly punished children are remembered, and increasingly, the education system as a whole has had to answer for the perception that "teachers are bad."

Individual police officers, such as Derek Chauvin (murderer of George Floyd), Betty Jo Shelby (who killed Terence Crutcher), or Stephen Rankin (who killed William Chapman II), have sparked outrage, and social movements such as "Black Lives Matter."

Some individual police officers, doctors, teachers, and other professionals have been held to account, but in other instances, such crimes have been ignored or dealt minor consequences, leading to the recognition of systemic racism: racism embedded in institutional assumptions and procedures. This is an area society is currently supporting for review.

The assumption that First Nations individuals are likely abusing substances underlay the incident in Winnipeg when Dr. Marcia Anderson DeCouteau had to advocate for the correct treatment of her own father when he arrived at the emergency department of the hospital where she was a resident: attending physicians failed to give him proper medication for his heart attack, believing he must be "another drunk Indian."

The practice of "starlight tours," when Saskatoon police officers arrested First Nations men for intoxication or disorderliness and abandoned them outside the city on winter nights, resulted in a series of suspicious deaths.

> **The Ferguson effect: Savagely beaten cop didn't draw gun for fear of media uproar, Chicago police chief says**
>
> A man on PCP allegedly struck a 43-year-old officer in the face, then repeatedly smashed her head against the pavement until she passed out
>
> —Washington Post

Curricula that fail to teach Aboriginal or Black history (for instance) and underfunding schools (which results in affluent parents fundraising when schools in poorer neighborhoods, many of which serve minority communities, cannot) are examples of systemic racism in the education system.

A snapshot of prison inmates reveals an over-representation of BIPOC people, while a snapshot of government, industry, and corporate boards shows an over-representation of white male people. Systemic racism, sexism, ableism, and many other "isms" exist.

De-policing—an officer choosing not to engage in

discretionary or proactive aspects of police duties—is a form of risk aversion. Some officers now weigh the costs of engaging with the public because "any interaction can carry with it the possibility of a racial profiling allegation, winding up in front of a disciplinary tribunal or human rights body, media scrutiny, a viral YouTube video or a judge finding they breached Charter rights" wrote the *Ottawa Citizen*. "These are the kinds of things that officers perceive cannot only ruin their careers, but their lives."

This is the fear front-line officers face today. Fear can make us risk-averse, and in the case of police officers, it can affect their proactive engagement with potential crime situations.

A good friend of mine spent the better part of his career focused on the development of himself and others—something, to this day, he is still very passionate about. An experienced and learned officer who'd worked in the firearms training unit, he eventually went on to enjoy a decade in Tac [SWAT], where he became a certified bomb technician and a valued team member. His career finished as a sergeant, dedicated to training frontline members in the skills they'd need to be safe and successful. Well-read and studious, he had this to say about living with risk:

"Risk can be listed in four quadrants. There are things we do in all policing operations that come at high frequency and low frequency, and there are things we do that are high risk and low risk. If you do something with a tremendous amount of frequency, you're probably pretty good at it through repetition. Any time you are doing something that's high risk and low frequency, you need to recognize it as such and say, 'This is a novel experience for me.' If I have discretionary time, I use it to call a friend, phone someone else, and just recognize it. Pump the brakes."

High Frequency Low Risk	High Frequency High Risk
Low Frequency Low Risk	Low Frequency High Risk

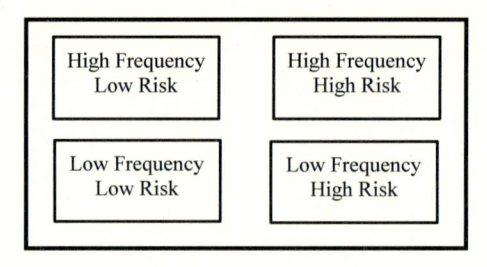

Recently, in our city, there was an incident that occurred in a suburban area, which brought the community to a standstill, a low-frequency, high-risk scenario that warranted the police to "pump the brakes" for almost thirty hours. In this case, police had attended the home of their suspect to execute a warrant to search for firearms. As police moved closer to the home, the subject inside detected their presence and opened fire before he could be safely apprehended. Over the next day and a half, more than one hundred rounds were shot by the suspect toward officers who were set around the residence. Thankfully, none of these members were hurt or killed during the standoff, which ended when the suspect emerged from the home, guns a-blazing, after efforts to have him peacefully surrender failed. He was shot and killed in a brief exchange of gunfire—not the outcome anyone involved hoped for. But an instance where "pumping the brakes" likely saved members of the public, and the officers who attended, any physical harm.

The other thing my Tac buddy identified: policy and procedures. They keep us out of trouble and should be followed in any risk management model. Supervisors who are active and engaged, ensuring each of us acts in accordance with well-thought-out previous experience (which makes up policy and procedures) help us stay out of trouble. If an officer is using their discretion too freely, the supervisor's job is to get them back on track so a small mistake doesn't snowball into a bigger mistake. This is the best way to handle risks that cannot be avoided.

Therefore, I believe the first step in managing risk is to recognize where it is coming from. If it is coming from fear *absent a true threat*, facing that fear and moving past it—if possible—may be the courageous response. Courageous people accept that risk is inherent in life, and strength and courage are required to move past fear versus being paralyzed by it.

Fear is a natural and common response to danger, prompting us to freeze, fight, or flee. There are circumstances under which each of these is adaptive, and some under which they are derailing.

Chapter 2—For F's Sake: Our Response to Fear

As humans, we have evolved a "fight or flight" response to potential dangers. It's what helped our hominid ancestors decide whether to do battle with predators or flee quick-sharp up a tree.

— Ellen Hoggard

When we're faced with a dangerous situation, our bodies are programmed to assess the level of threat against us. If we feel the threat is significant, we may *freeze*, either as an inborn strategy to become invisible, or to allow our adrenaline-fueled senses to better take in all details of the moment. Or both.

When the threat is serious, adrenaline courses through our bodies, our heart rate increases, and we may *fight*. If the threat is too monstrous, our body will galvanize us away from the danger and into *flight* or, in worst-case scenarios, may cause us to *faint*. Last, if we wish to de-fang the threat, some people will *fawn*—a submissive reaction to fear, which is often seen in abuse scenarios when one partner will fawn or dote over their abuser to maintain peace and keep rage at bay.

Multiple experts agree that the five fear responses *freeze, fight, flight, faint,* and *fawn* are the most common fear responses seen in humans. For the purposes of this chapter, we will talk at greater length about the three most familiar of the fear responses *fight, flight* and *freeze*.

Any of our fear responses can be triggered in everyday life and don't necessarily look like us throwing down thunder and lightning bolts from the heavens or scrambling up a tree. As a police officer, I saw the "fight" response play out in the streets and bar room floors countless times—sometimes leading to unimaginable brutality—but I also saw the flight and freeze responses regularly as well.

Police agencies describe the most common responses (*fight, flight,* and *freeze*) as engagement, disengagement, and containment. Uncommon people assess the threat and pick the appropriate response for that threat. Often, the reason they can do this comes down to what many fearless people pride themselves on doing—training, training, and more training. Before we go there, let's delve a little deeper into *fight, flight,* and *freeze*.

Fight

With the advancement of technology, police services around the globe are turning to the use of body-worn cameras. The internet is full of videos from these devices, and many of them depict police officers in *fight*. Although I am by no means a connoisseur of body-worn camera footage, from time to time I have found myself watching it.

One such video that caught my attention recently came from a school shooting in the US. The video captured the police response after it had been reported that a former student had entered the school with a gun and begun killing staff and students. What impressed me about the officers' responses to this unfolding tragedy was how deliberate and focused they were as they entered the school and began their search for the shooter.

On their body-worn cameras gunfire could be heard in the distance, coming from the second floor of the school. Pinpointing where they needed to go, officers moved without hesitation toward the stairwell and up to the second level. There, camera footage captured the police officers' movements down the hall. The sounds of gunfire grew louder, the echoes bouncing off the walls in all directions. They were clearly getting closer.

Their body-worn cameras also captured each officer's rapidly changing breath—adrenaline was coursing through their veins as they moved in on the suspect, who had positioned himself in a large open room just down the hall. In unison, police continued forward until they came to the opening of the large room.

Here, they engaged with the offender in a brief verbal exchange which resulted in gunfire. Officers returned fire, which ended in the former student being killed. None of the officers were injured. In this instance, the police and the suspect brought the fight to each other. In the case of the police, that bringing of the fight included both the heightened awareness and energy arising from the adrenaline of fear, combined with the discipline and training to use that focus and augmented physical response in a controlled, effective manner.

In other instances, the situation can be more one-sided, such as when a frightened suspect brings the fight to cops who are there in the role of peacemaker or rescuer and not expecting to bring a *fight* to the situation. Sometimes, such unanticipated turns of events are the result of a fleeing suspect turning to attack an officer; sometimes, the result of a suicidal person resisting officers' attempts to prevent self-harm; and sometimes, the result of a person acting irrationally under the influence of substances.

Early in my career, I remember vividly those times when, instead of turning to run from me, a suspect swiveled toward me and charged. I also remember the gulp of breath I'd take just before contact and the fight was on. Obviously, being able to write about it today means that in the half dozen times this happened to me, my training, physicality—and perhaps a guardian angel—allowed me to survive these ordeals relatively unscathed. I am, of course, not the only one to have been so lucky. Over the years, there have been hundreds of similar close calls involving the men and women I have worked alongside.

An example of the second scenario occurred on a sunny fall day a few years ago when two officers responded to the call of a suicidal man who'd stabbed himself in the chest and then ran into his detached garage at the back of his home, where he attempted to hang himself from a noose.

After clearing the home, these officers moved to the backyard and approached the locked garage. Through the garage window, constables could see the man hanging by a wire wrapped around his neck. Entering the garage was nearly impossible as the pedestrian door opened outward and couldn't be physically forced. Using his nightstick, one of the officers broke the garage window and entered the structure through the broken pane of glass. Immediately, he lifted the suspended male, holding him up to relieve the pressure on his throat, while the other officer ran back into the home to get wire cutters. Returning, the second officer cut the wire asphyxiating the man. This was when the situation turned bad.

Within seconds, the officers had to change course from saving the man to saving themselves. The critically injured man picked up a hammer. In a fight for their own lives, the officers wrestled with the bleeding man until he was finally in custody. In the end, despite the best efforts of officers and doctors, the suicidal man died in hospital as a result of his self-inflicted injuries. Thankfully, neither officer was seriously injured.

An example of the third scenario comes from almost a decade ago. It was a cold January night when police were dispatched to a call for help at a house party. According to the complainant, the man central to this story had been stabbed with a large, serrated knife. Following the assault, the intoxicated attacker fled but police found his victim just outside the house. The victim was suffering from a bleeding gash across his neck, which required immediate first aid if he had any chance of survival.

The officers began life-saving measures by placing pressure on the victim's wounds. However, instead of accepting officers' help, the inebriated man became assaultive, spitting blood into the face of one of the first responders. Nevertheless, the partners continued to help—no doubt adrenaline-fueled and "bringing the fight" to the situation—until medical services arrived.

Of course, not all officers are so lucky. A hard fact: in the past five years, between 2018 and 2023, twenty-one police officers have been killed in the line of duty in Canada while responding to another's emergency, according to the Police and Peace Officers' Memorial Ribbon Society.

Flight

Flight can be illustrated by the response some of us have in situations where we are walking down a sidewalk in a rough part of town and see someone who makes us uncomfortable coming the other way. To remove ourselves from the perceived threat, we will often adjust our behavior, even in subtle ways, to avoid them.

As an undercover police officer, I recall creating this response in others while I was in "costume": donning my very worst attire—old stained blue jeans, a beat-up hoody, and untied laces, and letting my beard and hair grow unkempt—I would proudly trudge off to work each day looking my very best for the world I was entering. Confirmation that I was doing my part came during my prowls around the city when I heard vehicle door locks click as I passed by, saw uneasy looks in people's eyes before they swiftly turned their heads, or observed a wary pedestrian lower their head and walk faster, shoulders hunched and fists in pockets, crossing to the south curb as I walked along the north.

As a recruit, I remember early lessons from my wiser senior partners, one being the most likely route of a suspect in flight after committing a crime. I was told then, and it makes sense to me now that—when you think about the suspect who has just robbed the local 7-Eleven and is fleeing to get away—their pattern of flight can be predicted. The first turn out of the store parking lot will likely be right. The right turn is away from traffic that may hold a suspect up. On the roadway, the next turn will also likely be right, followed by a quick left. I was told, If I could predict the pattern of flight behavior, then I had a better chance of catching up or even intercepting them. Although I am not aware of any formal studies on this passed-down knowledge, I've come to believe there's some truth or logic behind my old partners' assertions.

Most of us have used *flight* response to avoid conflict. I recall one situation when I was confronted about an issue and I could see no positive outcome resulting from that confrontation. Nothing I could say would change the other person's position, and more than likely, my words would result in unnecessary provocation. I choose to get up and, courteously, leave the room. The key words here, are unnecessary and courteously.

> If a situation is immediately dangerous "pumping the brakes" or backing away may be the best option in the moment. Later, find a beneficial way to address the issue, either through timing, persons involved, or skillful techniques.

The situation was this: I was invited to a small conference focused on raising awareness around intimate partner violence and abuse. I represented myself as a concerned citizen and not as a member of the police service.

While I was there, a guest speaker with a bone to pick began detailing her views about the organization I worked for and her belief that it was corrupt and racist toward the group for whom she was speaking. She was not afraid to reveal her true feelings about us cops. While I sat there, I grew particularly uncomfortable with her messages and misconstrued "facts." The whole time, thinking *if I had the same things to say about her group, I'd be hung by my toenails.* Regardless, I sat and listened as she described a case with which I was very familiar.

A young woman's head and torso had been found along a hillside pathway, but her arms and legs were never found. Because of this failure of the police, the victim could not be buried whole, and this failure—this unjust result (the speaker suggested)—was brought on by police bias. Because the victim, in this case, was not Caucasian.

I remembered the case well. I remembered how feverishly and tirelessly all investigators worked to identify a suspect quickly—and we did. I remembered that, following his arrest and the execution of a search warrant, we learned that the legs and arms of the victim had been disposed of in the trash, which had already been picked up and taken to the city landfill and buried.

Describing this case as an example of police bias, the speaker criticized the investigative team for not finding or locating the arms and legs, citing racism as the root cause. I wondered (as my arms crossed and I turned my body toward the door—a flight reaction) what the plethora of officers who had searched the dump for eight weeks in the heat of summer looking for said parts would have thought. I also wondered what the managers who provided the funds to search for the needles-in-a-haystack would have thought, as well—to this day, likely unaware of how muddy their reputations were made that night.

The speaker's assertion that evening that policing is two-tiered is a sentiment I do understand on some level, but not through my own experiences during my tenure in this office. Never once have I ever walked into a briefing room and heard the investigative group expressing any level of disinterest in solving a case because of the background, race, or socio-economic status of a victim. In fact, in the case described above, I remember how each of us clamored to find a vital position on the team that would allow us to be directly in the loop when new information came in so we could all be a part of what we hoped would be a successful conclusion to a very troubling crime. This reality nagged at me, and she continued her diatribe of misconstrued facts.

In the end, I choose to "tactfully disengage" from expressing my own opinion on it, to preserve the event and not succumb to her baiting just to try and prove a point. My decision (*flight*) likely was the right decision, the safest one for my organization and me that evening.

I didn't leave it there, though. I'm not one who is uncomfortable with having tough conversations with difficult people, but such a discussion would be more productive at a more appropriate time. When we did speak, I was able to address my concerns with her about the statements she had made. As expected, her response did not come with an apology, but at least the record was set straight.

Freeze

Often forgotten is the last of the fear responses: *freeze*.

The freeze response is exactly that: an actual stop, a stillness, often accompanied by either an inability to think, or conversely (usually for those who have been trained) a heightened sense of alertness. We stop in our tracks and assess.

During this response, thinking can become incredibly difficult because blood rushes from our brain to ready our muscles to fight or run. This very response can be seen to affect young officers just out of the academy who may hang back in bewilderment as they watch their partner engage physically with a suspect intent on harming the officer—until their training snaps them back to get in there and help. These momentary lapses of *freeze* for untrained or inexperienced individuals we coin "Going Code Black."

A few years ago, two officers became involved in a very serious incident after responding to an attempted suicide complaint. A victim had a self-inflicted stab wound to his chest and was dying as they arrived. The senior officer in the partnership, falling back on experience, jumped into first-responder mode and looked for something he could use to apply pressure to the victim's injury. Simultaneously, he noted that his trainee had fallen into a *freeze* response and needed reassurance and direction.

To get the partnership through the call and save the man's life, the experienced officer spoke to his partner, providing them with the direction they needed to get more help and assist in the administration of first aid. In the end, despite the victim dying multiple times on the way to the hospital, he was saved. No doubt this was, at least partially, due to the skill of that senior officer and his ability, through experience, to manage both the call and his recruit.

Uncommon people are mindful that each person's reaction to danger is not always what they wish it would be, and they learn from their missteps moving forward.

Training

Uncommon people know that learning and practice—in other words, training—can make a huge difference in an individual's response to fear; not only in evaluating the choices between *fight* and *flight*, but in modifying the *freeze* reaction.

Michael Rosenbaum believes the ability to pick the most

effective response to an emergent situation increases for individuals who are trained for confrontations and who have experience in dealing with violence. He also believes a trained individual is more apt to select the appropriate level of force than an untrained one. He states:

"For the inexperienced person, the danger signs often go unrecognized, hence they are surprised by the intensity of a confrontation or else ambushed by an attacker. Such mental dullness leads to panic, confusion, chaos, and sensory overload, along with an inappropriate response that can have fatal consequences for both victim and attacker alike."

> In his article "Fight, Flight or Freeze: Trained and Untrained Responses," Michael Rosenbaum speculates that the fight, flight or freeze syndrome dates to the Paleolithic era; that even then there were trained and untrained individuals who responded differently. For example, the seasoned hunter who stalked game day in and day out was very accustomed to fight, flight or freeze and may even have grown to enjoy the sensation, whereas his village-dwelling counterpart may have experienced sensory overload when facing danger.

How much does training factor into our responses in life-and-death situations? Rosenbaum would argue that training is a significant element in the *fight*, *flight*, and *freeze* responses. I would agree, and so would the friend of mine, who spent the better part of his career focused on the development of himself and others as a member of the tactical team, and first introduced back in chapter one.

Now retired, he recalled his time as a police officer and offered some of his memories from his decade in Tac. Here, he served in a unit that averaged about 250 calls a year, from high-risk warrant entries to barricaded gunmen and hostage rescue calls. During his tenure in Tac, his team handled a lot, and their day-to-day training helped ensure their many successes.

Something he shared with Susan and me as we wrote this book was a quote that resonated with him from a movie starring Denzel Washington—*Training Day*: "There are no hard people, just trained and untrained."

He went on to say, "I don't think you can overstate the value of training in any area, whether that's investigative or operational. In a crisis, you need responses to be as automatic as possible so you can free up the 'operating space in the computer' to make more conscious decisions. If you have not trained to an automatic standard, then you're not creating room in your 'computer (brain)' to come up with creative solutions to address high-stress dynamic situations."

Training automation is critical to high-functioning teams that are solving problems with high penalties for failure. He continues: "In stressful situations, it's difficult to be effective at decision making or evaluating and assessing what's going on around you if you have to also divert part of your thought process with where you're placing your feet, how you're moving through a building, or what direction your weapon system must be pointed."

When someone's highly trained, they're very competent, and when people are competent, they're confident—and that's critical. "Being confident results in more successful outcomes. Competence and confidence come from training."

During his time in the service, he had opportunities to observe people experience different fear responses in a myriad of ways, sometimes to his and his teammates' advantage. He recalled that about ninety percent of subjects they were looking to apprehend froze as the team made dynamic entry into these high-risk events. The freeze reaction gave him and his teammates the second or two they needed to successfully make the arrest and have a successful conclusion to the event they were there to manage.

Imagine you are a "bad guy" sitting at home after committing a crime you thought you'd got away with, when suddenly your front door smashes open, and a group of large armed men in uniforms enter in a deliberate and coordinated manner, yelling, "Police! Get down on the ground."

I suspect you, just like me, would fall into the ninety percent of people who would freeze in that moment as your mind began to digest what exactly was happening.

I remember being in situations like this as an undercover police officer where one moment I was sitting in a car in a planned arrest scenario, and in the next, the vehicle I was seated in was surrounded by the friendly neighborhood Tac team and I was being yanked from my seat faster than I could say, "I'll get out on my own."

Freeze.

I was not the only one. My colleague recalled a time when he momentarily froze while on the job at a high-risk event. In this case, he and his team had responded to a complaint involving a mentally disturbed gentleman threatening to kill himself and burn down his unit on the third floor of an apartment complex. Before my colleague's arrival, the original responding officers had already contained the man to his suite and were stationed at the door of the apartment in a darkened hallway, looking in. The distraught man had barricaded all the windows using mattresses from inside the apartment. The man's crisis seemed out of control.

After pulling into the parking lot, my colleague was approached by a bystander who said, "Are you here for this call? That's my brother. Just be careful; he's trained in martial arts."

When the negotiators, including my colleague, arrived at the apartment, they tried to verbally deescalate the situation, but unfortunately, he continued to act as a threat to himself and to the other tenants in the building.

My friend recalled, "We had been there for quite some time and we began to wonder where this guy was, when all of a sudden he appeared. He was about 6'5" and 280 pounds, wearing a pair of work out shorts and a Batman mask."

What?

"He was also holding two screwdrivers."

Despite his training, my colleague had never mentally prepared himself for that one. He froze while his brain computed what it had seen.

"Through the dark, I could see him jump from one side of the hallway to the other, and I said to the officer I was there with, 'Did you just see a giant guy in Tapout shorts and a Batman mask just jump across the hallway?'"

He gained control of the weak moment, and in the end, his freeze reaction didn't affect his performance, more than likely because his training kicked in. He and his team worked until the man could be taken to hospital, where he received the help he needed.

Police services, search and rescue societies, Border Services Agencies and Parks are not just training their two-legged officers to navigate through the big three F's. Our four-legged variety are also subjected to rigorous training to help them respond to the challenges of being a service animal.

A family member of Susan's who worked for many years as a dog handler for Parks Canada, Dale Portman, sat down to talk to us about his experiences working with dogs used primarily for national parks search and rescue operations. He and his working dog were trained together by the RCMP.

An important first step in dog candidate selection is to identify innate courage in the dogs destined to become police service dogs or park dogs. An initial test involves a person holding a bat, stick, or club who approaches the leashed dog while trainers note the dog's reaction: does the dog recoil and retreat, show aggression and attack, or just stand there and look at the guy? Either of the last two reactions (aggressive or noncommittal) qualifies the dog for further testing and training. Dogs that recoil or retreat are removed from the candidate pool and adopted out to loving homes as pets.

> "A lot of our dog handling work in the park was poaching cases and lost kids and drownings, but we also worked with the RCMP and the conservation officers and the park rangers in the provincial parks. But it was also a reciprocal deal because our dog handlers got trained by the RCMP for free and then we trained their officers who specialized in avalanche search and rescue, and free mountaineering training. It worked out pretty good for both outfits."
> —Dale Portman

Both the RCMP and Parks Canada consider two breeds of dogs to be good working patrol dogs: the German shepherd, which is known for its courage and working capabilities, and then the Belgian Malinois, a slightly smaller dog also known as a smart, eager working dog. For the police, retrievers made good drug, cadaver, and explosive scenting dogs where aggression is not needed.

Some of the courage required by a search and rescue dog is something the average person might not readily identify. Dale told us a lot of rescues occurred on glaciers. "We train the dog to search while on a rope so if he falls in a crevasse, I can get him out. None of my dogs were skittish about ice."

But search and rescue dogs face a lot of situations that are much more dramatic. For instance, back country adventurers can find themselves in need of help in deep hinterland environments. When time is of the essence, arriving in minutes rather than days can be critical.

Dale pointed out that courage requires overcoming fear—in the case of slinging under a helicopter, a fear of heights, which is inborn in humans and animals.

"To sling under the helicopter, we'd wear a big harness that's fairly skookum," Dale told us. "The dog is also in a harness connected to me by a carabiner. I'm squatted down, and he's standing right in front of me. When the helicopter lifts off, we're connected to the cable underneath the helicopter. He gets lifted off with me, and it's up to me to make sure the dog stays comfortable. Most dogs really do relax once they're suspended. They don't fight, which is good because we had to do a lot of slinging. There are places we had to get into where we had to search for bodies, and the only way you could access it was via helicopter."

"We did a climb one time up in Jasper with the dog, and on the way down, we had to rappel over a cliff. The dog was used to slinging under a helicopter in a harness, but he wasn't used to being pushed over a cliff. He didn't know what the hell was going on.

"We'd got it all figured out. We had him in his harness, and he was well set up. We decided the other park warden[1] would go down with the dog, so she rappelled off the cliff with him. Of course, the dog didn't want to have anything to do with it. I

---

[1] The Canadian (national) Park Warden is roughly equivalent to the American Park Ranger. In Canadian provincial parks, the title is Park Ranger.

had to push him off. Once he got suspended, he was fine, but he was knocking rocks down on the other warden while she was rappelling, so I guess the dog thought I'd gone crazy."

But Parks Canada rescue dogs have other duties as well. "We used to send projectiles up into avalanche areas to detonate slides before they came down unpredictably on a busy highway or a backcountry ski party. Some of the ordinances didn't explode, so in the summer, I'd use my dog to search for them before they blew up on a hiker or a mountain goat. The dogs were never scared—they didn't know what explosives could do."

Like humans, these working dogs exhibited inborn fears (of falling), but weren't afraid as long as they hadn't been traumatized or socialized to fear a thing (like explosives), and could do their work with confidence when they were trained (such as to sling under a helicopter).

Dogs used in policing do some similar work, such as searching for missing persons, explosives, or drugs, but they are mostly deployed in active arrest situations.

A good friend and classmate of mine was a dog trainer for years. When asked how a police service dog can be trained to have only one of two reactions while working (hold or engage) while discouraging the third response (fleeing), he had this to say: "First, it isn't training that stops a dog from fleeing. Like Parks Canada dogs, potential service dogs are selected for their inborn tendency to stand up to threat, rather than flee or become intimidated."

Once accepted to an agency and working with an officer, the dog would be exposed to as many different experiences as the trainer could create to build the dog's confidence in dealing with whatever situation could arise. Take stairs, for instance. Many dogs' first instinct when confronting a threat from above isn't to engage. Training prepares the dog for such scenarios. Training breeds confidence to face a real situation—but this is also a fine line; a dog's confidence can be broken if the trainer introduces a task that's too difficult, too early. It's imperative handlers allow their dogs to be successful in every step of their development.

In addition, learning a dog's hang-ups is an important first step. Some dogs, for instance, don't like tile or concrete floors. Others feel uncomfortable on stairs. Building the dog's confidence in these environments is the responsibility of the handler.

What about building a dog's confidence in the face of events that would shake almost all of us—gunfire?

At the time of feeding a dog, sounds of gunfire would be introduced in the distance. If the dog reacted the food would be taken away momentarily then returned, and the sound of gunfire reintroduced. Over time, as the dog stopped reacting, the sound of gunfire was brought closer.

Similar training prepares service animals for other life-and-death situations they may encounter while serving on the job.

A perfect case in point came several years ago, when members of my organization were involved in an aggressive situation with an individual high on drugs and determined to bring the *fight* to the cops. During the melee, one officer's gun was ripped from its holster, and the suspect escaped into the night with the stolen gun, his whereabouts unknown. A K9 unit was dispatched to assist. Officers contained the area, and the dog was deployed. Nose to the ground, the K9 unit began to track and within minutes located the assailant in a backyard, nervous and pointing the officer's gun.

Without hesitation, the dog fell back on its training, leaped forward and engaged the man, disarming the firearm from his grasp. His heroics saved the lives of the police officers in the area and saved his own, too.

Navigating the F's

According to my colleague and former Tac officer, in any tactical scenario, there are three options. You can penetrate (*fight*), disengage (*flee*), or hold in place (*freeze*). Selecting which of those three options is best for any given situation comes back to experience and training. "Being trained to switch gears is beneficial for officers going into these situations and much harder for the people who aren't trained," he said. For example, comparing the advantages of going in "loud," using overwhelming speed and surprise, versus being stealthier, which requires quiet and listening.

Selecting the right response for any given scenario comes down to the priorities of lives and policing operations. For example, officers making entry into a building to rescue a hostage will prioritize lives as follows:

- Victims, hostages, members of the public
- Police
- The offender

In other words, if an officer makes entry for a hostage rescue and one of their teammates is shot, the officer will step over their teammate because they are lower on the list of priorities than the hostage. To do this requires training and a rock-solid resolve.

In instances where they are entering a home with overwhelming speed and surprise and deploying distraction devices, police officers must consider the subjects' reactive mode. If a distraction device is deployed or a Taser is used, there will be a delay in the subject's ability to react to officers' commands, such as, "Show me your hands." They may not be willfully obstinate but simply still processing their *freeze* response.

Here, again, is where training is critical. Rosenbaum says when the *fight* response is activated in a trained individual, their physical movements become more precise than those of the untrained person, who may be uncoordinated and flailing. Through repetition, the brain pathways for coordinated action are strengthened and kick in automatically. A tactically trained SWAT member with hundreds of hours of training in how to clear a building will enter any room with precision and decisiveness, regardless of potential threats within. The trained individual can strategically stalk the threat like prey, while the untrained individual's actions are governed by doubt. A trained person's mindset is calmer, while an untrained individual, facing a situation new to them and needing to think through all possible actions and ramifications, will be more flustered, hyper, unfocused, and over—or under—acting. Similarly, I believe—and I have witnessed—that acclimatization to uncomfortable or unpleasant scenes also allows the seasoned death investigator to remain calmer and more in control than the fresh-faced recruit, at a violent death scene.

Rosenbaum's descriptors of the trained person in *fight*-response mode remind me of two situations involving heroic officers I met almost a decade ago.

A phone call came in to 911 from a concerned wife and mother of two who told the call taker she was worried her husband was acting strangely. She requested officers meet her at the family home so they could check on him, as well as the two children the couple shared. Police officers were on their way when a second call came from the same residence.

On the second call a woman could be heard screaming for help. When first-responding officers arrived at the scene, they noted a warm vehicle parked in the driveway, unoccupied, and a purse left open on the front passenger seat. As officers approached the front door of the two-story home, they saw one set of footprints in the freshly fallen snow.

At the door, officers called into the residence: "Police!"

They received no answer.

The officers made their way into the house. Training kicked in. They started on the main floor, checking all rooms before making their way into the basement. They descended the wooden stairs to a poorly lit area of the home, a concrete-walled space scattered with stored furniture, boxes, and shelving. A bundle of yellow rope hung from the stair railing.

A small boy was dead.

The radio recording to dispatch from one of the officers came in without any deflection or shake to his voice. He stated: "We got an insecure door at the front here on this 43 (check on welfare). We checked the basement. There's a 10-32 (deceased person) in the basement of the residence. We're just going to clear the upper floor as well."

"Acknowledged."

Silence followed this radio transmission. Additional units began to book onto the call and respond to the scene to assist their colleagues.

The basement was cleared, disclosing no further victims or threats. The officers moved to the second story. They entered the bedroom of the youngest child, a young girl who was maybe six years old. She was dead under the pink covers of her bed.

Then the officers on scene heard it: faint muffles and the

sounds of struggle from the master bedroom.

The officers moved toward these sounds. Just outside the master bathroom door, a pair of broken glasses marked the location of the violence. The junior officer swung the door to the bathroom open.

A man had his arms in a dry bathtub, in the final throes of taking his wife's life. A rope was wrapped around her neck.

The officers sprang into the room, wrestling with the offender, pulling him from the victim, and freeing her from the stranglehold. His body was covered in scratches, and a rope burn marked the bridge of his nose. He'd shuffled her into the bathroom to muffle her screams.

The man was arrested, cuffed, and removed to the officers' vehicle. The victim was checked for injuries, and an ambulance was called. The radio crackled again. "We have one in custody. There are two 32s in this house now. Both children. And we interrupted him, I believe, attempting (to kill) his wife."

This is an example of the officers doing exactly as Rosenbaum would have expected trained professionals to do: they remained calm and coordinated through the response, despite the potential danger and unpleasantries they faced; despite the adrenaline flooding the officers' systems from the potential and real threats they faced.

Rosenbaum's descriptors also reminded me of this next officer, who, to this day, still amazes me. While working without a partner one afternoon, he responded to reports of a man swinging a black, stick-like object on the platform of a metro train station.

Upon arrival, the officer discovered the subject (of now multiple calls) was no longer on the train station platform. The officer searched the area and spotted him walking through the parking lot toward a busy mall. As the officer approached, the offender dodged and ran toward one of the mall entrances. The officer remained on his tail, calling for backup.

Inside the mall, security cameras scanning the aisles of a major department store captured the incident as it unfolded. The offender was recorded in full stride, reaching down the front of this pants to pull out a large, black machete. In that same moment the officer was shown readying his Taser, which he deployed but did not hit his target.

Bystanders screamed and took cover as the offender turned with the machete in a full overhead swing.

The officer transitioned to his service firearm, but not before the blade struck the top of his shoulder, severely gashing his arm. Unbelievably, now in a fight for his life, the officer moved past the partial amputation to draw and fire his gun. The offender collapsed, wounded, and dropped his weapon. Backup units arrived, and the situation was contained.

In both cases, these trained officers showed the wherewithal to keep their composure in very difficult situations and to rely upon their training to bring both incidents to the best possible conclusion, with no further threat to the public. In both cases, neither offender was killed, and both were later convicted of their crimes.

Similarly, the *flight* response differs between a trained and an untrained individual. According to Rosenbaum, a trained individual in *flight* would disengage from the threat tactfully without escalating the risk, while the untrained person might run from the threat, unrestrained, possibly initiating pursuit. The trained individual would be aware of the situation and the surrounding environment, while the untrained individual would be unaware of their surroundings. For this reason, the trained individual would be more mentally focused than the untrained person in a panic state.

My colleague would also agree, although *unrestrained flight* would not be expected from members of their team, it was something they always made contingency plans to address when dealing with a frightened suspect who might try to flee apprehension: *if we go in through the front door, we better have someone covering the back.*

On the other hand, officers did prepare for instances where they might encounter something unexpected like an improvised explosive device (IED), which could require them to temporarily disengage from their mission. In such cases, tactical officers were prepared to implement an emergency evacuation, but this wouldn't be unrestrained running away from the threat but deliberate, tactical disengagement without escalating risk.

In Rosenbaum's assessment of the *freeze* response, he notes that the trained individual who freezes will take on a hunter's crouch position, whereas the untrained individual will become paralyzed. The trained individual's responses to all stimuli in his or her environment will become heightened, while the untrained person may go numb and unable to think ("Code Black"). Last, the trained individual will prepare to ready their weapon for fight, while an untrained person will become submissive.

When discussing a trained *freeze* response, my tactical colleague related a strategy he would use to gain information about a structure he and his team intended to enter. For instance, they might breach the doorway, then hold their position and use this time to assess. From the entryway, they would watch, listen, or consider introducing a canine or a robotic platform to get the information they needed before making the final entry. "If it's trained, *freeze* can be an appropriate response."

An experienced officer once encapsulated the concept of using the trained *freeze* response following a foot chase where the bad guy almost got away after I ran past him.

I vividly remember the night: running through alleys and over fences, my lungs burning, as I huffed and puffed, chasing down a car prowler until he just—disappeared.

"It was at this exact time," my senior partner later told me, "you needed to stop in your tracks, listen, and *freeze*. Listen for the snap of a tree limb or the scrape of a jacket scuttling under a vehicle on a gravel pad, the crunch of snow, or the exhalation of breath. Once those audible clues give away your suspect's location, you can resume your pursuit or begin your search for them in the area you last saw them."

"The truth," he explained, "is this. They are not much faster than us. When they disappear, they are likely closer than you think. And for this reason, you always risk running past them after they go to ground; you believe they are that much further ahead." From his perspective, freezing really turns the chase from "tag" to "hide and seek."

Training prepares us to face fear with greater confidence and understanding.

Empowerment

The very best police officers I know can understand, empathize, and empower people through their fears. By doing so, I believe they create more positive outcomes in their interactions with the public than officers who don't. For this reason, the ability to empower others to work through the things holding them back is a virtue found in uncommon people.

In a police environment, empowerment first requires active listening on the part of the officer. By doing so, an officer will likely hear what a person is afraid of and what may be preventing them from taking action. As was stated in chapter one, most people who have difficulty moving forward over-estimate risk and underestimate opportunity. When it comes to those who fall under the scope of a police investigation, what do you think these individuals fear? And how do you think an officer may address those fears?

Witnesses' Fears

As discussed earlier, witnesses often fear stitches. Some fear going to court, or not being believed, or being wrong about what they have seen. They may fear that the perpetrator will not be found guilty and that there will be repercussions for themselves or others. They may fear damage to their reputation. Also—witnesses come from all backgrounds, so criminal witnesses may worry about going back to their community and how the evidence they give may affect their life and relationships after the fact.

As a homicide detective, I've seen countless examples of the inner conflict people experience when contemplating doing what's right versus doing nothing at all, especially in cases where one individual holds dark secrets for another.

Such secrets, if shared, could mean the betrayal of a friend, a family member, a lover, or a spouse. Yet, failing to share such information can lead to an unjust result for victims or ongoing pain for families seeking answers and closure. The choice is not easy. The act of speaking up takes strength and must come from a place of courage. Such courageous people must be supported, and we must recognize that they may be placing themselves in jeopardy. The truth is, almost every case that goes "cold" in our office is the result of someone afraid of the consequences of sharing a secret.

Infamous serial killer Ted Bundy, who was believed to have killed at least thirty women in five different states, first appeared on police radar when his girlfriend reported her suspicions about him to authorities. Her willingness to do the right thing, to say something, and to share her concerns likely saved many other women from Bundy's clutches throughout the 1970s. However, her courage is not unlike many others I have met in police interview suites and back hallways since joining the Homicide unit.

Brave people like this witness, who came forward to police following a tragic shooting in the city's downtown core:

"I don't know where to begin," her 911 call began. "Last night, I was at the club with a few of my friends, and we met a group of guys. We were all leaving the bar together when one of them pulled out a gun and began shooting. I was so scared. But after he was done shooting, he jumped into the back seat of my car with his buddies. I dropped them off at a hotel up the street. They told me if I ever said anything, they'd find me. But I must tell someone. A person died."

What, in the end, were the consequences of her sharing this secret? There were many. One result was that she went through a deep process of rethinking her priorities; she took an inventory of her life and realized she needed to re-evaluate her choice of friends and lifestyle. To achieve this, she moved closer to her family. She cut back on extra-curricular activities and focused more on finishing school. Eventually, she started her career. In the end, she emerged as a fearless warrior in the eyes of the victim's family.

What didn't happen as a consequence? She was never intimidated, threatened, or harassed for her decision to come forward. And she will never have to live with the blame she could put on herself if the offender had ever done this again.

Not every person is this courageous, and not every result is as positive.

I suspect, if you ask most police officers, they will tell you there are a few cases that haunt them. The next is one of mine.

Years ago, I investigated the suicide of a child, a young girl who—heartbroken over the rejection of a boy—decided to take her own life. But before she did, she reached out. She told a friend about her decision, and her friend—a child himself—did what he had always been told to do. He told an adult.

But this secret was uncomfortable to hear. It was also bad timing, as it arrived on the first day of a family vacation. The boy's parents could not absorb and sort through what to do. The girl was only twelve. Surely, this disclosure was just a call for help, an overreaction. They told him they would deal with it when they reached the other side of the mountains.

But that was too late. By then, the girl was dead.

Perhaps the thought of having to have a difficult conversation with another parent would be uncomfortable. Perhaps they didn't believe the message truly meant what it meant. For whatever reason, the secret was not disclosed, and a young person went on to die by her own hand.

Holding onto information for someone else was a factor in the next two stories, as well.

One of my first cases in Homicide began in the early summer of 2009. The evening had been hot, and two men were sitting in the living room of a quiet suburban bungalow with one of the men's girlfriends, playing video games and throwing back shooters. An argument broke out that escalated until one man pulled out a knife and stabbed the other multiple times.

The key witness to the event was the offender's girlfriend, who witnessed the whole thing. However, to this day, I believe she constructed a story of self-defense to help mitigate her abusive boyfriend's role in the homicide. Why? Fear, no doubt. But her unwavering and untruthful account asserted that the victim, fueled by alcohol, violently attacked the love of her life, who could do nothing to protect himself except pick up a knife and begin stabbing. Despite contradicting evidence, her tale hurt the prosecution's case immensely. As a result, the offender entered a guilty plea to the lesser charge of manslaughter and received a sentence of only a few years in custody.

Time passed.

Then, one afternoon, out of the blue, the offender's girlfriend contacted me to say she was frightened for her own safety. The reason? The convicted offender was going to be released from custody, and she believed he would expect to return to their previous abusive relationship. Had she chosen to be courageous and truthful in her statements regarding his responsibility in the original murder, he would have been gone for a significant length of time, long enough for her life to move on.

Of course, speaking out truthfully is not easy to do. I understand. Nevertheless, if asked today, I suspect this young lady would say that the hell of that night paled in comparison to the fear she felt on hearing about her boyfriend's release from custody. Indeed, her fear was so profound, she uprooted herself from her family to start over in a new home far away from her troublesome ex.

The second story is similar.

It was spring in the city. A husband became enraged when he discovered his wife was having an affair and immediately began plotting revenge. He told his wife to contact the lover to lure him to their home. She refused, but he threatened her. The wife tried to call for help, but her husband hung up her cell phone before she could tell 911 operators where she was and what was wrong. The emergency call center repeatedly attempted to call her back but failed to regain a connection with the victim. But her adult daughter, who was present, did answer the phone.

And then proceeded to lie.

She lied about the phone's location and about what was happening. "Everything is okay over here," she said. "We're just having a party." By this time, the father had tied up his wife in the basement and begun several hours of brutal beatings.

Back when this offense occurred, the tracking of cellular phones was very new and had its failings. Pinpointing an exact location was the biggest one, but the inability to get subscriber information immediately was a second. Therefore, without more direction from the daughter, it took several hours to locate the victim, and when we did, she was near death and could not be saved.

I have no doubt the daughter of this murdered mother relives this regrettable outcome every day.

These two cases tragically demonstrate what happens when fear triumphs over courage.

Victims' Fears

Similar to the fears of witnesses, victims can also have a wide range of fears. *Will the perpetrator return and hurt them again?* is a central question, and certainly one common among women who have reported their abuser to the police.

Families victimized by break-and-enters are left with a pervasive uneasiness and often outright fear that the culprit may return. Children are particularly susceptible to this type of fear, and I remember vividly this question being raised by the children in one family who had been targeted in a break-and-enter, back when I was in uniform. My partner and I had been dispatched to a break-and-enter in progress after a family of four returned home to find the suspect still inside their house. Upon arriving on scene, we learned from the terrorized victims waiting outside that the offender had not been able to escape because their unit in the fourplex did not have a back door, and the front door had been blocked by the family patriarch.

My partner and I called into the home. "Police. We are coming inside. Make your way to the front door."

The sound of scuttling from the home's basement did not seem like it was moving toward the front door. In fact, the scuttling sounded more like someone preparing to barricade themself in. My partner and I barreled down the stairs. Using the beams of our flashlights, we moved, room to room, closer to the noises until we found the room we believed our suspect to be. The dazzle of my flashlight caught the young man by surprise in the corner behind a large child's dollhouse. He brandished what appeared to be a box cutter. In moments, my partner and I disarmed him and took him into custody.

Once the suspect was securely in our police vehicle, we returned to the family to collect statements, speak with the kids, and offer our victim services program. It was clear both youngsters were terrified that the man who had been in their playroom would return. My partner made a promise that we would return for the next few nights, flash our lights, and check on them. Their relief was clearly captured in their words and on their faces. We followed through on that promise for several weeks, off and on, until the family eventually moved from their home.

Some victims may fear being judged, not believed, or not taken seriously. This type of fear is very common, not unreasonably, among women who have come forward to report sexual assault—likely the driver behind why so many of these types of incidents go unreported in Canada. According to our Government of Canada website, "Sexual assault is among the crimes which are least likely to be reported." An antiquated 1999 General Social Survey found that 78% of sexual assaults were not reported to the police: 51% because the respondents did not feel the police could help them; 19% because they feared revenge by their perpetrator. Although these statistics are historical, it is my belief under reporting is still a problem. But such statistics, if still relevant, demonstrate the need for the criminal justice system to improve, and demonstrate the need to remove the fear of reporting these very serious violent crimes.

Other victims may fear not getting their day in court or never receiving an answer to who perpetrated the crime. More than once in my career, I recall being woken up from a dead sleep to answer my phone so that a victim's family member could express this very concern. In some instances, I knew the answer would come soon, but in others, I knew the answer would have to wait, as no conclusion could be reached until we had incontrovertible evidence to prove the "who."

One such case I was involved in began on Christmas Eve when a young man who had made a series of bad decisions in life now stared down the barrel of a gun. In the darkened alley, a thief was intent on robbing him for money and drugs. But the young man struggled and was beaten savagely with the butt end of the offender's pistol until he succumbed to his injuries and died in the back seat of his vehicle. When the young man did not return home for Christmas Day festivities, his mother reported him missing. It was several days later when her son's body was found after a neighbor reported a "suspicious vehicle" parked in the alley that had not moved.

From the outset, this case was going to be tough. The evidence collected in those first few days was extremely limited. The alley had no cameras. Because the victim was a drug trafficker, the suspect list was extremely long. Nevertheless, we trudged forward, slowly making progress as the investigation went from weeks to months and then to years.

As each milestone and anniversary passed, one thing never changed—the mother's desire to find out who did this to her son. I remember the awkwardness of each conversation with her as I balanced the needs of the investigation with her desire to know what was happening. More than once, she expressed her fear: is my son's case cold? And each time, I would have to answer *no*. She would inquire about what investigative steps had been taken and if I had talked with this person or that one. In that first year, I likely spoke with this concerned mom on more than seventy-five occasions—many times after office hours—and each time her fear was palpable.

Finally, after three years, the answers to her questions finally came. A former drug customer was identified. I remember the day I called this mother and told her we had made an arrest. She was incredibly relieved. But now a new fear arose that a court would find the suspect *not guilty*. Thankfully, they found the suspect guilty six years later.

Perpetrators' Fears

What do you think a perpetrator fears? Certainly, discovery. This is why so many people who commit crimes do their very best to backtrack after the crime has been committed to obliterate evidence they believe could identify them. For example, a recent trend in organized crime homicides is advance planning: the culprit acquires a stolen vehicle in the days before the planned homicide. Following the murder, the stolen getaway vehicle is driven directly from the scene to a rural area just outside the city to be burned. This dramatically decreases the chances that fingerprints or DNA, which could assist us in identifying the killer, will be found. But arson is not the only technique "bad guys" use to avoid discovery. Some may use "burner" phones, which are destroyed following the commission of the crime. Some perpetrators wear masks or disguises to avoid identification.

I remember years ago, while working in the drug unit, approaching a woman whom we had watched dealing cocaine. She matched the description of a person the homicide unit wanted to arrest for the brutal murder of another sex trade worker. My job was to confirm whether she was indeed their suspect and, while I was at it, attempt to purchase cocaine from her.

As I approached, something seemed off. Parts of her appearance appeared consistent with the old mugshot photo I'd seen of her, but something wasn't quite right. Engaging her in a quick "drug convo," I was able to purchase a small amount of cocaine, and following this, it seemed reasonable to me that a uniform car be sent to identify her and confirm whether she was the woman Homicide was looking for. At the very least, they could arrest her for the drug crime she had just committed.

The uniform car entered the area, and officers placed her in custody. Suddenly, a male she was with bolted from the arresting officers, running toward the river, directing much of their attention onto him. The second officer scuttled the handcuffed female into the back of a locked police car then joined her partner in a foot chase after the fleeing man. Returning moments later with the apprehended male, the officers found the back window of their car broken, a wig on the back seat, and the female suspect running down the street, still wearing handcuffs. An amusing scene. Apprehended for a second time she was ultimately identified as the suspect Homicide was searching for—even though her disguise had originally made me question it.

Perpetrators also fear going to jail.

Recently, I sat across the room from a young fellow accused of murdering a kid who was just out at the baseball diamond, playing some ball. I listened intently to what this youngster was saying. He asked questions like, "Will I have my own cell, or will there be someone in the cell with me? How often am I allowed out of my cell, and will there be other inmates around? Can I stay in my cell if I don't want to leave it?"

What fear did I need to address, and what words could I use to empower this kid to move past his fear? The young man was telling me he feared for his safety while incarcerated.

To do this, I explained that in jail, many staff are employed to ensure the safety of all inmates, that there are protocols and procedures to keep certain inmates away from other inmates, and that corrections officers work tirelessly to ensure each person in jail is provided the protections they need. All the units are monitored twenty-four hours a day by officers and by cameras manned by officers. If an inmate is having a problem with someone, it's okay to speak to staff about it so that they can address those concerns and perhaps move an inmate to another area within the jail.

The truth is that jail can be a scary place, but people who have crossed the line and need a reset can find a period of incarceration useful. There are opportunities for self-improvement and change. With that, the young man became more at ease and ultimately made the decision to tell me his version of what had happened the afternoon of the murder.

Finally, perpetrators may fear the perceptions of others and damage to their reputation. Some may fear their side of the story will not be heard; some may fear returning to a criminal gang where they will have lost trust and be punished for having been arrested—for potentially having given up group secrets. Some may fear trying to create a new life without the support of their gang, particularly if they have poorly developed occupational skills. They may have fears the investigator can barely guess at. Depending on the background and experiences of the arrested individual, it may be difficult for the investigator to discover what these fears are.

Bottom line, if an interviewer can identify what the suspect is afraid of through active listening, and if they can address each by providing an empowering alternative perspective, they will be more successful in obtaining a statement and getting closer to the truth.

An interviewer might point out, for instance, "Everyone in your situation wants to have their story told. There are always two sides. The time to do that is now because people who own up to their mistakes early are viewed as more courageous than those who try to do it years from now. This is your opportunity to tell me what happened. If you don't, it will be left for the evidence to speak for you, and I am sure you would agree this evidence does not look good."

Or, "I understand the concept of being incarcerated is scary to you, but there is a life to be had in jail, opportunities to help you and others. Alcohol and drugs can change people and make them act in pretty bad ways. Society understands this now. Is this what happened to you? If this was more like an error in judgment rather than a premeditated attack, that is really important information to know."

Recognizing a suspect's fears and empowering them to move through these is an important role of the interviewer in any interrogation room.

Police Officers' Fears

Police officers, too, have fears: the fear of not getting the correct criminal behind bars, or not getting the investigation right so the criminal walks free—or a family is not afforded proper justice.

These fears certainly spurred me on over my fourteen-year career in Homicide. Never did I want to let the family of a victim down or be wrong about someone that I was about to throw in jail. Working through these fears led me to realize that the best way to ensure these concerns were never realized was to do two things. First, to conduct all investigations professionally from beginning to end, which meant following the evidence and facts as they were uncovered and staying away from the temptation of theories. This included recognizing the limitations of evidence and never overstating the significance of one piece of information. Second was to put trust in my teammates, to listen to their unique perspectives and opinions, and by doing so, to avoid the bane of almost all wrongful convictions: tunnel vision.

I remember several years ago being on an investigative team where the lead investigator had a similar philosophy to mine—in fact I think we all did, which made working in this environment easier most days than not. This was a good thing because it empowered each of us to speak up when we knew something did not feel right in the case we were working on.

In this investigation the victim had attended a small apartment gathering with only three other people in attendance, two being witnesses and one being the offender. Everyone in the apartment this evening knew each other casually, that is, by nicknames or first names only.

The night started off like one would expect—but after dozens of beers, tension began to brew between two of the guests, a nephew and an uncle who started to quibble. As the night went on, quibbles turned to insults, to wrestling, to the nephew brandishing a knife from the kitchen and chasing his uncle out of the apartment. In the stairwell, the uncle and nephew's argument heated and the nephew attacked, killing his uncle—in fact, slicing his throat so deeply he was almost decapitated.

Called in to investigate, our team interviewed the witnesses. In a photo lineup, both witnesses identified the nephew as the person responsible for the murder. We also had CCTV footage of what appeared to be the same man entering, and later leaving the apartment building after the murder. Damning evidence to be sure. A few hours later the nephew was found, arrested, and brought back to headquarters for an interview.

As the assigned interviewer, I was aware going in that the case against the nephew was strong. There had been a history of similar disturbances between the pair leading up to this night, especially when alcohol was involved. As the interview began, I remember how stoic the nephew remained, saying nothing to implicate himself further. But something did not feel right—call it intuition or call it a gut feeling based on thousands of hours of interview experience. Through the first few hours, I could see the young man had something he wanted to say but was afraid.

I changed my questioning tactic from "Did you do it?" to "Prove you didn't do it." Things began to open a little in our conversation. But the cat still had his tongue. Finally, I decided to leave the room for a few minutes to express my general sense of this lack of progress with the primary investigator. *Something feels wrong.* The lead investigator heard and understood all too well because, as it turned out, in a room a few doors down from my interrogation suite, the young man's family had been brought in to ask them to convince the suspect to come clean about killing his uncle.

But there was a twist. A big one.

The young man's older brother, the spitting image of the fellow I was interviewing, was wearing a yellow jacket like the one described by the two independent witnesses and caught on CCTV video as the perpetrator left the apartment. Was it possible we were interviewing the wrong nephew?

We were.

Despite having been identified by two independent witnesses through photo lineups, we had the wrong man.

Armed with this new information, I returned to the interview suite and spent the next several hours going through how the man we had in custody could be alibied. To do this, I had to empower him to look at the totality of evidence that had led to his arrest—including the photo lineups and video evidence—and then ask him to be brave enough to speak on his own behalf even though by doing so he would end up placing his brother in the line of our inquiry.

The young man saw that if he did not provide further details on his own activities that evening, suspicion about his role in the murder would remain. He did what was asked. He provided indisputable proof that he was not the man we were looking for;

it was his "look-alike" brother who had come to the office to plead to him to "do the right thing" and confess to killing his uncle.

Phew. That was a close one, and I think the closest I ever came to having one of my fears realized.

Outside letting down the community, other officers fear letting down their teammates by not pulling their weight or by doing something that puts members of their team at risk. As one officer put it, "I fear knowing that I did something, or I failed to do something, that got a teammate hurt or killed, or a victim or a hostage hurt or killed. These are absolutely unacceptable outcomes."

One thing most officers do not fear, outwardly at least, is a threat to their own mortality in the line of duty. I believe for most of us, this is something we reconcile in our own minds long before we ever put in our application to serve. With that said, even though we have come to terms with our own mortality and accept that this could be an outcome of our service, many of us still fear leaving spouses, children, and other family and friends alone should something ever happen to us.

That is why training in scenarios as close as possible to the worst-case event an officer would encounter is so important: it empowers officers with the confidence to deal with whatever is in front of them. On-the-job vigilance, developing strong working teams, having a healthy support network of family and friends, and accessing available professional mental health services are some of the other strategies police officers may use to empower themselves through the things they face as fears.

Whether it is an accused, a witness, a victim, or an investigator, all of us have fear. People we view as brave challenge their fears. They may be cautious and aware; they may have a respect for dangerous things, but they are not immediately stopped by them either. They evaluate the threat, as well as their own competence in facing that threat, then get in front of those fears to move through life undaunted in spite of those fears.

In the chapters that follow, you will be introduced to individuals who were able to move past their learned fears or make use of their fear responses to do something remarkable. Let their stories inspire you so that you, too, can be brave enough to unlock the front door and take that first step outside your comfort zone.

It's in all of us to be brave.

Chapter 3—Ethos: Ethical Change

> *Sometimes standing against evil is more important than defeating it. The greatest heroes stand because it is right to do so, not because they believe they will walk away with their lives. Such selfless courage is a victory in itself.*
> — N.D. Wilson, *Dandelion Fire*

In today's world of policing, ethical considerations form much of what a police officer or an investigator must deliberate on before taking a particular course of action. The answers to the question *should I or shouldn't I?* are at the heart of any ethical consideration and must consider not only personal values and comfort but also public shock and the legal ramifications of taking a particular course of action—or of doing nothing at all.

For reputable police agencies across the globe, ethics are woven through all major cases and police operations. The fact of the matter is that the reputation of any agency can plummet if the actions of officers are not in alignment with accepted standards and expectations.

Sir William Peel wrote as one of his nine principles of policing: "To recognize always that the power of the police to fulfill their functions and duties is dependent on public approval of their existence, actions, and behavior, and on their ability to secure and maintain public respect."

What is ethically right? For example, in the political arena:

Do you think it's okay to make profits from people who haven't fully understood their contract or risks, as long as no laws are broken?

Do you think it's okay to confiscate a person's home and all their worldly possessions because that home happens to be a tent on public property?

Do you think it's okay to disrupt the lives of people living in a community with protest noise and intimidation if you disagree strongly enough with an elected government's position on an issue?

Or in the policing arena:

Do you believe the police should notify the public when a dangerous offender is released from custody?

Do you believe an investigator should be allowed to torture a suspect believed to be involved in the kidnapping and possible trafficking of a child?

What would you do if you were the first responding police officer to an injury accident and found your colleague drunk and behind the wheel?

Do you think a police officer should be able to lie to a suspect in an interrogation room? Or purposefully mislead the public to protect the integrity of an ongoing investigation?

I believe, the answer to these questions and others like them will vary from person to person and will ultimately be dependent on two things: A person's core values, and how they define their purpose—both concepts we will expand on throughout this chapter.

This is why defining what is ethically right can be tricky, and therefore, it will not be the scope of this chapter to try to define moral correctness. Instead, what we hope to do is to introduce you to people who exemplify moral courage in a variety of ways, whether through championing others or themselves, taking the initiative to act when they observe something they believe is wrong, or having the integrity to remain true to their purpose and act accordingly.

Championing

Championing, standing up for yourself or another and speaking out against a status quo based on faulty assumptions, takes courage.

But does loyalty to your authentic self-mean arbitrarily taking a stand and acting on it without considering historical wisdom? No. There is value in the insights that led to "the way things are," as well as context, evolving circumstances, differing perspectives, and all other available information. This includes listening to other viewpoints and feeling empathy for another's situation. Unless a situation is urgent—someone could be hurt—the decision to act comes after consideration of all sides of the issue. When people don't consider all viewpoints, their choices often fall short of the virtue of "standing up for the right."

The integrity to stand up for what is right.

Taking into account all sides of a situation is one key to justice. In Western judicial systems, the right of an accused person to be heard is sacred. On a more modest scale, Susan has adjudicated hundreds of playground disputes in her role as a teacher and school administrator. Although there is no such thing as a school without bullying, in most cases, responsibility for a disagreement is shared. Susan says, "I don't know how many times I've seen this: once the two students each tell their side of the story and realize each has hurt the other in some way, a look of surprise comes over both faces, and they say, 'I didn't mean to hurt my friend!' Then, with guidance, they resolve the situation and carry on—as friends." A summary punishment of one based on the complaints of the other only leads to a situation where resentments fester and grow.

Susan's story reminds me of a time when, following a gangland shooting where two young men were rushed to hospital with life-threatening injuries and a third was shot in the hand, a partner of mine came up with a controversial plan. Following the arrest of two of the gang members, one from each side of the conflict, he said at our team meeting, "This gang war has been going on for years now, so long that—do you think either side even remembers how it began?" The rest of the investigative team agreed. The gang members' attitudes had become: "shoot on sight of a rival."

He asked, "What would happen if we bring both sides together while we have them in our custody? Place both in an interview room and try to figure it out? Let each see the human across the table. Ask each to explain their actions to the other?" The idea had merit. Of course, we would be in there too. And yes, both would be handcuffed. I was impressed by his confidence. The truth was, nothing had worked prior to this. So I thought, "Why not?"

And so it happened. Both sides were brought into one room, where a discussion began.

"Who is this?" one gangster asked us when he saw the other. His eyes bulged.

"Yeah, man. Who is this? I don't know this guy," the other stuttered.

"Well, fellas, a couple of hours ago, you were each trying to kill the other," my partner said. "So what's that about?"

Bewildered, shocked and totally confused by this tactic, each just glared into the eyes of the other. But they were uncomfortable, shifting in their chairs. At five feet apart, each could see the other's beating heart, see the fear in the other's eye, see what the other was. Human. Each was forced to acknowledge a broader view: to consider new information. To consider the humanity of the other person.

Did this work? Perhaps not. The conflict between the two gangs raged on for another year. But despite this fact, as I write about it today, I know neither of these two men was ever suspected of shooting again—and both still live to this day. So that is something.

I would argue that standing up for yourself or your group—or in this case, gang—is only a courageous ethical stance when context is considered.

But given that the individual has taken this necessary first step, championing what is right is a quality that weaves into many public service careers, and it is a virtue I have observed in many amazing people over the course of mine. People who have stood up to bullies and stood up for the little guy. People who have stood up for their morals and principles. If taking a stand means an almost certain increase in personal jeopardy, then the person who is choosing this action is exemplifying moral courage—something that is rarely easy to do.

One of the most publicized and cruel stories to ever be told in our city occurred what seems now many moons ago.

The little girl was six years old and full of life. Home videos showed her dancing and singing. With her long blond hair, cute smile, and youthful energy, it was not hard to fall in love with this little one, and our community did.

It was autumn when 911 operators received a phone call from her house. An adult female cried, "I need an ambulance! My daughter fell down the stairs! She's not conscious, she's not awake, she's not breathing—"

EMS crews raced to the scene, and when they arrived, they found the young girl in serious medical distress. A day later, she died from her injuries, but these were not from a fall down the stairs. They were an accumulation of injuries she had received through a week of abuse at the hands of her stepmother and biological father. Both were convicted for their crimes a few years later.

Grappling with grief from their unimaginable loss, the child's biological mother and stepfather searched for understanding. One day, landing on a website promoting a biker group originating out of the United States, both parents were drawn to their mission and message: *We empower children to find strength they don't know they have when they become victims of abuse and neglect.*

Inspired by this cause, the couple brought the first chapter of its kind (out of 320 worldwide) to our community. Over the past five years, members of this chapter have been involved in supporting dozens of children who've had to face their own abusers in a courtroom and who required support not covered within the current systems.

A group of uncommon people who have become advocates for children who face abuse and neglect at the hands of an adult: rough-around-the-edges biker types with hearts of gold who bring with them a powerful message: *We have your back, and we're here when you need it.*

And I can attest that they are. More than once, I've stood on the steps of the courthouse and witnessed twenty bikes roll up to the front doors to greet the child they were there to support. Rumbling motors, scruffy-bearded faces, and leather—all part of their deportment—and the little persons they are there to support grin from ear to ear when they know that these big, burly fellas are there for them.

Sadly, not all outcomes are positive—although they may be no less courageous—when championing another.

A few years ago, a young mother of a five-year-old was making ends meet as a waitress at a local restaurant. Her daughter was the love of her life, and when the mom was not working, her attention was always on the little girl.

She was also a loyal friend. When she learned her bestie's abusive boyfriend was trying to force her into prostitution, the young woman stepped up. She suggested her friend get help and leave this extremely unhealthy relationship. But the man found out—and came to the conclusion that her meddling would affect his bottom line. Tragically, her decision to champion her friend cost both her and her daughter their lives.

On another occasion, about five years ago, 911 operators received a chilling call.

"Hi, I just killed my parents in their home. You will also find my girlfriend's body in her apartment. I am at the corner near the 7-Eleven and will be waiting for your arrival," the caller said.

What ensued was a tragic and brutal triple homicide investigation, which left all of us to puzzle "but why?" A question we believed we ultimately came to answer under the leadership of a dedicated investigator well known for her ability to dig into the truth.

This was what we pieced together:

A week prior to that chilling 911 call, the caller had become embroiled in a heated argument with his girlfriend, which resulted in her murder. He left her apartment undetected and carried on with his week as if nothing happened. But people began to notice her obvious absence from his life—people including his mother, who wanted to understand why she hadn't heard anything about the missing woman. Evidence from the crime scene suggested that just before he murdered his mom, the pair had sat down at the kitchen table where, over a cup of coffee, I believe the mom challenged her son, perhaps insisting he come clean about what he might know about his missing girlfriend.

Feeling trapped and unable to explain what occurred, I believe the son did the unthinkable. Rising from the kitchen table, he armed himself with a knife and savagely attacked his mother. Her screams awakened the suspect's father, who rushed down the stairs and came face to face with his homicidal son. The attack on his father was as brutal as any I have seen during my time in Homicide.

Championing the most vulnerable in our society is a cause shared by a fellow officer who has inspired me ever since I first heard his story.

"My father was an alcoholic, an illness with a long history in my family. Although he did not turn into a 'monster' or do bad things when he was drunk, he was not there for me." As a child, Tad's parents divorced and his father married a woman who brought in new rules for the family. First, Tad had to stay alone in the basement. "I was told many times over the years that 'kids don't belong upstairs.'"

He was not allowed to have toys, computers, cell phones, PVRs or even a DVD player, but for whatever reason, he was allowed a small black and white television with an antenna. The basement consisted of four cold, cement walls, a cement floor with a damp, musty smell, a single light and three windows which were mostly covered up. He could never see the outside. "I always felt my dad and his new wife were ashamed by me."

His stepmother would yell at him, talk down to him, and call him names. All he wanted was to be accepted or liked, even if only for a few minutes. "I was truly afraid of her. I hated being home, I hated how she made me feel, and I hated that my dad never did anything to help me."

At times, Tad would cry uncontrollably, unable to speak and unable to explain his emotions, a situation that spilled over into school. And on top of these emotional challenges, he knew he was different from other boys; he was gay. "I knew being gay was not something I could control, but at the same time, I never understood what was happening or why I was gay. At that time, there were no gay characters on television, role models, or support groups in school."

Tad kept his confusion over his sexuality hidden and certainly never acted on his feelings. "My friendships with boys were concentrated, involved, and intense—I can't tell you the number of 'crushes' I had while growing up. I *can* tell you, however, that each and every one of them ended in heartache."

Because he was extremely introverted and would never stand up for himself, Tad was a target at school. "I would always cry. That was the way my body coped with pressure or stress."

Many times he was pushed, had books knocked from his hands, tripped, had his hair pulled out, or was punched. One day in high school, a group of boys followed him home, calling him names. They spit on the front door to his house, and Tad had to clean it up. But he was afraid that reaching out would only make everything worse.

At the time, Tad felt that this was happening only to him.

He thought the world hated him. "I mean, I was locked in a basement by night and targeted at school by day. Day after day, I only hoped life would get better on its own, like magic."

And to top all of this off, over a period of several years, he was sexually abused by an older man—something he kept locked away in his mind until recently.

During his last year of high school, Tad began to dream of being a police officer. "But I made a mistake. I never acted on my dream because I believed it was just a dream, that dreams weren't meant to be achieved. I never looked into becoming an officer."

Tad struggled with mental illness for years. When he was twenty-one, he attempted suicide. "This is still tough for me to talk about, but I'm glad I didn't succeed. When I woke the morning after my attempt, I was incredibly angry with myself. I realized immediately that suicide is NOT an option." Tad promised himself to live healthier and to get the help he needed *and deserved*. Reaching out would not be a sign of weakness; it would be a sign of strength.

Travel during his twenties gave Tad the opportunity to learn about himself, learn how to be social, and slowly become more extroverted. To accept the reality that he was gay.

He decided to call his birth mom and tell her. "I gathered up all of the strength I had, sat on my bed (with my friend beside me) and made the call. I was twenty-five years old."

Her response? "I know!"

"I was floored. I asked her to be angry simply because I had always envisioned that she would be. At least, disappointed. But no! Mom shared stories about how she always knew, and that it was great that I was telling her." She ended the conversation as they always did, by telling Tad she loved him.

"I remember hanging up, looking at my friend, and feeling

as if the world had lifted from my shoulders."

Tad's mom later told him she went to her bedroom where Tad's stepdad was resting to tell him Tad's message. His stepdad said, "That's nice," and went back to sleep.

"After all those years of beating myself up inside, nearly giving up, and keeping the true *me* hidden, my life felt brand new again."

To this day, Tad reports never having had a negative reaction when sharing the fact that he was gay. Sadly, this is not the same for everyone.

It was not until Tad was thirty-two years old that he made another life-changing decision. He was playing on a baseball team, and a new player joined the team. Tad remembered what it was like to be new, and when he saw the new player enter the room, he introduced himself. After a short chat, Tad asked about his career, and he told Tad he was a police officer. Tad told him how that was his dream job. The new player convinced Tad to at least apply—after all, he had nothing to lose.

"Since I was five years old, I'd dreamed about becoming a police officer. Today, that dream is a reality. Ultimately, I didn't let my sexual orientation stand in the way of living out this dream. I didn't let the negativity I experienced while growing up stop me. I always wanted to help people, and today, I am lucky enough to be in that position."

In October 2011, Tad read a news article about a young man from Ottawa who'd taken his own life because of years of relentless bullying and struggles with mental illness. The bullying started because he was a figure skater and later continued because he was gay.

"Reading Jamie's story reminded me about myself, being that five-year-old boy who had a dream to become a police officer because I wanted to help people." Tad felt helpless, knowing that Jamie had gone through such torment for so many years.

"Because of Jamie's story, I made a choice to 'do my part' to help those who need it most. On my own time and at my own expense, I began speaking at schools and sharing my story, along with Jamie's. It took a tragedy for me to act, but I will work as hard as I can in an attempt to prevent further tragedies."

Constable Tad Milmine's story is exceptional, and it has had a positive impact on the thousands of people with whom he has shared it since he began to champion his cause, "Bullying Ends Here." Tad embodies championing. By facing his own abuse and traumas he became a champion for himself first, and an advocate for so many others who face bullying.

People willing to champion themselves or others, regardless of their outcome, share an important takeaway.

How we stand up for others reflects how we see purpose in ourselves.

Initiative

The things many ethically courageous people share as a virtue, outside of standing up for what's right, is their willingness to take initiative to act on what they observe.

Annually, my policing organization holds a gala and awards ceremony to honor the contributions of people who step up to the plate when they are thrust into situations where they have a choice to either act on their observations or not. Over the years, there have been many great examples of common people doing uncommon things and acting fearlessly when they see a need to perform their duty as a citizen.

Willingness to act on observance

Take the situation that occurred one November when a young woman saw a man approach her special needs daughter at a local library and touch her inappropriately. The mother came to the aid of her daughter and confronted the man, who then fled the library. An older gentleman who heard the mother's screams gave chase and cornered the offender in a nearby yard. Feeling trapped, the offender, not ready to give up, armed himself with a metal watering wand, and a struggle ensued. The courageous intervener emerged from the backyard, gripping the bad guy by his biceps, returned him to the library, and locked him in a bathroom until police arrived.

Another example. On a cold January morning in 2015, a psychiatric patient left the hospital grounds and, confused, began to wander around the nearby community. Dressed only in a hospital gown, her body temperature dropped, and soon she found herself in a medical emergency—hypothermia. A passerby in the area pulled her car to the curb to check on her. Through chattering teeth, the patient said, "I think I'm going to die."

"Let me wrap my arms around you," the driver said, and with that, the patient fell into her arms. The driver carried the patient to her vehicle and drove her back to the hospital, where she could be treated. In the emergency room, doctors discovered the patient's core temperature had dropped to a dangerously low 30° Celsius. If it hadn't been for the passerby, she would have surely frozen to death.

Finally, one September day, on her way home from school, a fourteen-year-old girl came across a man hitting a woman. The young girl confronted the man and told him to stop, all the while calling 911 on her phone. The couple walked away, but the young hero followed them, updating police on their whereabouts. When the offender realized the young witness was still following, he turned to confront her. With admirable presence of mind, the girl went to a nearby residence for help. Though many people would not have become involved, this young woman followed her own strong sense of right and wrong, and did.

Noticing what needs to be done can range from a small act of kindness to a life-saving intervention.

I am proud to say I am a part of an initiative doing just that. For me, it all began one Christmas Eve several years ago. The sadness and cruelty of the night and the inspiration born from it will be with me forever.

When parents are separated, special holidays spent with children must be shared. On this Christmas Eve, it was my turn to have the kids, something I had been looking forward to for some time. But of course, in my world, along with that family joy, there's always something plotting against it—emergency work interruptions. It never fails.

On this night, it was the discovery of an infant in a dumpster not far from where I lived.

The call pulled me away from my plans moments after setting up the stockings and presents by the fireplace to be opened Christmas morning. As the kids slept peacefully in their beds, a call to grandma for assistance saved the day and I hurried to the scene, hoping I could make it back in time for Christmas morning—and I did, but with a head and heart full of questions.

Who could have done such a thing? Leaving a baby to succumb to frigid temperatures? What was the mom's life like, that she would decide to abandon her baby in such a way? Why would she not have accessed the services available in our community? Surely this was one of the reasons we have children's services and hospitals? How many other infants have met the same fate hours after entering this world? After all, what are the odds that babies abandoned this way are ever found at all?

These questions dogged me for weeks following this crime as we searched for the mother. Those weeks turned into years. Eventually, a determined and committed investigator reviewing the case caught something on video that had been missed. A woman who appeared to be mildly distressed entered a convenience store nearby the scene just after midnight, purchasing hygiene products, Gatorade, and ibuprofen. The significance of this moment jumped out at the new lead investigator and, using this snippet of video, tracked down this twenty-something gal and eventually identified her through DNA as the child's mother. Truly remarkable and brilliant police work.

And this moment seeded in me the germ of an idea: a truly remarkable and brilliant opportunity to make a difference, to put services in place so no other wee one would have to be abandoned this way. Thanks to the persistence of many who shared this vision, our city now has an anonymous baby surrender program run by some of the kindest souls on our planet who heard this story and wanted to honor this baby girl's death by partnering with fire departments and other agencies in our community. Hope's Cradle allows mothers contemplating giving up their infant to do so anonymously, without fear of discovery. In this way, the baby can be taken care of and raised by a family who can provide the things the young life needs.

Along the same vein, one officer I know recognized (through his work with infants who had been born into vulnerable situations) that there existed a gap for expectant moms deemed to be at risk: no pre-natal support programs for high-risk mothers to assist them through their pregnancies and then with the babies once they were born.

Today, this officer's vision can be seen in the Prenatal Support Team, a collaborative team made up of a police officer, a registered nurse, and two support workers, whose mission is to reduce incidents of risk to infants not yet born.

Initiatives like Hope's Cradle and the Prenatal Support Team are important in our community so we can avoid tragic stories like this: Several years ago, a man was on his way to a convenience store close to his home when he heard what sounded like the faint cries of an infant coming from a garbage bin. Could it be? He made his way closer to the source of those unmistakable cries. In the dumpster, between a few cardboard boxes and garbage bags, he found a newborn infant discarded as if their life never mattered. Taking the baby in his arms, he cradled him until police arrived.

But.

As the investigation proceeded, police identified the suspected mother, who, in a twist of fate, happened to be the rescuer's girlfriend. The baby he saved was his own, and in the arrest and interview that followed, investigators learned this was the third infant that she had discarded in this manner. The other two were never found.

It is not just actions taken by members within the police and the community that can affect change. There are also amazing families who have been so deeply impacted by the loss of a loved one that, after taking the time to understand the tragedy, they looked for an opportunity to fill the hole that led to their misfortune. They do this selflessly to—hopefully—prevent another family from suffering the same fate. Their actions make our community safer for all.

Constable John Petropoulos's widow is one such person.

At 5:40 a.m. on September 29, 2000, Constable Petropoulos and his partner were dispatched to investigate an alarm at a business in the south end of town, where it was suspected someone had broken into the building. While searching the premises, Constable Petropoulos stepped through a false ceiling, falling nine feet into the room below. He was rushed to hospital with severe head injuries and pronounced dead later that afternoon. In the analysis of the incident that followed, investigators determined there was no safety railing to warn him of the danger.

Following his death, the John Petropoulos Memorial Fund was established by his widow and several of his closest colleagues. Their goal was to eliminate preventable workplace fatalities and injuries to emergency responders by educating the public about its role in helping to keep these essential workers safe on the job.

The death of Constable Rick Sonnenberg led to the institutionalization of a different service, not only for our city but for our province.

In the early morning of October 8, 1993, Constable Sonnenberg and his partner were alerted to the theft of a vehicle and a subsequent pursuit by other responding units. As the vehicle traveled south toward their containment point, Constable Sonnenberg attempted to lay down a spike belt. The speeding car swerved into his lane, striking him. He died instantly.

A youth out on bail was convicted of criminal negligence causing death, hit and run, and possession of a stolen vehicle. Following the death, Constable Sonnenberg's sister pointed out the dangers inherent in the spike belt strategy and led a campaign to raise funds for our city's first police helicopter. By having an eye in the sky, a helicopter could monitor and track offenders intent on fleeing police while allowing ground units to maintain a safe distance. In July 1995, the police service acquired its very first police helicopter, and since the implementation of this program, police effectiveness in apprehending fleeing offenders has increased tenfold.

It's not just police families who have taken on initiatives for the betterment of all through the grief of their own circumstances. In September of 2021, the country was horrified to learn that a young mother, Mchale Busch, and her son, Noah, were murdered in Hinton, Alberta, by a sexual predator who should never have been out of custody—but was. Since that time, Mchale's partner and the father of young Noah has become the driving force behind Noah's Law, a law that, if enacted, will require convicted sexual offenders to mandatorily report any changes of residence and allow communities to be alerted when a sexual offender has moved in. But perhaps most importantly, Noah's Law also seeks wide-sweeping changes to sentencing restrictions. Although the bill has not yet been passed into law, the initiative to make our communities safer has been taken.

I believe Sir Robert Peel was right when he said, "Police are the public and public are the police; the police being the only members of the public who are paid to give full-time attention to duties which are incumbent on *every* citizen in the interests of community welfare and existence."

I feel we all have a responsibility to each other and to ourselves, to pay attention, to care, and to avoid apathy. We should not expect someone else to notice something that needs noticing. We have a responsibility to do our part to keep our communities and each other as strong, safe, vibrant, and healthy as possible. That means we must not turn a blind eye; we must not pretend we don't notice the swollen lip and black eye of the kid who just walked past; we must be brave enough to act on our own observations. We must all do our part when we are called to do so, to be more like those we have just met in the stories above.

> How many times can a man turn his head, and pretend that he just doesn't see?
> —Bob Dylan

When you see a situation that doesn't involve you but you know is not right, it's easy not to get involved. It's easy to say, "Someone else will help," or worry that without knowing the context of the situation, you could be putting your nose in and making things worse—and getting yourself into hot water as a result. Of course, as we pointed out at the opening of this section, understanding context can be critical. But situations where people will be hurt need to be questioned. It takes courage to step out of your circumscribed lane and get involved.

It takes courage to take a path that others may not choose. Uncommon people do their best not to dwell on the "what ifs" and instead take the initiative to make a change or do what others are not willing to do.

For example, I am impressed with officers who respond to reports of children playing "street hockey" on a roadway or basketball off the end of a driveway and, when they arrive, have the courage to *take* the complaint that's likely coming and instead join into the game. And yes, this has happened.

Years ago, a police officer in my organization identified conflicts between some of our young people from diverse communities. Troubled by this finding, he did more than file the report away or increase punitive policing against instigators in cultural squabbles; he came up with an unconventional solution. Together, this officer and affected community leaders used a collaborative process to identify that sport—specifically soccer—could be a unifying strategy. They proposed an annual tournament for youth from a wide range of religious and cultural backgrounds. To make this momentous task successful, many hours were required to arrange for sponsors, volunteers, marketing, registration, uniforms, facilities, and the scheduling of teams. The result created positive impacts on hundreds of youths from diverse communities.

Taking initiative is the key. These next few cases illustrate this point.

In August 2015, a cab pulled into a convenience store parking lot, and the two female passengers saw a confrontation taking place among a group of men. Leaving the cab to enter the convenience store, both women noticed a man lying on the pavement with a large gaping wound in his abdomen, his intestines outside his body. The women called 911 and yelled at the men, who were now beating a second victim. Their actions stopped the assault on the second victim and the group fled, leaving both victims behind. While waiting for emergency crews, the women provided first aid to the injured men, keeping both talking and applying pressure to their wounds. The women helped save their lives. Unbelievably, security camera footage from the convenience store showed that the first victim had lain on the ground for a full two minutes before the girls arrived, and multiple people had just walked past or over him.

One February day in 2016, a young man was walking down a well-traveled roadway when he came across a man sitting on the railing of an overpass contemplating his own demise. The passerby had recently lost a close friend to suicide. He called 911 and then attempted to talk to the man, but the distressed man would not listen. So when the time felt right and necessary, the rescuer grabbed him from the railing and pulled him back onto the sidewalk. When police arrived, a suicide note was found in the man's pocket, and he was taken to the hospital. If this young person had not intervened, he could have died. Many others had already driven past or walked by the unfolding scene.

In April 2015, four young people were skateboarding in the car park of a local mall when a well-dressed man holding up an inebriated and distraught female caught their eye. For them, things did not feel right, and they did what no one else had done in the mall that day. They stopped the pair and asked questions of the man to ascertain whether the girl was safe. The man did his best to alleviate the boys' concerns and showed them his phone, telling them he had been trying to get hold of this young lady's father without luck. The boys bought the story and watched him as he and the young female entered a car park stairwell. But something still didn't sit right. After doing another lap with their skateboards, the young men went to the stairwell and witnessed the offender sexually assaulting the woman. They slammed open the stairwell door, and the man fled. One of the boys called 911 and remained with the victim while the others chased him down, initiating a physical confrontation. Moments later, police arrived, and the suspect was arrested.

Doing what nobody else in the mall had done that day, the boys challenged the offender when things didn't feel right. They saved the young victim from further assault while demonstrating an important principle of initiative:

> Being part of a vibrant village requires us to speak up and take action.

Integrity

Recently, I was involved in a case where an older brother made the very difficult decision to tell the truth about his younger brother. The younger brother had confided that he had been involved in a murder, providing undisputable and undeniable details of the offense in his confession.

This placed the older brother in an agonizing position. The right thing was to tell investigators what he knew. However, in doing so, the elder brother risked the loss of a family member forever. But the younger brother was not just a family member; he was the older brother's *only* family. After suffering unfathomable abuses as children, both had been removed from their mother's home and grew up together in a number of foster homes. Both battled addictions along the way. One got sober, found love, and married, and the other did not. But still they remained close.

Despite their closeness, though, the older brother stood up for what he viewed as the right thing. He told detectives what he knew—knowing he would later become a witness for the police. He chose to do this because it was authentic to his inner moral compass—to do otherwise would have compromised his own integrity.

But a second example of courage came into play here. Empathizing with the brother's plight and his decision to speak out, the lead investigator grappled with how best to proceed with the information. His solution? The investigator worked tirelessly to gather *more* evidence so he did not have to rely solely on one brother's statement against the other. The investigator went beyond what was strictly necessary to go to court: he looked to forensics, to other witnesses, and to phone analytics, all in an effort to take the spotlight away from the older brother and focus the case on the other sources for the facts. Due to this diligence, the offender was convicted, but in the process, the investigative team was able to insulate the older brother from blame.

When people act in accordance with a standard moral and ethical code of conduct they are defining two other important virtues of moral courage for themselves: the integrity to match actions and words with core values and beliefs, and the discipline to set appropriate boundaries. In other words, actions you choose to take, and limits you set for yourself, demonstrate your true inner values.

Values are cornerstones you can go back to and build from during difficult times. When a person or organization can inwardly identify those values and articulate them, their ability to choose action and to set boundaries becomes conscious. Analyzing one's beliefs to discover what core principles one holds is a valuable step in this process.

But principles must be continually defended and upheld.

> The culture of any organization is shaped by the worst behavior the leader is willing to tolerate.
>
> —Gruenert and Whitaker

When we think of this in terms of a policing organization, for example, if the leadership is okay with, and turns a blind eye to, their officers beating up bad guys in alleys as part of the administration of justice, does it really matter how many good things that same organization did? They could have solved ninety-five percent of the homicides, saved countless victims from imminent harm or death, and rescued children and animals from hot cars, but at the end of the day, the organization will still be known for its worst-tolerated behavior: thuggery in the back alleys. Therefore, boundary-setting around core values within leadership is immensely important.

What will and will not be tolerated is defined through accountability. This, of course, is not easy to do. And it takes courage to do so. Over the years, I have seen leaders both excel and fail in this quagmire of reinforcing boundaries.

The note in the text box to the right is true: police officers will almost always work in environments where sin is present—even the norm, such as when working in undercover drug

> He must know where all the sin is and not partake.
> —Paul Harvey

communities—but they can never participate in any of it. This is not hard for officers who understand their core values and beliefs. More than once in my twenty years, I have been in situations where I have been around tens of thousands of dollars in cash in some drug trafficker's home and known without a doubt that not one penny of that money would go missing during the police investigation. This is because, despite the temptation this could create for some, for the highly skilled and responsible people I worked around, "stealing" did not line up with those core values. It fell outside the boundaries we set for ourselves.

I have a friend. She is one of the most amazing individuals I have ever known, a beautiful soul with a generous smile. But even more important, kindness, love, and compassion cascade out of her every pore. She has scars, yet she is an inspiration. She is an abuse survivor. She is the founder of an organization that empowers women who have left their abusers. She has a strong set of core values and an unwavering commitment to staying within the boundaries of those beliefs.

I first met this friend through a family who had lost a daughter to intimate partner violence. The family I was supporting at the time thought it would be good if we met because they knew we shared similar lofty goals—ending the cycle of domestic abuse. You see, there come times in every person's life when the opportunity presented fits. For me, this came when I was growing tired of always only *reacting* to the fatal outcomes of domestic violence. I was tired of scraping up the bodies of women from a sidewalk or carpark who had died violently at the hands of an intimate partner. I was looking to do my part to help right this listing ship.

And so, one spring day, I met a young woman for coffee, and she shared her story. Growing up in a family of limited means was at times difficult—very difficult. Sometimes, she and her family did not even have what most would consider basic needs. One Christmas, she and her siblings wished to overcome some of the struggles they saw their mother going through, and they decided they would pool together their limited resources and collectively buy her the most beautiful item they could afford. It was an antique-looking bracelet encrusted with clear, tiny gemstones (likely glass).

From the moment they bought it, they were excited to give it to her. My friend recalled that Christmas morning, when her mom opened the gift, she beamed, cried, and then the biggest smile came over her. From that day forward, each time the mother wore it, she also put on makeup, did her hair, and wore her best clothes. This tiny thing had reconnected her with being a woman and an individual, which were things she had lost touch with while struggling to support her three children for so many years.

Inspired by her mother's reaction, my friend—now a young adult—decided she would try to give that feeling to women in situations similar to those her mom had experienced. She wished to give them a boost by reconnecting them with being a woman and an individual, and to show them they had not been forgotten.

My friend's organization began in 2015 as a Christmas Jewelry Drive, in which women in the community were asked to donate their gently used jewelry. It would then be cleaned, packaged, and given as a Christmas gift to a woman who had experienced abuse and was residing in an emergency shelter. The first year, her organization was able to give 436 women a gift of jewelry, and since then, thousands more gifts were given to women across our country and even overseas.

Over time, the organization has also expanded to include public speaking events meant to raise awareness and provide support and empowerment to the survivors of intimate partner violence. It also now includes a scholarship program. Of course, like every charitable foundation, money and volunteer resources are central to its effectiveness and its ability to bring about change and hope, and to impact the community. This organization is no different.

Because of who my friend is, what she stands for, and what her messages are, she has never been short on support; she is adored and loved by many. But she is also committed to ensuring that each person who joins her team supports the organization's—and her—core values and beliefs, especially as they relate to the empowerment of women. To that end, despite what some may be able to bring to the table financially, I have watched her exercise her discretion several different times and politely say "no" to someone whom she feels may not align with what her foundation stands for.

And sometimes this is not easy. I recall one such instance where a very qualified, well-thought-of person wished to throw support into the cause she so believed in. But when a quick search of social media posts and memes revealed certain ideological differences, my friend politely said no—giving up potential financial benefits—to keep her organization's core values intact. This, too, is a kind of moral courage.

> Aligning actions, words, and beliefs reveals integrity.

People who act on their integrity align themselves with their core values and demonstrate a final virtue filtered into their moral being. That virtue, I believe, is having a clearly defined purpose.

Purpose

In today's world, many people who seek to define their life's purpose turn back to a concept that was first introduced by Aristotle: writing a personal ethos. Putting pen to paper, this practice helps some people crystalize their values, ideologies, and boundaries. The struggle to define such important but ethereal concepts in written form sharpens our understanding of ourselves, and I believe it's something uncommon people are well aligned to, within themselves. Such concrete statements allow their authors to more intentionally align their vision with action.

Often our purpose can change over time. Thinking back to when I was a twenty-something police officer, I must bashfully admit my purpose was to drive fast, kick-ass, serve my community, build my reputation within my organization, and look good doing it.

As a thirty-something police officer my purpose began to

change: do right by my family, my children, and my wife at the time; serve the community with integrity and do nothing to embarrass myself or the ones I loved. Work hard.

Today my purpose is completely different: to do today things I might consider putting off until tomorrow; to work on my legacy—my written words, memories I create with those I love, things I build; to be remembered as a person who lived a life that mattered. This purpose is in alignment with how I have matured overtime even though my core values have remained the same.

In many ways, the fundamental core values of most people have significant similarities, but there can be differences, if not in absolute values, then in priorities among our values. Having differences is normal and for the most part provides the diversity that helps society thrive. However, our adherence to our own purpose and core values, although valiant, can never be used as an excuse for harming other people.

Sadly, in our city, there have been more than a few cases in which this has occurred. Some are cases where parents have overridden the needs of their own children because of beliefs they had about Western medicines.

One of the most notorious examples of this came about ten years ago when investigators were called to look into the death of a fifteen-year-old boy who, as a child, was diagnosed with Type 1 diabetes. His parents did not accept this diagnosis and made a choice to ignore doctors' health recommendations. They believed his body did not need insulin to survive; instead, they believed that "air" was his food as God had decided. Their decision resulted in them losing custody of their son at the age of six after he had been taken to hospital in medical distress, emaciated, and in poor nutritional health. Over the following year, this boy lived with a family who fostered him until the day came when his parents were given a second chance.

The family moved to our province where they reverted to ignoring their son's medical needs. Unbelievably, by the time this young man passed away at the age of fifteen, he had lost four pounds (since he was apprehended at the age of six) and weighed only thirty-eight pounds at the time of his death. Ironically, investigative searches of the home found prescription drugs to which his mom, dad, and his siblings had access, but we never found insulin for him. Both parents were convicted of the first-degree murder of their son, whom they allowed, over a number of years, to starve to death. This was a brutal instance of adherence to a set of core values that harmed a person. Their child.

His is not the only case. I remember another investigation where a family opted to treat their infant's massive infection by freezing his feet in the snow behind the family's home—something they had read on the internet—instead of taking him to a doctor. This child suffered some of the worst frostbitten toes I had ever seen on a human being at an autopsy.

The examples above are drastic but emphasize how ethical decision making can go askew.

For some, especially those who struggle with finding direction and aligning their moral compasses, writing a simple statement—or several—can be a valuable exercise, even monumental. For example, part of Master Yoda's personal ethos is no doubt, *Do or do not; there is no try.* Simple and to the point: a personal ethos should not be vague.

My philosophy for living is set around the knowledge that one day, I will die. We all will. This means the impacts I make in this life and the experiences I have today must be as meaningful as possible—not so I can guarantee salvation in some utopia that may one day come, but so I can have the best things this life has to offer and make the greatest positive outcomes in the lives of others.

The things I want to do one day should, in fact, be the things I am doing today because, as I have been reminded so many times before, tomorrow is not promised to any of us. With that wisdom, I am going to continue to work on my legacy. I will use my written words, the memories I create with those I love, and the things I build so I can be remembered as a person who lived a life that mattered. Love people.

I believe people who live within their purpose and values will also be remembered as people who lived a life that mattered.

Live a life that matters.

Chapter 4—Frank: Social Courage

Speak your mind, even if your voice shakes.
— Maggie Kuhn, Social Activist

It was a warm September day in 1959 when the New York City Police Department welcomed a new batch of probationary patrolmen to their ranks. Among those chosen to serve was the son of an Italian policeman—Frank Serpico.

Frank began his police career in uniform, but by 1967, his career path had led him to plainclothes undercover work targeting vice, drugs, and racketeering offenses in Brooklyn, the Bronx, and Manhattan. Frank was shocked and dismayed at what he saw there: police officers receiving payoffs for turning a blind eye to crime in an effort to keep the lucrative red-light districts and drug trafficking networks protected and organized crime syndicates profitable.

So, Frank did what he believed he must: he reported what he was seeing to his superior officers, who, in turn—dismissed his concerns. I can't even imagine this today, but back in the time of boogey nights and bell bottoms, Frank must have felt the whole egg was rotten—and he wasn't wrong. That was, until February 1970. Forced by police partners who did not trust a clean cop—officers who made it plain they would make his life hard—he felt driven to contribute to a front-page story in *The New York Times* in order to see action. Frank's story, reporting on the widespread corruption he'd been witnessing, drew national media attention and compelled politicians to act. A five-member panel (now known as the Knapp Commission) was tasked with investigating accusations of police corruption.

Frank's courage did not go unnoticed amongst the rank and file of the NYPD, and by 1971, he was certainly not being invited as guest of honor to any police Christmas parties. In fact, I imagine he likely was feeling tremendous pressure from his fellow officers who'd not only lost significant income but faced discipline—all at the hands of this one *snitch*.

In February of that year, Frank and three other officers received a tip that a drug deal was about to take place in a third-floor apartment in Brooklyn. As the team set up to observe the building, Frank saw two men leave the apartment. He reported what he had seen to the other members of the team, who intercepted the pair and found a quantity of heroin on both. After arresting the two, one of Frank's fellow officers stayed with the suspects but suggested that, since Frank spoke Spanish, they go to the third-floor apartment and Frank gain entrance to the suite.

Frank agreed. He knocked, and as the door opened, he wedged his way in while calling for the officers behind him to help. The officers failed to come. Frank was shot in the face by the drug dealer. Frank shot back, hitting his assailant.

As he lay on the floor bleeding, Frank's colleagues chose not to report to dispatch that an officer had been shot. In fact, Frank's only savior on this day was an elderly man who lived in the apartment nearby, who called 911 and stayed with him. When help arrived, it was more police officers who transported Frank to hospital in the back of a police car—not an ambulance.

Frank survived the shooting, but speculation that the event was an elaborate plot to kill him persists.

Serpico's courage was the inspiration behind a book and a movie that came out two years later—*Serpico*. Al Pacino, who played Frank Serpico in the movie, reportedly asked Frank during the filming why he decided to blow the whistle (Frank called it "lamp lighting") on his colleagues. Frank said, "Well, Al, I don't know. I guess I would have to say it would be because if I didn't, who would I be when I listened to a piece of music?"

> Never doubt that a small group of thoughtful committed individuals can change the world. In fact, it's the only thing that ever has.
> —Margaret Mead

Most of us are governed to some degree by the opinions of others. People are social animals who, from childhood, depend on the group. From the time we are young, we are taught that saying *no*, particularly when there is an imbalance in power, is rude. The unasked-for sociological experiment of social isolation brought on by the COVID-19 pandemic has shown how fundamental group interaction and acceptance is to human mental health and quality of life.

So, when someone speaks out against a social group, risking exclusion or rejection, they do so at great peril. To oppose group consensus requires a different sort of courage: social courage. A single voice opposing the majority can lend courage to others of like-mindedness to join them and potentially effect monumental change.

Challenge

The strength to respectfully disagree or challenge is a key virtue in social courage. I have observed that this ability is very much a part of the Type A personality often seen in the homicide detectives I have worked with. This may be in part because of the environment in which we work and the willingness of all of us, and our supervisors, to remain open-minded. It may also, in part, be because we are wired this way.

Within our own briefing rooms, we exploit this virtue in every new investigation by assigning the position of *Devil's Advocate* as part of our team. This is a person placed on the investigative team to challenge the thinking of the moment, the strategies being discussed, the direction, and the focus. It is this person's role to respectfully provide an opposing view to the ones present in any case so the decisions we make are carefully considered before action is taken, but also to ensure they can be well articulated and defended before they ever are needed in a courtroom.

Another expression of social courage is the courage to say "no." For many of us it's not easy to say no—and so we have created three types of yesses. Two of the yesses are in fact dressed up versions of "no" with the third being the only affirmative version of this word.

Courage to say no.

The counterfeit *yes* is one in which you use the word *yes* as an escape route to avoid being rude—to avoid saying no. For example, we have all had an experience at one time or another of bumping into an old friend in the mall, and after some small talk, they say, "We should go and do coffee sometime," to which we reply, "Yes, that would be nice," all the while knowing we actually have no intention of carrying on this relationship over a coffee.

The confirmation *yes* is a more genuine response, but it lacks commitment. When the old friend says, "We should go for coffee sometime," we think, *geez, you know a coffee would be lovely*, and so we agree. We even go as far as exchanging numbers, but because there is no commitment, there's no follow-through to actually set up the coffee date.

> According to public speaker, ex-hostage negotiator, and author of *Never Split the Difference,* Chris Voss, the three types of yeses are:
> - The counterfeit yes
> - The confirmation yes
> - The commitment yes

The last *yes* is the commitment yes. This is the yes that, as a negotiator, you want to get to when dealing with a hostile situation such as a hostage negotiation. The commitment *yes* is the real deal. Back in the mall, when we bump into an old friend and say "yes," we pull out our phone, exchange numbers, and set a date in our calendar for that steamy cup of java. This *yes* results in action.

An insincere *yes* can have worse consequences than a missed connection with an old friend. Many bad decisions individuals make come from an inability to say *no*. "No, I won't drive with you because you are drunk," or "No, I won't share a cigarette because I don't want to become addicted" are types of statements that often require courage to say no.

As much as doing what is right in the face of a group's—or an entire society's—assumptions that certain things should be done in a certain way can be an admirable stance, there are some situations in which the entire burden of saying no is placed on individuals, and we as a society must work to lift that burden. Specifically, the expectation that a woman must say no to unwanted advances assumes that such advances are acceptable if the woman does not specifically deny them with a word "no". This can place a significant weight of responsibility on an individual—particularly young women emerging from adolescence and experiencing tricky social freedoms for the first time.

The phrase, "No means no," puts the issue of consent on women. Rather, men must understand that "no" can take many forms. *Pulling a shirt closed* is a "no." *You are a really nice guy but I'm not ready yet* is a "no." Taking the onus off victims who find it difficult to say no is a task every member of our society should be working toward.

In Canada, by the age of eighteen, twenty percent of girls will have experienced intimate partner violence, which includes sexual assault. But as much as violent crimes such as rape can grab headlines, women face many forms of harassment and intimidation from the macro to the micro on a frequent basis. The task of continual vigilance dictates many women's choices and behaviors, such as limiting where she can feel safe in her own city or neighborhood after dark, how she walks down a street alone at night (away from openings between buildings), which office mates she must avoid, and which jokes and comments she must endure or confront.

How has this assumption that women can be bullied come about, and what maintains it? Certainly, a history in many cultures of patriarchy and power in male hands is one factor. Another is the sense of loss and threat some men may feel as women's roles in society have shifted over the past hundred years to increase personal and group power. A third has to do with images, specifically those illustrating the relationships between men and women in our media and entertainment.

One articulate YouTube essay, *Predatory Romance in Harrison Ford Movies*, outlines how romantic action heroes, such as Han Solo, Indiana Jones, and Rick Deckard, provide a powerful example to young boys growing up about what it means to be a man. Princess Leia, Willie, Elsa, and Rachel back away, push him away, say "no" explicitly, say "stop," shake their heads, or fail to respond to his advances, yet in each of these films, the loveable rogue who takes what he wants—including women—is framed as the good guy, and the audience is shown that women's anger isn't real; that they secretly want men to force themselves on them. With powerful messaging like this—often unremarked upon—is it any wonder boys grow up thinking it's okay to press women beyond their comfort level? It is for this reason men need to step up and work collaboratively with women if we are ever to eradicate sexual harassment and abuse. Honestly, such widely accepted messaging is one of the biggest parts of the problem.

This media and social environment requires all of us to have conversations with our sons, co-workers, friends, and associates when we hear or see things we know are not right, and this is not always easy. It requires courage.

It also requires us to have conversations with our daughters, instilling in them the strength of knowing their consent is their own if ever they are to be the unfortunate one-in-four women to face abuse.

Last, it requires men to lead by example to show both our sons and daughters what healthy loving relationships should look like, so they may learn from our example.

Challenge.

If you were you to ask me what career in the criminal justice system epitomizes social courage the most, my answer may surprise you. It is a career within the system that requires those that do it to be hated, thought poorly of, and targeted in the public for their "lack of a moral compass." It is the role of defense lawyer.

Defense law is a career that functions as an important part of a democratic society, a society for which our grandparents and great grandparents fought wars, so we might enjoy our freedoms. Every day, courtrooms and lawyers' lounges across the country fill with these folks who stand ready to ensure the tyranny of the majority does not overstep the needs of the voiceless and vulnerable. For this reason, I believe defense lawyers put the exclamation point on the virtue of challenge.

One counsel I have come to deeply respect and admire over the years has been doing defense work for almost as long as I've been a police officer. Because she defends individuals whom some consider "the worst of the worst," victims of crime or their advocates—in pain—have targeted her and other defenders like her. She shared with me some of the things people have said about her over the years. There is the standard, "How do you sleep at night?" or the common insult of "Bottom feeder," and of course, at times, there have been the low, low comments left on an office voicemail, "I hope he rapes you next."

But despite these daily facts, she goes to work, in her words, "to try and make the system better." She is clear in her mind she doesn't want to live in a world where people are victimized, but she also does not want to live in a country where innocent people are convicted either. "The consequences of being convicted of something a person didn't do—jail time, a criminal record, re-integration processes, and all the fallout from these—is so severe that it's important an innocent person is not convicted." She views her role as an accountability mechanism for fairness.

Her aspirations toward this career began back in university, where she majored in women's studies, embracing a feminist identity. One of the courses she took was a criminal law class she struggled to enjoy because she felt her instructor was sexist, an opinion she expressed and challenged him on. His response changed her trajectory forever. "I would've thought because you talk like a feminist, that you would've understood that criminal law is about equity for everyone, not just women." This was her eureka moment.

She'd grown up in a conservative home with lots of rules, had a chance to see the world, and rebelled in high school. There, she found herself in difficult situations and reflects now that she could easily have slid into criminal behavior and drug addiction. She believes most people have a devious side. But she was lucky to have good parents and a good foundation of values. She chose criminal law instead of criminality.

When she started, very few women took law. However, on graduation she had no difficulty acquiring clients because she treated people well. She does not condone crime or violence, but she can see brokenness in people, and she's aware of her own imperfections, too. All people are imperfect, but some have been dealt a raw hand from the beginning. A baby does not choose to be born into poverty, into a house with addictions, or into a family culture that teaches disdain for schooling. Yet many enter daycare, preschool, grade school, and high school with a string of anchors tied to their ankles, and it is the rare, strong individual who—usually with the help of a significant positive relationship such as a teacher or counselor—transcends such difficulties.

This defense lawyer recognizes some people need to be separated from society. But everyone needs to be treated as human. One client has her name as "mom" on his phone because she has been there, through it all, with him.

She really believes the justice system can work. "If you believe a client is innocent, then it's a hard job. It weighs on your shoulders. Your best work is done when you don't have a personal belief of guilt or innocence, knowing you are making *all* players accountable."

She states, "The intellectual part of me says this: the crown, the court, and the police must

> Susan taught for five years in a school for emotionally disturbed children. Her classes included one boy who was born in prison, addicted to cocaine. Another of her students was apprehended from his parents eight times before the age of six. A third was taken into care from a van parked in a store parking lot where his parents were shopping; his baby sister's diaper had frozen to the van floor. A fourth student was gang raped at fourteen and returned to the school a few months later to show off her baby—of a different racial background—whom she was unable to breastfeed. Susan never learned whether most of her students went on to successful lives or not, because of privacy legislation, but later in life, she would occasionally run into one as a successful adult, or see the untimely death of one under violent circumstances reported in the news.

be held accountable for doing their jobs." It's a slippery slope, allowing the forces of policing and justice to get convictions on slipshod evidence and procedures—that's the path to a totalitarian state where the rights of individuals, particularly minorities, are nonexistent. "It is my profound concern that everyone is treated fairly."

"At its heart, [our system] works better than many systems of justice around the world." She wants to keep it that way.

> Finding the strength to respectfully disagree unveils unquestionable assumptions.

Humility

Another form of social courage is the ability to admit mistakes and apologize. Because the positive regard of the group is so powerful, it is embarrassing, even humiliating, to face others when we have done something to break this trust, and often it seems easier to avoid or bluff it out.

To right such a wrong is equally powerful because it takes immense courage to do so. Related to this is the ability to draw negative attention to oneself—take the hit—in order to maintain greater team cohesion. As Rocky Balboa said, "It ain't about how hard you hit. It's about how hard you can get hit and keep moving forward."

An officer I worked with who trains police phrased it this way: "If someone isn't successful in training they have to be willing to admit it. If you're resistant to feedback, if you're resistant to new ways of

> **Humility to take the hit, admit mistakes, and apologize.**

doing things, and you lack that humility to get feedback and to improve, then you will probably get into trouble out there real quick."

People often demand police accountability, both in the public arena when the actions of officers require inquiry, and in a courtroom. Anyone who has ever worn a uniform will at some point feel the scrutiny of the public. When warranted, for that matter, all professions must admit their mistakes, apologize, and make the necessary changes to ensure mistakes and abuses don't happen in the future, and to work toward rectifying systemic abuse. This takes social courage.

And, in many places, often in response to public outcry, this is finally happening. Within policing organizations across the globe, efforts are being made by specialized units, uniformed officers, investigators, and police brass to continue to improve. Improvement is a constant within my police organization. A few months before I retired and in a one-week interval, I participated in training to improve the quality of video systems in an interview suite, received training on a new portable DNA system our service acquired, learned about a new 3D video system used to detail crime scenes, and attended an eagle feather ceremony involving one of our Indigenous communities.

Do police make mistakes? Yes. They are human. And, unfortunately, a mistake made by a police officer can have huge ramifications, both because they deal with life-and-death situations, and because they are potent symbols—for good, or ill. Hence, the need for policing teams to hold themselves to a very high standard, and to examine their own actions after every event of consequence, whether that event turned out well for those involved, or not.

The debriefings in my former police service were our

platform to discuss issues, to admit when we were wrong, and to improve as we go. They were required to strengthen teams and make individuals within those teams more effective and more humane in their application of discretion.

When a person—a police officer, a lawbreaker, an everyday person—has the courage to admit their error and apologize, this act has the ability to help the person they harmed heal. Of course, there are many circumstances where an apology can never give full restitution. Murder is a heinous crime that can have effects that transcend generations, and no apology can ever bring back a life. The cost is high and repercussions unknowable when someone takes the life of another, and although it may be difficult to fathom, there have been occasions where I have seen a murderer, of their own free will, confess and apologize. There have also been instances where a murderer's apology has led to remarkable healing.

The story of Margot Van Sluytman and Glen Flett is one such example. Flett murdered Van Sluytman's father unintentionally during a Brinks robbery when Van Sluytman was a teenager. Flett served fourteen years before achieving parole, but after four years of his sentence, fed up with his life, he opened himself up to a Christian friend and had a transformative experience. Twenty-nine years after the murder, he learned about Van Sluytman's poetry and donated to her publication—which was the first step in their subsequent connection. Flett had been waiting all these years to have the opportunity to apologize, and when Van Sluytman received his letter, she described it as "a very authentic, clear, beautiful letter." Flett said he had a desire "to somehow not just say I was sorry but to show I was sorry to the people I'd harmed." When he left prison, he worked to support people recently released from prison.

After an exchange of emails, the two met. Van Sluytman described her feelings while anticipating the meeting: Flett was "the last human being who saw my dad alive. I was terrified, but I had gratitude because it was going to happen, and then I could die in peace." She described their actual meeting: "We just hugged each other, and he said, 'I'm sorry.' He was crying, and I was crying. He said, 'I'm sorry, I'm sorry, I'm sorry.' I said, 'I know. It's okay.' And it was very powerful." Ten years later, they maintain their relationship and, in fact, speak together in prisons about restorative justice.

Although Flett and Van Sluytman did not go through a formal restorative justice program, such alternatives to our traditional punitive justice system has seen worldwide growth since the 1990s.

> Based on traditional approaches of First Nations people in Canada and the US, and Maori in New Zealand, restorative justice differs significantly from justice systems inherited from Europe. European-rooted justice systems focus on what laws have been broken and how the offender should be punished. Restorative justice focusses on how the victim and others in the community have been hurt and what the offender needs to do to put things right. It usually involves a community-witnessed circle in which each party is given space and time to say what happened and how they felt, and a time for individuals and the group to reflect on what actions are needed for harmony to be restored. The restorative actions can include restitution by the offender to the victim such as money, service, apologies, or other appropriate actions. The ultimate goal is for the victim to feel a greater sense of empowerment, and for the offender to earn his or her way back into the community's good graces. Handled with skill, such practices can be very powerful.

A program Susan was involved with when she worked as a school principal used the principles of restorative justice—

though the program may have been operating under a different name—with two young girls who were involved in a serious conflict that escalated to become emotionally distressful for both. Two skilled social workers managed the intervention.

First, each of the girls and their parents were interviewed separately. This not only allowed the social workers to get a handle on the details but also allowed each participant the opportunity to feel heard and to organize their thoughts. Then both girls, their parents, and the social workers—as well as Susan as the school representative—convened to outline what had happened, to allow each participant to express what they hoped the result would be, for each participant to accept responsibility or apologize where appropriate and for the team to create a plan to move forward.

The result was outstanding, insofar as the girls (and their parents) not only were able to overcome their lingering feelings of distrust but to gain new skills and new perspectives to take into their lives.

Restorative justice is an opportunity for the offender to redeem themself and allows the victim to have an active role in the process. Studies have suggested such programs make offenders less likely to re-offend and that they have a higher rate of victim satisfaction than traditional (Western) methods of justice delivery.

The sister of a victim I know talked with me at length about her back-and-forth decision to seek a form of restorative justice from her sister's killer—her former brother-in-law, who is coming up for parole. She told me that perhaps the biggest thing that could hold her back is the thought of the pain she could unleash in family members who still nurse anger through her own quest to move past grief by resolving her relationship with her brother-in-law.

But even with those reservations, she believes facing him could be a good thing if his response is sincere, if she can believe it's not manipulated to advance his parole. She doesn't want him to suffer forever. She understands there is a realistic expectation he will get out, and she will have to face him then. Resolving the emotions before then will be best for everyone. Such a process could give her peace of mind and possibly help him to forgive himself. Ultimately, it will help her let go of some of the hurt and help him let go of some of the guilt. She hopes he can give back to society and his situation does not

> **Steps in an Apology**
>
> Most people believe the words, "I'm sorry" are all that an apology involves, but this phrase alone is hollow. Apologies should contain four elements:
>
> "I'm sorry": When sincere, this phrase can be very powerful to the person hearing it, and most people would feel that an apology that doesn't use these exact words is incomplete. However, if the words are not sincere, the apology collapses.
>
> Take responsibility: The offending person should describe what it was they did to cause harm and how that affected the victim. An apology that begins "I'm sorry *you* felt …" shifts the blame to the victim and the offender fails to show understanding of the harms they caused.
>
> Plan: The offending person should reassure the victim that they (and others) are safe; that the offender has an alternative way to face a similar situation in the future.
>
> Restitution: Although the harm caused can never be undone, the offending person should make an attempt to take a positive action toward the victim to reduce the harm as much as possible. Repairing or replacing a damaged object, a hug, community service, or a donation to a charity could all be forms of restitution. In Glen Flett's situation, he worked toward helping those leaving prison to rehabilitate.

have to be a waste of his life.

All of these are admirable—and potentially achievable—goals. A lot of work, but worth it if done with skill and caring.

I recently watched a man convicted of murder stand in front of a courtroom packed with people who hated him and hated what he had done, deliver a statement to the court that was heartfelt, sincere and apologetic. Isn't it true a sincere, "I am sorry" is one of the most powerful phrases within the English language? It can even create an empathetic response from those who choose to accept it.

When a person accused of a crime like murder walks into an interview with the intention of owning up to their actions, some are trying to influence their own trajectory. In Canada, a murder conviction means a life sentence, with a to-be-determined parole eligibility date—and only thirty percent of offenders who are convicted of murder ever actually get parole; the other seventy percent stay in jail until literally their heart stops beating. So with that on the line, when an accused does have the courage to "face the music"—if they can muster the strength or have remorse to do so—their acceptance of responsibility, they believe, can weigh significantly in their favor. I have seen this play out many times during my career and with many different types of accused.

One of my colleagues (I believe) still holds the record for the fastest confession to ever come out of one of our interview suites. It was about six years ago when a woman who had been human trafficked was found murdered inside a vehicle with her underwear wrapped around her neck. Following this awful discovery, it did not take long for us to put the pieces together, in part because she had been found on the passenger side of a vehicle associated with our suspect. Sometimes it just isn't rocket science.

Once the suspect was in custody, it was the interviewer's responsibility to learn what happened. So, our interviewer readied himself for what we believed was going to be a long night, pulling together the interview material he would present to our arrestee.

In the end, the interview and confession sounded like this: *knock, knock, knock*; the interviewer enters the room and begins to shuffle toward his chair; the accused clears his throat and begins, "I really didn't mean to choke that girl." He spoke before the clock hit the thirty-second mark. The only thing left was collecting the details.

The reverse of having the courage to apologize is having the courage to forgive. People who have been wronged—people in pain—can find this extremely difficult. It takes time to heal from loss, and as Elisabeth Kübler-Ross famously theorized, people in grief typically face denial, anger, bargaining, depression, and even acceptance—sometimes repeatedly—before they can come to an ultimate and enduring acceptance of their loss. In some cases, people become stuck in one or more of these stages and have a great deal of difficulty moving on; yet as Reverend Dale Lang, father of Jason Lang (student shot in the W. R. Myers High School shooting in Taber, Alberta, in 1999) said: "To hold anger within yourself damages you more than it damages the person with whom you are angry."

To find the strength to let go of anger and grief, and to forgive, is its own special kind of courage. Sometimes the person you must forgive is yourself.

In the 1980s, attending grade school in an upper-middle-class neighborhood, one of my classmates was very different from the majority of children from more privileged backgrounds. She was awkward, introverted, and didn't dress the same or come from a family with the same spiritual beliefs as others in our class. She was not allowed to celebrate birthdays, Halloween, Christmas, or other holiday events, and she would have to sit such things out when they came up in school. She was the kid with the thick-rimmed glasses who wore heavy leotards and heavy woolen clothes.

As she got older, she was not allowed to experiment with makeup and certainly was never permitted to attend a school dance; her clumsiness would never have allowed her to make a school sports team. This, of course, led to bullying, which, back then, was left relatively unchecked. As we all grew older, this bullying magnified.

I knew what was happening to her was wrong. I saw people knock books out of her hands in the hallways and laugh; I saw people blow spitballs into her hair. I felt bad, but back then I did not have the strength to stand up to those who were doing it. Some were my friends and others were cute girls I wanted to make my friends. But in the end, I choose to do nothing publicly to address the wrong things that were happening.

I didn't completely ignore it, though. After school, I knew we walked home the same way and so one day I decided to wait for her about a half block from the school, offering to walk her the rest of the way home.

Our after-school walks and talks lasted for about two weeks in my grade eight year. That was until the "mean girls" got a hold of her one day. "Who do you like?" they repeatedly asked as she was pinned against a set of hallway lockers. Eventually giving into the pressure, her voice quivered as she said, "Dave Sweet."

Oh my god. You have just ruined my life, I thought as her response spread around the school like wildfire. Now, in full damage control, I painted my regret at that moment. I told her, "I don't like you, and we can't be friends anymore. No more walks, no more talks." And that, right there, was the end of it.

Damn. As I write this, I still feel the ugly emotions that overtook me in an effort to maintain self-preservation that day. My damage was short-lived as, no doubt, some new piece of gossip trumped mine a day later, but the damage was done. I imagine her isolation lasted a long time afterward. While researching her on Google recently, I came across her obituary. She'd died suddenly at the age of forty-one. In life, she'd become a personal care assistant in Home Care, and never married.

And, as this story illustrates, forgiving oneself is hard; it is a type of courage I still struggle with. But I'm working on it.

Finding the strength to apologize, to forgive, or to forgive yourself is a rare gift.

Synergy

It was mid-April when our city encountered another sad case of a missing mother and child, both presumed murdered even though their bodies had yet to be found. A suspect at the time told the interviewer he was "the last person to have seen them alive." As the case began to narrow in on him, the mystery was: where he had discarded the bodies?

Weeks had gone by, and we were hampered by snow that blanketed the search area where we believed we would find their remains. Cadaver dogs and teams of searchers failed to locate either victim in the vast wilderness just west of the city.

Then it happened. We got the break we needed to locate the missing victims. Our offender decided he needed to tell someone what he had done; he boasted to two men he had just met, unbelievably agreeing to take them to the location of the remains. The two men, of course, were plainclothes officers.

> **A willingness to put trust in others. To trust your team.**

But, to obtain the location, the surveillance teams assigned to support the two undercover operators had to make some major concessions in the risk management department. As our suspect and his new friends headed out of the city toward the foothills, cellular phone reception became non-existent, and roads became remote. The surveillance teams in the city had no ability to hear or see what was going on. We all held our breath and waited. An hour went by.

Now ...

Imagine you have just met someone suspected of killing two people without any real cause. Imagine this person has agreed to take you to a lonely and desolate place to show you where he buried the victims. Imagine the guts required to agree to such a plan.

Imagine, on the way out to this desolate location, you notice the killer has a knife on the front seat of the car.

You've parked on a gravel logging road overhung by dense spruce trees, and the silence of the night is the only thing you can hear. Well, that and the crunching of the snow under your feet as you and your partner leave the car and walk into the woods with this man.

It's now three o'clock in the morning as you approach the burial location. Under the forest canopy, the snow is thinner, and in places, the underbrush is bare. Imagine how your heart must be racing, knowing you are seconds away from being brought into the dark secret of a murderer, the only light guiding you beneath the canopy of spruce boughs coming from your cell phone.

I should also mention that you are unarmed.

You hear the words, "It's right there."

Now, in the dark, your eyes must strain to try and identify the disturbed earth of the grave site under the camouflaging brush and forest debris. The killer marks it by throwing a cigarette onto the dried mulch that covers the victims' final resting place, and all you can think about is how to extinguish the cigarette before the trees catch fire—without raising suspicion that you have this care.

After you are shown the site, you must remain composed for your long drive back to the city with your new killer friend so you can inform the team of the morbid find. Imagine that you did all this only three hundred meters from a grizzly's den.

This, in the end, was the reality faced by two amazingly talented undercover police officers. Because of their ability to put trust in their training, each other, and their team, they were able to successfully locate and return these missing victims to the family.

This is a dramatic example of how two officers had no one to trust but each other and about how the surveillance team, hamstrung by an inability to follow and support them, had to trust the two officers to keep themselves safe.

But there are other, less dramatic, occasions where trusting the team is key.

In policing, sometimes we get to pick our teammates but sometimes it's the "spares off the bench" who become our temporary team mates. Many examples of valor come from putting trust in the spares off the bench.

In January 2009, two investigators went to the probation office to assist in the arrest of a disruptive offender on behalf of the offender's probation officer. When the offender spotted the two police officers entering the front door of the probation office, he became agitated. Within minutes, the fight was on. Having difficulty subduing the man, the officers barked for the probation officer to use his portable radio to call for help: "Officer in trouble."

And they were: the offender was fighting vigorously to disarm one of the two members. The commotion caught the attention of another probation officer, who joined in the fray. Now, three people were involved in this man's arrest, and he was not giving up easily. The quick-thinking probation officer sounded the office's internal alarm, which brought more help. In the end, the offender was arrested—but only after fighting with police for almost five minutes (a long time for a fight, despite what you might think from the movies), and all survived with a few bruises and one broken ankle. An example of synergy cobbled from team members who had never met.

Although these are examples of people trusting others because they must—they were thrown into situations where there was no choice—and because they could rely on certain role and training expectations, most trusting relationships are built over time. Trust comes from a person demonstrating, usually in small but consistent ways, that they will follow through on promises. It develops in spite of knowing that, to put your trust in someone, you must open yourself up to be vulnerable to being hurt. Anyone who has trusted unwisely and experienced this knows the fear that can result. This is one of the reasons making a promise is a serious commitment. This is especially true when making a promise to a child, as children are by the nature of their inexperience, more vulnerable.

But in situations where people come through with trust, the resulting joy ranges from pleasurable to ecstatic. Loving spousal relationships build synergy over time through small and large promises and dependability.

Some relationships develop quickly out of need. An actor on a stage trusts the other actors to fill their role, and being part of a great performance is a heady rush. A mountaineer puts incredible trust in the members of their rope team—even if they've never met before—because they are literally putting their lives on the line.

And breaking trust—failing to keep a promise, whether explicit or implied—can leave lifelong scars. Re-building broken relationships can take years and, in some instances, can never be fully healed. To trust again after experiencing the pain of broken trust can take tremendous courage.

In October of 2014, while driving her regular route, a bus driver pulled her bus to the curb to pick up a passenger who paid his fare, but when he moved to the back of the bus she heard a commotion. The man and another passenger had begun to argue. The new passenger yelled, "I have a knife! Get all the men off the bus. Call police!"

The driver pulled to the side of the road and opened the side door. She asked the ten male passengers to leave (which they were happy to do), but not the four female passengers. The man stopped them as they tried to leave, then turned his focus on the bus driver herself. The driver, remaining calm, negotiated with him to allow the women to leave, to which he eventually agreed. Threatening her, he demanded she drive him downtown.

"You asked me to call the police," she replied, "so we should wait for them as you requested. They are on their way."

And they were. When the police arrived, they opened a dialog with the offender. At the same time, nonverbally, they directed the bus driver to the back of the bus. The driver and police, in a coordinated effort, were able to isolate the man at the front of the bus. That was when the tactical team entered and took the man into custody.

Teamwork plus trust adds up to the virtue of synergy.

> Teamwork recognizes the whole will always be greater than the sum of its individual parts. It takes courage to trust the strength of the team.

Leadership

Susan worked for many years as a teacher, and for the last eleven years of her work with our city's major school board, was an elementary school principal. One initiative pursued by the board used the catch phrase, "courageous leadership."

What is courageous leadership? It is the sum of the elements of social courage outlined here. The strength to respectfully disagree can apply to helping parents understand board initiatives or helping teachers understand parents' desires, as well as the ability to become a devil's advocate within the larger school system. The courage to say no to any of these groups must be guided by what is best for children. Humility to take the hit, admit mistakes, and apologize is an important step in any plan to improve student learning because not every initiative we try will be successful. Honoring loyalty must be tempered with personal integrity when multiple groups—parents, teachers, students, administrators—each have a different view of what might constitute the greatest good; the principal's loyalty and integrity must align with what is best for children. Taking initiative is a key element of courageous leadership. Trusting your team means giving teachers the space to be the best they can be, recognizing that parents want the best for their children, and appreciating that senior leadership's moves to initiate change are based on having their fingers on the pulse of cutting-edge understandings in educational research.

All theoretical? Maybe, but there are times when the rubber hits the road. Having the courage to face a stricken first-year teacher with an evaluation stating she is not meeting the standards needed to acquire a tenured position despite multiple attempts to help her improve is key to ensuring the learning needs of many classes of students who would learn from her over the years of her career. Challenging the assumptions of an entrenched teacher in a social situation when he badmouths his employer. Helping an angry parent who wants to scapegoat a child with poor social skills to understand that the school is there for all children, not just her own. These are all face-to-face encounters where it might be easier to be a wishy-washy leader who agrees with everyone and stands for nothing.

As Susan shared what she believed courageous leadership meant to her, it struck a chord in me. For years, I have spoken to a variety of groups both within and outside of policing. One of my favorite exercises to do with smaller groups is to challenge them to come up with five key attributes of a great leader. Those attributes have been remarkably consistent across groups. People believe great leaders are transparent, accountable, trustworthy or honest, fair and equitable, knowledgeable, and supportive.

Never have I seen a group say that one of the qualities of being a leader comes from rank or position within an organization. You could be a sergeant, a chief, a principal, or a manager but if you do not possess those attributes people admire then you are not a leader, and this is why people may resist you and what you are trying to achieve. Leadership has nothing to do with rank, and has everything to do with the qualities a person possesses. Good food for thought.

I believe courageous leaders are those who go out every day and pave a path forward for others to follow. Sometimes leading from the front and sometimes from behind.

One exceptional example in my field comes from the first women who pioneered policing; the ones who faced barriers—structural, social, emotional, even physical—but trudged forward to pave a path for others to follow.

Back in 1998, I received my badge from the first woman chief in our organization's history. She had been hired from an outside agency only a couple of years earlier and had come to our city to implement change in the culture of our organization. First working systemically, dismantling the "old boys' club," she led a series of progressive initiatives, particularly in the area of intimate partner abuse and violence. Under her supervision, the newly formed Domestic Conflict Unit was one such example which remains today.

But the truth is, women in early policing who were trying to pave the path forward faced situations that, by today's standards, would be intolerable: "There were bullies in the unit, and my partner and I were targeted," one veteran officer reported in a documentary series shown at the Calgary Police Interpretive Centre called *Policewoman*.

"We were doing some really good work, and we were selected to go to Homicide for a six-month secondment, and there was jealousy. It led to some very unprofessional behavior, talking behind our backs, criticizing our work, criticizing even the way we dressed. It was just ridiculous. I worked with some remarkable men, but these clowns were a small percentage."

"We had snaps on our shirts when I first joined the job," another female police officer said. "One guy just walked up and ripped my shirt open. I punched him in the nose. 'I just wanted to see if you were wearing a vest. Ha, ha, ha.' Everybody laughed. Oh well. I punched him."

"Even as a junior officer, I said to myself, *I have to get to a position where I could change these things*," a third policewoman said. "I had to get into a position where I could remove the barriers that existed. My last few years were tough because I was working on gender equity. It was really hard to be that loud, pounding-on-the-table voice saying, 'We have to do this. We can't do that because it is unfair. We can't treat people that way.' I was pretty unpopular. There were a number of times I considered quitting. But I didn't."

Sometimes, the courageous leadership focused on what might seem like a very small thing—like women wearing the same uniform as the men. But it wasn't small. First, women couldn't do proper policework hampered by silly clothing or without the correct equipment, but second, the symbolism of the clothing could hamper their authority:

"We were doing the same work," the veteran officer said, "but when I first started policing, they put me in a skirt. 'Don't even bother,' I said. 'I'm never going to wear it. Waste of money.'"

"We carried a snub-nosed revolver in our *purse*." The reminiscing policewoman shook her head. "We'd go to a car or a complaint or an incident, and invariably, the person we stopped would defer to the man because he had the uniform that looked like a policeman. I looked like the mail lady."

"They must have put us through twenty different styles of hats," another chuckled. "The men would always be doing something with your hat. Flatten it and stick it in a pigeon hole, hide it. And they'd charge us for a new hat. It took years to fight that war to get the same type of hat as what was issued to the men."

"At the time, one of the officers' boyfriends was a leatherworker, so he made us a gun belt," a policewoman said. "I walk in, and the chief says, 'The pants I approved. I don't think I approved the equipment belt.' 'Well, sir,' I said, 'maybe you should.' And by the end of the meeting, it was approved. It might seem like a small step, but once you have the same uniform, it's clearer that you are equal."

Social courage is courageous leadership.

Chapter 5—Galileo: Intellectual Courage

Man cannot discover new oceans unless he has courage to lose sight of the shore.

— Lord Chesterfield

I grew up in a family that valued science and education. My father was a well-respected paleontologist. My mother was a teacher. Among the many dinner guests at our table on a Saturday or Sunday evening over the course of my childhood were people like the professor who told me birds could be descended from dinosaurs or another who entertained me with stories of dinosaur flatulence. As a kid, I heard many amazing theories of science from some incredibly smart people.

I clearly remember my dad's respect for one scientist, particularly as a result of some of the challenges he faced and overcame early in his career. As a young scientist, he pursued evidence of the cataclysmic event that ushered in the end of the Cretaceous period. The Chicxulub crater in the Gulf of Mexico provided evidence to support what he believed was the impact site of a large asteroid event, which ultimately wiped out seventy-five percent of species when it hit the earth sixty-six million years ago.

He'd pitched his theory to a room full of colleagues, many

of whom dismissed his findings outright. Some would have taken the censure as a reason to abandon his ideas, but not this man. Undeterred, he continued to collect, publish, and speak about the evidence he collected from the Chicxulub crater despite ongoing opposition. But his perseverance ultimately paid off, and now, thirty years later, his theory is almost unanimously accepted as scientifically sound.

Intellectual courage.

When people choose to deny evidence supporting new ideas or perspectives, it may be for many reasons. Scientists tend to be conservative by nature and may demand experimental replication or other types of supporting evidence. However, rejection of new theories may occur because of bias or because the new evidence contradicts one's own cherished thoughts. A sense that another has "won" may lead some to feel their own work, sometimes over years or decades, is now considered useless. Such rejection of evidence can be dangerous in the pursuit of the truth.

In policing, denial of evidence can lead to the wrongful conviction of an innocent person. In science, the dismissal of evidence could prevent a major breakthrough that could benefit millions of people. Openness to accepting new ideas, perspectives, and insights as new evidence is discovered is a good thing; certainty resides among the foolish. Even courts, in assessing guilt, recognize this: there is no requirement for guilt to be *certain*, but it must be likely *beyond a reasonable doubt*.

Without the willingness to accept new perspectives, ideas, or insights, and without people who are brave enough to promote them, we would still believe the earth is flat, and that our planet is the only one, with the universe revolving around it. Lawyers advocating for those who are wrongfully convicted would be out of work, and cold case homicide offices would not need to exist.

Good science is evidence-based, just like good police work. The use of logic can change the way we think and interact with the world around us and inspire others to think differently.

Expertise

In the case of one policewoman I know, Picasso's mantra could not ring truer. It was the late '90s when she received a call from the police recruiting unit saying, "Congratulations, you are the newest member of Recruit Class 123." From that day on, she was set on her path—ultimately becoming an influencer within our organization through her lifelong calling and passion to protect and work with children.

> The meaning of life is to find your gift. The purpose of life is to give it away.
> —Pablo Picasso

Her journey into law enforcement was not conventional. As a child, she never dreamed about wanting to be a police officer; she wanted to work with kids and be a positive influence in their lives. She started her postgraduate studies focused on this goal, but her family felt her educational pursuits would not provide her with the means to support herself. Then, a friend suggested policing could perhaps be a better choice, with a more stable income, career flexibility, and a better pension than what she expected from academia. Influenced by her friend's comments, she decided that policing could be the "real job" that her family wished for her, so she mustered the courage to change directions and applied. In her mind's eye, it did not hurt that the police had always had a relationship with education and with child protection.

As a young, uniformed patrol officer, more often than not, she would get the nod from her teammates whenever an assignment came up at a local school to have a police officer attend a career day or classroom. The police force was happy to send their fresh-faced recruit into the fray to speak with wide-eyed students about safety and the role of police in the community. During this time, she recognized a void in this informal practice of responding to school requests that could be improved—an opportunity to make these visits more impactful and more meaningful. Inspired, she created a unique program for students across the city that would ultimately influence the culture of our whole organization.

Most people remember times when police officers came to the classroom or auditorium to talk about their careers. Somehow, unsupported by curriculum expectations, many officers found themselves falling back on sharing stories of the craziest foot chase they ever had or the fastest car chase they were a part of. Cops love to tell stories. At times, these "war stories" likely went darker. "What was the worst thing you have ever seen?" is a common question I've often heard a youngster ask from their blanket of naivety. Answering truthfully would be like throwing a hand grenade into a developing young mind. Unfortunately, this question has likely been answered by some, even if it should not have been.

But my colleague recognized these pitfalls; how police officers, trying to be the good guys on a career day or a classroom visit—telling scary stories, showing pictures of a person in the evolution of meth addiction, or locking a kid up in a jail cell—could, in the end, be doing more harm than good.

No one learns in an environment of fear or trauma. She

believed that campaigns such as "Just Say No to Drugs" or "Scared Straight" were attempting to do just that—educate children through fear—even though there was no evidence to suggest these types of programs worked.

She shared an analogy she learned from a mentor and child psychologist about dandelions and orchids (see box) and wondered, "Is there something that can be done to develop better resiliency in children? To prepare them for our often-hard world by providing them with some of the tools they will need to make good choices moving forward? As an organization that had already developed a good relationship with youth education and the schools, was there something more we could do to make our visits to schools more impactful and more meaningful?"

Her ideas around this caught the attention of a visionary police chief who believed in community policing, and who believed people with ideas were the engines of any organization. He gave her the green light to develop a program. So, she began working with several wonderful community partners to create a strength-based series of modules for students from kindergarten to grade six. For example, instead of talking about domestic violence to a class of grade three students, police officers could instead

> Children come in two flowers—dandelions and orchids. Dandelion kids constitute 80% of all kids, and they can flourish in almost any environment: they can grow through cracks, they can grow in poor soil—they really can grow anywhere; they are resilient. Orchid kids need the right set of environmental conditions to flourish. They require the right amount of light, warmth, and care.
>
> —Dr. Thomas Boyce

work with students through discussion points, activities, and reading materials that spoke about healthy relationships, respecting boundaries, working through disagreements, and how healthy relationships feel. The program honored the principle of *do no harm*, while creating positive interactions between police and students—ultimately leading to a win for the police and the students alike.

This framework also allowed for something more. Now, trained police officers working with educators could more easily identify those children who were already in need of help or support, were being victimized or exploited, or who were living in environments of risk. Once identified, those students could then be recommended to partnerships between police and social workers in support of the healthy development of children.

For her efforts, dedication, and passion for improving the quality of life for all children living in our community, this colleague was awarded our service's highest honor: the Chief's Award Of Merit For Community Service. Her visionary leadership demonstrated what I believe is another key attribute of the uncommon person: the confidence to be exceptional and hold yourself out to be an expert.

> **The confidence to be exceptional.**

For some people the word "confidence" can imply arrogance, conceit, or even closed-mindedness. But confidence is none of these things. Speaking out, even when one is an authority on a subject, is not an easy thing for many people to do. Agreeing to take on a leadership role and become an expert can mean becoming a target.

Intellectually strong people must have the courage to ignore their naysayers, listen to the valid points of those who honestly bring a different perspective, and clearly articulate their own expertise supported by evidence and logic in a world where expertise can come at a cost.

This was the case for my colleague referenced above, who developed police school programs. What she was able to accomplish in the schools with the help of a dedicated group of experts and partners did not come without criticism from some of the members of our organization—and early on, I was one of them.

Why? At that time, it seemed to me that sending police into schools to read to children or talk to them about healthy choices was us not staying in our lane—not even close. I believed this was the job of a teacher or a guidance counselor, not a cop who was needed dearly in other places—like the street where calls for service seemed to increase exponentially every day.

But she saw it differently, and so did the chief. Intercepting and diverting high risk children into supportive programs could ultimately reduce the number of calls to service into the future—and reduce the personal heartache that accompanied the road to police apprehension. My colleague's—and the chief's—courageous leadership promoted the idea that by helping kids who were at higher risk develop into positive, contributing members of our community was a very powerful crime reduction strategy.

But the problem was and will continue to be entrenchment. Not only in the police force (Susan certainly experienced it in the school system), but in any walk of life, a person touted as an expert, whether they be a school principal, the developer of a new program, or the chief of police, will be viewed by some as an upstart. "Why should I change?" "Isn't my work good enough—you want me to do things differently?" "You don't understand what I'm dealing with—I've done things this way for a long time, and they work." "Those fancy university studies are out of touch with real life." And—"Go ahead and talk during your boring meeting. I'll go back to my classroom—or go on my school police visit—and do things the same old way." My colleague faced these issues.

For the health and survival of this—or any—new program, the person who becomes an expert must not only demonstrate the new idea's validity but also bring others onside. Cops wanted to know the statistical impact of such a program on crime *now*. But the truth is, the answer to that question is still a generation away—and the program needs to run, and run according to its parameters, over a sufficient time for an impact to be felt. At this writing, it will be up to other like-minded leaders to support her vision into the future. If they do, however, I have no doubt that the final answer could be remarkably significant. Yes, I have now drunk the Kool-Aid and believe. Uncommon people—their vision, dreams, and passion—can be infectious.

I think many people would agree they have—or need—a "person in their corner, their go-to" at work. A trusted work partner provides a much-needed perspective or solution to everyday problems in the office. They can even provide guidance personally. For me, one of those people is a talented woman for whom I have great respect and had the pleasure of working with for many years. She is someone I've known for over a decade and someone I've always trusted to be my greatest resource in any investigation. She holds the distinction of being the longest-serving civilian member of the Homicide Unit's 137-year history. With just over fourteen years in the unit, I hold the same distinction on the sworn side.

Always impeccably styled, with blue eyes and long blond

hair, she isn't necessarily what you would think a twenty-year veteran in the Homicide Unit would look like. Competent and confident in her abilities, she always welcomes you with a "What's up?" and an eagerness to support our investigations. Often one of the first in on an early morning call-out, her ponytail can be seen just above two large computer screens in our unit's briefing room as she pounds out the answers to our greatest questions from the multitude of databases she searches whenever a new murder has occurred.

Growing up, she always had an interest in becoming either a police officer or a lawyer, but as she neared the end of college, police services across the country were putting freezes on hiring. It wasn't until an instructor at the school she was attending encouraged her to consider a position as a crime analyst that she even gave this route much thought. What she knew for sure was that she did not want a career where you punched a clock, where it was the same thing every day, five days a week. So, the thought of being an analyst was tempting.

Her first placement was in the organized crime section, a fast-paced environment where she was required to track gang trends through the analysis of already completed investigative work. She was expected to possess an immense amount of knowledge of the who's who in the underworld. But—after only a few short years, the Homicide Unit came knocking on her door.

She vividly remembers, early on in her career, spending as much time helping some of the more senior, computer-illiterate investigators with their computer skills as she did her analytical work. However, as younger officers came on board and police computer literacy improved, more of her time was spent doing what she was really hired to do: sift large amounts of data to support investigations.

It was also during this time that she carved out her purpose and found her niche. She became the analyst for a very complex investigation into a well-orchestrated organized crime hit, which occurred one night outside a downtown bar. For weeks, she poured over spreadsheets of phone data gathered through countless court orders and warrants, looking for that needle in the haystack that would prove our suspects' phones were in communication with one another—and in the same geographical area as each other at the time of the murder. Eventually—frazzled and thankful—she found it, but after going through the ordeal of that experience, she thought there had to be a better way to analyze cellphone data. With that in mind, she began the process of building a better mouse trap.

She began by learning about the software tools of the trade, taking courses, both on her own time and on the company's. She studied mapping software and its application in cellphone analysis. She learned the lingo and definitions cellphone providers use: beam, azimuth, radius, and sector, to name a few. She developed key contacts within the cellphone provider companies.

Why did she put in this kind of effort? First, she wanted to make the analytical work easier. Second, there were very few analysts working in this field, and only a small number of courses available to take on the subject, leaving the power of forensic analysis relatively untapped.

Today, this colleague has created and teaches the courses she desperately wanted all those years ago. Now considered an expert in cellphone analysis, she has traveled across the country and around the world, teaching crime analysts and investigators about cellphone analytics. Her dedication and willingness to explore this valuable tool have had immeasurable impacts on modern police investigations she has been a part of.

Like back in 2015 when a concerned family reported a loved one, a young man, had gone missing. His last sighting had been in our city, though the family home was located in a nearby bedroom community. His loved ones knew that when he was depressed, he would often travel back to that area. However, although rural cellphone locals may appear small on a map, in reality, they represent vast expanses of space, which require logistics and a bit of guesswork on the part of searchers combing fields and forests. This is where any extra help is always welcome.

In this particular case, investigators were able to acquire the despondent man's cellular phone data. Through a humanitarian exemption in the law, they also obtained cellular tower locations, which were then turned over to our crime analyst. An analysis of this data made her realize the search efforts were occurring on the wrong side of the river. Within hours of re-deployment, searchers came across the man—deceased. Although the outcome was hard for the family, the recovery of his remains provided them with some degree of closure.

In this test case, this type of phone analysis was proven to be a legitimate tool for use by investigators.

Later that same year, a young man was abducted from the city following a child custody dispute between himself and his ex-wife. Although, early on, three suspects were identified through surveillance camera video, all efforts to locate the victim had failed. Then, a helpful engineer provided cellular phone tower data, and our analyst plugged in a software tool to create a propagation map that got us closer to marking an "x" on the spot. The remains of the young man were found a month later in a burned-out oil barrel. Three people were eventually arrested and charged with his murder—one of those being the mother of his child, who was the alleged mastermind of it all.

But perhaps the most notable of her investigations is also one that captured the hearts of our entire community and country. It occurred in the summer of 2016 when the young mother of a four-year-old girl was found deceased in her home. Family members checking on the mother found her stuffed into a closet laundry hamper, and the grisly discovery prompted an immediate call to the police. When cops on scene found no trace of her daughter, shock waves rippled through our community, and the investigation ramped up to a feverish pace.

Fifty investigators assigned to the case saturated the area of the child's home, looking for any clue that could assist us in identifying where she might be. Pouring over video collected from homes and businesses in the area, investigators turned up evidence from a surveillance video that depicted our young victim walking hand in hand with an unidentified man. In the video, it was clear the youngster was crying. She was led to a dark sedan parked not far from her mother's home. Our hearts sank.

It didn't take long to identify a suspect as a man known to the mother, as well as to find a phone number for him. Surveillance teams observed the man's home, but no sightings of the little girl were made. As he left his residence alone, he was arrested and brought back to our office for an interview.

Where was the little one?

This question weighed heavily on our minds and even heavier when a search of the suspect's home failed to find her.

As the first interviewer assigned to speak with the suspect, I wrestled with the question of how much pressure was too much to get a guy talking. How far should I—and *could* I—push the boundaries? He didn't say a word. Was torture off the table? Some would say yes—others no. What I did know was that we all hoped to find this beautiful little girl alive, and any statements from him about her whereabouts would go a long way toward that goal. Still nothing, and we didn't have enough evidence to hold the guy.

It was Day 7 by now and national news. We were working well into the night, going home, getting a few hours' sleep, and coming back to beat our brains out over it all over again.

Then.

One o'clock in the morning. The analyst working on phone use records and mapping software saw a pattern. And she knew.

The suspect had used his phone multiple times in quick succession, his texts pinging from cell tower to cell tower in the hour immediately after he'd picked up the child. A straight line out of town. A five-minute silence. A straight line back to town.

She gave herself a moment—just got up and left the room, went to the printer, and printed off the map. The primary investigator happened by at that moment. "Are you okay?"

"We have to talk. I have something you need to see."

She took him back to the boardroom and put the map down, expecting to talk just to the primary investigator, but she turned around and saw a ring of officers crowded behind her. So she put the map down. "I think she's dead, and I think she's going to be out here, east of the city." The analyst pointed to a map. "He took a quick trip just outside the city's east side. This is where you will find her. Because of the turnaround time, she will likely be found not too far off the road. Likely under the cover of some bushes."

It was 01:30 and pouring rain, pitch dark, and everybody—*everybody*—in that room was like, "Tell us where we need to go. We need to do something." I don't know how many cars went out with flashlights just to check and see if they could find any sign of her. Obviously, nothing.

But when the sun rose, we recovered the body. As the

analyst predicted, it was just off the road and under some brush in the area she'd told us to look.

The suspect was convicted for the murder of both mom and daughter and received a life sentence with no eligibility for parole for twenty-five years.

It takes courage to become an expert—to hold yourself to a higher standard than others—to learn new things, and to put in the time to eventually hold this rank. Putting time into your expertise means you are not spending it on other things. Without our analyst's commitment to service and desire to be as effective as she could, it's quite likely that at least one of the people in the cases highlighted earlier would never have been found.

A dear friend and colleague of mine found his calling in the area of child death investigation. Not unlike our analyst, he worked to sharpen his expertise after going through a trying investigation of his own—but unlike our analyst, this one involved a young child. Following the conclusion of that emotionally difficult investigation, he went through his own self-analysis and realized that he and the rest of us were limited in the skill-specific expertise that an investigator should possess when it came to investigating the death of the child. His recognition of his own limitations and initiative to seek out feedback and new opportunities for improvement and learning is an attribute of courage displayed by the most uncommon of people.

He recognized, as I do now (thanks to his efforts) that child death cases are much more complicated in their pathology than, say, the death investigation of a teen or adult. This is because often, the cause of a wee one's death lies under the surface—it is not as easily detectable as it is in an adult victim. Thankfully, it is rare to see an infant die as a result of stabbing or shooting, but shaking is not that uncommon—and not always obvious on an external examination because the evidence lies inside the body. Inside the brain.

Why do police, as a collective, not possess the type of expertise this investigator sought out? The answer is not hard to imagine. Few cops wake up in the morning hoping to become involved in the death investigation of an infant or child. These cases are sad, troubling, and not easy on the mind. Regardless, their resolution is necessary: children do die on occasion, and they do die at the hands of another.

As an expert in child death investigation, my colleague became keenly aware of how important those initial interviews are and what questions should be asked. He learned about what to look for at a scene, and he learned the lingo and terminology doctors used so he could better understand what their descriptions and reports meant. And, he shared his newfound knowledge with the rest of us—he didn't guard or hoard it to himself.

His willingness to become engaged in such difficult subject matter, to attend conferences, meet with other experts in the field, and develop connections made him an invaluable asset to our team. The day he resigned, the unit was left with a void, which remains unfilled.

Honest self-understanding can give the confidence to be exceptional.

Seeking Growth

We admire people who recognize their own limitations. This is not always an easy thing to do—it makes us vulnerable. For this reason, many people mask their limitations or try to work around them instead of simply asking for assistance. Concerns over what others might think because we don't know something prevents some of us from raising our hands. So, when an investigator comes, hat in hand, to ask a question or seek advice, one must listen. Over my career, I have always been impressed by those who do.

One very young officer I met a decade ago came looking for advice in relation to the sudden death of a sixty-year-old woman found one February morning in her recliner. In this case, nothing seemed untoward, and both the medical examiner and first responding officers felt her death was likely cardiac-related. Then, months later, that finding was flipped on its back when toxicological testing showed she had, in fact, died from a methadone overdose. This came out of left field for her two distraught daughters—the victim had no history of opioid dependencies.

Had the victim been poisoned—murdered? Or had she taken the fatal drug unknowingly? This question weighed on the mind of the young officer who had originally attended the scene and who was now tasked by the medical examiner to follow up and report back what she found. If she was going to be thorough with her task, she thought, *I am going to need some help and outside expertise to do so.* The willingness to take this path led her to our office and, ultimately, to a short secondment into the Homicide Unit, where she was exposed to a larger think-tank of talented investigators who helped guide her through her next steps.

Sadly, despite all her efforts, how the methadone was ingested remains a mystery to this day. However, the officer's eagerness to find the truth exposed her to the collective wisdom of many others and every time I see her now, wearing her own investigator's cap and mentoring others, I think her career trajectory was, in part, likely due to this early experience and her willingness to accept her own limitations when it came to investigating this type of occurrence. The insights she gleaned came because she sought them out.

Her actions remind me of two more seasoned officers from a smaller municipal agency who found themselves embroiled in a murder mystery of their own. It was spring about seven years ago when first-responding officers were called to the scene of a violent murder: an elderly woman who lived alone in a quaint community far from the hustle and bustle (and murder rates) of the city.

Diligent and studious, the officers identified a suspect in the case early—the victim's daughter—but without sufficient evidence to support their hunch, the pair knew they would not be able to meet the court's test for a conviction.

Policing in a small city has its advantages. I imagine it's easier for officers to develop relationships within the community, allowing the police to stay more informed about events and about citizens' concerns regarding crime. Also, living without congested city streets during rush hour, having shorter commute times, and enjoying lower housing costs give the peacekeepers of these towns important advantages. But I also imagine that policing in a smaller center comes with its challenges.

Most large municipal police services have deeper pockets, access to better technologies, and specialists with advanced crime-solving strategies. Wiretaps, for instance, are difficult to resource for many smaller centers, and therefore, when the use of such a technique is required, the smaller agency must look to a larger one for the use of their resource, as well as for their experience and expertise regarding how to use this tool successfully. For instance, before the wiretap even goes up, the plan for how to intercept the suspect's communications must be well thought-out and even scripted—wiretaps are an art form all to themselves.

Investigators who have the best results with phone taps are highly experienced and understand the principles of cause and effect and the influence of these on behavior better than most. They understand how to use these principles to get someone talking about an offense over a tapped line because they understand how to create those loose lips through stress. That's why when someone familiar with the technology but inexperienced in technique comes knocking on the door for help—the only right thing is to step up and do so.

Working with a more experienced investigator in the use of this—or any—technique is critical. In this case, the two agencies came together to script and deliver a series of events which ultimately led to the target of their investigation "giving it up," both on the wiretap and later in an interview when the suspect was presented with the evidence painstakingly collected by the two investigators who—despite their years of proud service—were not afraid to ask for help when they knew they needed it.

On a larger scale, when an organization can recognize its own limitations, systemic change can happen. For example, one officer I know took it upon himself to start an in-service training program specifically dealing with death notifications after learning how poorly one had been delivered to a family regarding the terrible news of their son's workplace accident. This officer's efforts led to an overhaul of our agency's notification process and the implementation of new organizational policies. The organization was willing to stand up and say, "We can do better," and they have.

Similarly, during a tragic firearms training accident, one of our officers was killed. His death led to an overhaul of training procedures, which are still in place—and still effective—twenty years later.

Columbine changed everything when it came to the way policing institutions responded to mass shooting events.

On April 20, 1999, at Columbine High School in Columbine, Colorado, two twelfth-grade students, Dylan Klebold and Eric Harris, entered their school with bombs, guns, and a plan to kill as many students as possible. What ensued was, at the time, America's worst mass school shooting. In the wake of the chaos, ten students were killed in the school's library, and twenty-one additional people were injured by gunfire. Several bombs brought to the school failed to detonate, or by all accounts, the casualty numbers would have increased exponentially. Both Klebold and Harris took their own lives.

At the time of this shooting, police responded as they had always done. First, responding officers set up containment points around the school to ensure the "threat" inside the school didn't get away. But this tactic, although useful in some hostage-type scenarios, caused the police response to the school to be extremely impeded and arguably risk averse. This is one of the reasons some believe the casualty count was so high. Klebold and Harris had more time to carry out their plan.

In the analysis of the incident afterward, police services looked closely at their own protocols to come up with better practices regarding how to deal with an active shooter situation.

As a result, they developed new training and tactics to deploy resources into a school more rapidly. It did not take long for the tragedy of Columbine to wake everyone up, and within months of this tragedy, I received my first training in Rapid Intervention Response.

I remember that day well. Training was set up in an old school that was scheduled to be torn down. Armed with simulation pistols, we learned how to move as a team of first responders through a school in a rapid deployment model. Although this was only an exercise, I remember how eerie that day felt as the trainers blasted over the school's PA system, the sounds of people panicking and screaming. Actors (shooters and quarries) moved around corridors and classrooms, some firing blank rounds as other participants lay on floors pretending to be dead. The whole experience hit home hard.

> Uncommon people recognize their own limitations. They are willing to learn.
> They have commitment and they persevere.
> They put in the time and work.
> They possess confidence in themselves to be able to achieve their goals.

This new model eliminated containment points on the outside corners and front doors of a school and directed officers to face risk directly and aggressively, fighting their own natural instincts to hold and contain. By learning from the tragedy at Columbine High School, policing organizations the world over demonstrated the intellectual courage described here: the willingness to recognize their own limitations, the eagerness to learn; the commitment to persevere; the readiness to put in the time and work; and the confidence to be able to achieve worthwhile goals.

Implementation of new procedures is ongoing, not only

when a policing organization has experienced a major incident—and in the analysis of that incident recognizes it requires a new initiative or resource to prevent a similar tragedy in the future—but also through actively seeking to grow by staying current with policing best practices.

Like the tragedy at Columbine High School, the story of what is infamously known in my circles as Black Friday was a devastation that led to the inception of our city's tactical team today.

On December 20, 1974, police were dispatched to a report of a theft. According to the complainant, a man had entered his grocery store and stolen airplane glue, likely for sniffing. The officer involved told the story on a recent documentary. In his words:

"I received a dispatch call because there was a guy coming in stealing between ten to fifteen tubes of model airplane glue. It was a low-profile call at the time. I'm sitting outside in the patrol car, and this guy comes outside and spotted us. He started running. I chased him.

"A gentleman on the street said, 'He went into that garage over there.' I called for backup, and a patrol car came from downtown. Two other constables came to assist me, so I thought, *okay, we'll be all right.*

"One of those officers opened the window and said, 'Come on out. We just want to talk to you,' and the guy hollered, 'I'm not coming out. You come in and get me.' Well, back in those days that's what you did. You get an invitation to come and get you, well, we'll come in and get you. So two of us went in one door, while another officer went in the other door. Now things start to go wrong.

"'He's got a rifle,' one of the officers inside the garage yells.

"As soon as I hear that, I grab my radio. I hollered, 'This is a code red: man with a rifle.' All of a sudden, I can see him. He's got the rifle aimed at me. Next thing you know, it's hard to explain, but you don't hear the bang. You hear nothing. All you see is a puff of smoke."

Another officer picked up the tale. "I was attending a meeting with the chief at the time, and some individual came running in and said, 'Chief! Chief! You've got to get out here. We've got a shooting of some kind.' As we're hurrying down the hall, we hear a frantic call. 'We're running out of ammunition. We're pinned down. We have no ammo. Someone get ammo.' So I ran back to the property room, and I got a couple of cases of .38 special. I remember one officer, Detective Boyd Davidson, with a shotgun running down the hall, almost bowling me over, then he was out the door. The next thing you know, there are policemen coming from all over to help. Thank God.

"We'd only been there a few minutes. I'm starting to get worried. This doesn't look good at all. All of a sudden, there was a concussion. I felt it, and I got this spray in my eyes. One of the fellows had taken a high-caliber round. I couldn't believe this could actually happen. I thought *this just happened in movies*.

"As soon as I saw what had happened to him, I thought, *this is really serious*. Because if he hadn't had that suit of armor on, he'd've been totally dead right there on the spot. There's no question in my mind.

"Then things went from bad to worse. Another officer comes running up to the police car, and I'm looking at him, and I'm thinking, *Geez, don't do that* as he gets up and he's peeking up, and—boom. The bad guy shot.

"The officer's head went back and a giant plume of bright red blood went flying off his head. And down he went.

"And I thought, *Oh, my God, he's dead*. I saw another officer come up and put himself over top of the wounded comrade. And I can still hear him hollering, 'You son of a bitch, don't die yet. Don't die! Aw, you son of a bitch, don't die!' It was just, well, it was upsetting that you could watch this, and yet that guy was still in there. 'This has to stop. This has to stop. He just killed a member.'

"Fortunately, the officer didn't die. He was an Irishman. You couldn't kill him by shooting him in the head, that's for sure.

"The wounded officer was rushed to the hospital. This was at two o'clock in the afternoon."

The guy in the garage had a plan to kill a police officer. There was a volley of shots from the garage, and I heard somebody say, 'Boyd Davidson had been shot.'

"I was a fortunate one. I got a graze. Some people got it in their hands. Some people got it in the head. One officer got it in the neck."

The story continues from a different constable: "We're hearing something on the radio about a tank coming down. The city police had called in the military. This armored personnel carrier comes up the lane and does a hard right turn. I couldn't see it, but I heard this huge roar and *boom*. The tank is right inside, and then in reverse, and out again. The building shook, and after a second or two, there was another huge roar, and the building shook again. I said, 'Go right through it if you can.' The driver went right through the bloody garage. The tracks were spinning, there was wood flying, shingles flying, and it just blew the one corner right out of the garage.

"I had my gun out, and I got down on one knee, and I braced beside the building. I looked up and saw the door move. I shouted, 'He's coming out! He's coming out! Get ready!' He had a rifle in each hand at the hip, and as he ran, he was firing into the police officers to the south of him. I lifted that shotgun, and I shot. The blast just stood the man right up straight. He froze in mid-air for a second.

"And you know my emotions were unbelievable. I was flat. There was no feeling. There was no fear, there were no nerves, I was just flat.

"Boyd was a bit of a legend. Boyd was not tall but he was wide. He was 320 pounds. And they said he was a marvel to watch kick down a door, because most guys back up and kick it with their foot, well Boyd had this great big barrel of a chest. But he could run, faster than anybody could think. He hit that door and it just disintegrated.

"He would be the perfect guy to be the office Santa Claus cause he was built like that. He had a twinkle in his eye and a nice smile. If something was going on and you needed somebody, Boyd would be there to help.

"Policing was everything to him. It was no surprise he'd be the first to be out there with a shotgun. One hell of a detective. Good man. Good person. God, he would be a perfect grandfather, but he never lived to be a grandfather. Damn it, he was such a nice guy, and he had a wife and children that loved him so much. He didn't have to die. There was nothing to be gained by Boyd dying. That hurts me. That really hurts. Maybe by him dying, maybe we prevented another dozen men from being shot, or God only knows what.

"So I went back, turned in my stuff at the station headquarters, resumed my duty and worked until eleven o'clock that night. That's pretty much the way the day went for me.

"When I went home, I saw my wife's car in the driveway. I can remember walking through the kitchen, and she looked at me, and she said, 'Are you okay?'

"And I said, 'Oh, yeah, I'm okay. Not to worry. I'm okay.' She came up the stairs and I grabbed her and the two of us stood there and cried and cried and cried. I figured that was the end for us.

"I went back to work the next day. I had to. I couldn't sit at home and stew about it. Like the inspector told me, "If you don't, you'll probably end up quitting." And I'm glad I did. It was a harrowing experience, but we learned a world of things that day. This sort of incident should never happen again. That's the best thing that came out of it. Knowing how much things have progressed over the years, the difference between then and now is like night and day.

"With the training we have today, it's one hell of a lot better than it ever used to be. And look what they've got on this force now. Probably the best Tac team you can find in the world. At least in Canada, for sure. I'm sure proud of being a part of it. Yep.

"Looking back, I can say that I truly loved my job. I'm part of this huge family called the police service. Every day was a big adventure. Yep. It used to be an imposition to take a day off because I loved what I was doing. I could never leave my home city. A lot of police officers leave here after they retire, but I could never leave.

"I wish I was twenty years old. I'd dash down and sign up and do it all over again."

Wow. Some story.

When organizations or individuals within an organization recognize their own limitations and create change, they demonstrate the courage to put their egos aside and seek growth.

> People who seek growth recognize their limitations and open themselves to new insights.

Reasoning

A colleague of mine is admired across our organization for his ability to think both inside and outside the box during challenging investigations, using logic, reasoning, and new techniques he has researched, to solve cold case homicides. In fact, he was once described over a wiretapped conversation between two suspects as "the best detective in North America."

With significant advancements in DNA technology over the last few years, he was one of the first officers in Canada to research and begin using genetic genealogy to solve some of our oldest cold cases. In the course of this research, he met a woman who had been doing a lot of work on genetic genealogical research on her own, mapping out her family tree. The pair forged a partnership to tackle some of our city's oldest cold cases.

Now a semi-permanent fixture in our unit, the former retired businesswoman has become a detective-of-sorts with her own workspace in the office. She pours over family trees of people who may be related to a killer. After a number of early successes, they were joined by a second detective and a genetic genealogist from Newfoundland.

How do they do it? Genetic genealogy databases in the US

accept DNA samples from people who create their own genealogical trees and consent to their DNA being compared with law enforcement forensic samples. Samples of what such law enforcement agencies believe to be offender DNA are processed through this database to see if any links to the unknown profile appear. If a hit is generated, the teams try to ascertain the identity of this person through reasoning and logic; they build a family tree.

How successful have they been? Very. Since tapping into this new resource, teams have cracked several stalled historic homicides and unidentified human remains cases that never would have been solved without their efforts.

The ability to use logic to reason is revered within the police world. The best detectives I know have the ability to use logic to engineer creative new approaches to everyday problems. This is a big skill to have in any organization that prides itself in being progressive.

Using effective reasoning to solve crime may not sound novel; most people believe this is a detective's *job*—and they wouldn't be wrong. Reasoning and the use of logic to tie evidence together is something every detective should be able to do.

But the reality is that many people can fall prey to tunnel vision, especially if they let a theory or a wish for a fast arrest dictate how they weigh evidence. This has been seen tragically in the past, for example, in the Steven Truscott case—a fourteen-year-old boy wrongfully convicted in 1959 for the rape and murder of a classmate. For the most complicated challenges, not all can see the forest for the trees. For this reason, when someone can offer up a fresh new perspective on an old-school investigative technique, their talents are applauded by all of us.

Here is a case in point. Years ago, a man out for an evening walk ventured into a darkened alley where two angry, aggressive, and confrontational thugs beat him to death for no reason but "just because."

In the investigation that followed, several pieces of evidence were collected from the scene that helped identify two suspects: CCTV video, which captured both suspects near the area about an hour before the murder, and some cigarette butts in the alley, which were later found to contain their DNA. Another less obvious piece of evidence was a freshly discarded can of red spray paint.

At the victim's autopsy the following day, members of the Crime Scenes Unit seized the victim's bloodied clothing and scrapings from his fingernails. Officers noticed two specks of red paint on his jacket. Hmm. Could the victim have been in contact with wet paint at the time of his murder?

Pouring back over their crime scene photos, officers noticed what on Day One was discounted as alley art. Written on the wall near where the victim had fallen were several graffiti tags in red paint. The officers surmised if they could prove that the paint from the can, the paint on the wall, and the paint on the jacket were all forensically matched, it could give the exact time the victim was in the alley: by studying the dry time of paint.

The idea was if we could prove the suspects were the ones "tagging" the wall, then we could also show through the dry times of paint how long it was between the time of the tagging and the time of the murder, something DNA on cigarette butts wouldn't be able to do. Without this evidence, the argument could be made that the cigarette butts had been discarded at a different time from the time of the offense.

Samples from the wall, the paint can, and the jacket were

sent to the crime lab. A match. The paint manufacturer was contacted and reported that the dry time of their paint was between seven to nine minutes, a finding also tested and later confirmed by us. We could now say that the offenders had been tagging the wall within seven to nine minutes of the victim entering, and therefore, the cigarette butts were likely also left behind around this same time.

Now, we just needed to prove the offenders were the taggers. Our suspects.

Over the next several weeks, surveillance teams followed the suspected tagger murderers around the city and captured both men on numerous occasions "tagging" various walls with the same tags seen at the original crime scene.

Gotcha, as we say in the business.

Let me share one more story where logic was required to tie pieces of evidence together.

A few years ago, gunfire erupted from the front of a downtown bar, leaving one man dead on the sidewalk with a single gunshot wound to his chest: a brazen killing that put the public at significant risk.

Eleven shots were fired from two different shooters. Witnesses at the scene described the chaos and provided descriptions of both offenders. One of the suspects was most easily identifiable by a large gold medallion that hung around his neck. The second suspect was shorter and stockier. So, which one killed the victim? This was going to be a difficult question to answer as both offenders had fled the scene prior to police arriving, and both had been seen in possession of, and shooting, a gun.

Looking at statements provided by witnesses, there were several common denominators. Prior to the guns being leveled toward the crowd, all of the witnesses observed the male with the gold medallion shooting the gun up into the air multiple times, like warning shots. It stood to reason that if we could find ballistic evidence of the warning shot rounds in the surrounding buildings, we could compare these to the bullet in the victim's body. We would be able to conclude whether or not the male wearing the gold medal was the one responsible for the murder or that the other shooter (by process of elimination) was, in fact, the killer.

To recover the rounds fired into the surrounding buildings would be like finding needles in a haystack. But good luck and a lot of perseverance paid off. Six different rounds, which had been fired through windows and into walls around the scene, were recovered, and all matched to one gun—the gun we believed was being shot by the offender wearing the gold medallion.

It was confirmed: the bullet that took this victim's life was fired from the gun in possession of the male with the gold medallion. Within a few days, he was tracked down and arrested for his role in the murder.

Now, it is your turn to challenge your reasoning with a few examples. The answers can be found in the appendices at the back of the book.

Challenge 1

Here is a well-known but still challenging logic puzzle that is not much different from how a crime dilemma might be solved. If we were to ask you how to connect all nine dots together using just four lines without lifting your pencil off the paper—how would you do it?

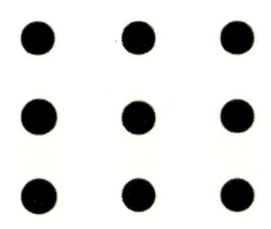

• • •

• • •

• • •

Challenge 2

If I told you about a case where, following the murder of a victim inside her home, the culprit dropped a flashlight on his way out her window, leaving it for crime scene investigators to collect later, how could you use this flashlight to help identify a suspect when fingerprinting the body of flashlight yields no results? When swabbing the flashlight's body for DNA

Use logic and reasoning to think differently, both inside and outside the box.

leaves no results? When identifying a store where the flashlight could have been purchased leads to the discovery that it's been sold a hundred thousand times before from outlets across the country. Yet this flashlight holds the key to your suspect's identity. How?

Challenge 3

You have been called to a home for a suspicious death. After entering the house, you find a male deceased in a back bedroom. His face is covered with a tea towel, and a noose is wrapped around his neck and affixed to a grommet in the wall behind the bed's headboard. The man's feet have been tied to the foot of the bed, and his hands are tied behind his back with slip knots.

In deliberating with colleagues and from the victim's history, the case appears to be consistent with a suicide, but there is a problem. How could someone take their own life if their hands are tied behind their back?

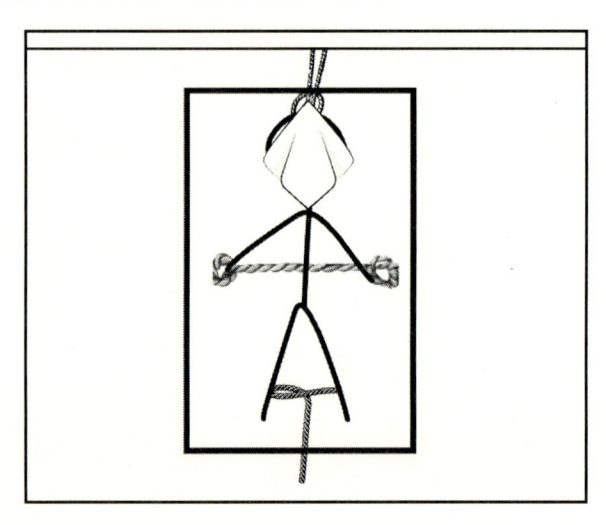

Challenge 4

You are a criminology student, and you have been asked to pick one type of crime that could be used to measure the health of a community. What type of crime would you pick and why?

Whether you're a contestant in our mini challenge or a homicide investigator, the ability to use reasoning often comes down to this:

Complex problems or dilemmas can be solved by thinking one of three ways: inside the box, outside the box, or from an entirely different box on the other side of the room.

Ingenuity

Cunning is a word that some believe is synonymous with sneaky or deceptive and perhaps in some ways that description isn't far off. But is that necessarily a bad thing? I guess the answer to that depends on what cunning or ingenuity are used for.

Within the hallways and boardrooms of our own homicide office, being ingenious can be necessary to catch a murderer.

Investigating crime is like a game of cat and mouse or a chess match. The collective think tank assembles to find inventive ways to advance our investigations, all the while being mindful of what the law allows. Here are a few examples where the use of logic, cunning, and initiative were put on center stage following think tank sessions:

Several years ago, myself and other members of the team became embroiled in an awful murder mystery. Two people had gone missing and were presumed murdered based on evidence we had collected from the crime scene. We had also come to believe the victims would likely be found in a huge, forested provincial park west of our city—but until this point, they hadn't.

It was spring when this troubling set of circumstances revealed themselves to us. In Canada, that meant bears were just coming out of hibernation and would be feeding after their long winter slumber. Acting on this, one member of the team suggested we contact the Parks Department and inquire whether it would be possible to track the bears through their GPS collars to see where they were going at night to feed. Using them like tracking dogs, we hoped they might lead us to the bodies.

At the end of the day, did it work? No. But it was a great idea and demonstration of ingenuity.

In another case I was involved in, the suspects had beaten a man to death by kicking and stomping on him. After the killing, they left the scene wearing their boots, which we theorized had to have been bloodied by the attack. Fortunately, it did not take long to figure out who we thought they were and that they lived very close by. As the investigation continued, one thing none of us wished to do was alert the suspects of our investigation, out of fear that they could destroy potential evidence or put up their guard, making future investigative efforts more futile.

Instead we investigated quietly around them. We realized, because of their close proximity to the scene, after they fled from the area, returning home, they likely stepped on a front entry carpet—and by doing so, may have deposited biological material onto that carpet.

So we struck a deal with the landlord. We offered to replace the carpet in the front entry and down the stairs for no charge because, according to him, it needed to be replaced anyway.

And that's exactly what happened. Under the authority of a special type of warrant, two plainclothes police officers, who had installed and removed carpet in the past, went in wearing their Sunday best work clothes and in plain sight of the suspects (who thought they were just carpet installers), seized the bloodied carpets from inside the building. Brilliant, as that and several other pieces of evidence ultimately led to them being arrested.

Then there was the case of a five-year-old little fella who had been brought to Canada from Mexico to live with his grandparents and their three adult children. But in his new home, the child was subjected to abuse by all of the adults—particularly the child's father. Over a two-month period, the once vibrant youngster deteriorated at the hands of the family, his suffering documented in pictures taken while he lived with them.

Then, one day, it happened. After calling 911 to report that the boy had fallen down a flight of stairs, emergency responders rushed the boy to the hospital, where he died as a result of the injuries he had received—none of them consistent with the family's version of a stair fall. In the investigation that ensued, the challenge for all of us was collecting the evidence to identify which adult had caused the injuries.

We learned through wiretaps in the home that this family was very spiritual. They were into witch doctors and Voodoo, a smorgasbord of beliefs and systems. We also learned they were concerned this little fella's spirit could come back and visit, and that oil and black paint were signs of the devil. So, we used cunning to hatch a plan.

To prepare, first we brought one of our members' daughters into the unit, who was five at the time. Here we cast her hands in plaster to create two five-year-old hand impressions. Then we moved onto phase two. In the dead of night, several teammates descended on the family's home to stamp the cast impressions on the home's windows and exterior walls using black oil. Slipping away, the only thing left for investigators to do was wait to measure the reaction of the family.

Over the following days, the father, convinced the spirit of the youngster was disturbed and restless, cried out to God to save him and asked for forgiveness for killing the little boy. His recorded words over a wiretap helped obtain his conviction.

Ingenuity is a trump card.

Chapter 6—Transcendent: Spiritual Cougage

A man of courage is also full of faith.
— Marcus Tullius Cicero

Spiritual courage fortifies us when we grapple with questions about our purpose, meaning, and perhaps our faith. Spirituality is not religion, and being religious is not necessarily spirituality. Spirituality takes many forms. For some, it involves prayer. For others, meditation, and yet for others, it may mean none of the above. Inner peace may come from a belief that nothing exists for any of us after death—therefore ensuring we live each day fully, living it for ourselves and for the ones we love.

> Spiritual courage, embedded in inner reflection and tested against temptation, fortifies us when we grapple with questions about our purpose.

In many ways, our own personal ethos will intersect with

our spirituality, a person's connection to both their deepest essence and their conception of the vastness of the universal. Spiritual self-understanding, whether following a recognized set of beliefs, entity, or institution, or whether purely self-developed, can result in inner peace and acceptance—even love—for everything around. I believe it is journey-focused, that there is no point at which we can say, "I've arrived."

Spiritual courage begins with the exploration of one's own personal beliefs.

Belief

A person's inner beliefs are their own, and this book will not attempt to answer theological or philosophical questions about whether god or gods exist or not; whether there is a heaven, hell, or someplace else; or claim one belief system is superior to another. Our aim is to introduce you to people who have used their own experiences with spirituality to help them find purpose or meaning in life—especially when terrible things have happened to them.

No matter what your thoughts, opinions, or beliefs are, if they bring you peace and they don't hurt other people, embrace them. From deeply held belief can flow an inner peace or a deeper meaning that can provide comfort, particularly in life's most difficult moments, such as facing one's own death or that of a loved one.

Conversely, speaking out about one's beliefs can be fraught with condemnation, isolation, ridicule, and even hate and violence. So it is no wonder people can find it difficult to express their beliefs, and it is all the more reason for us to recognize the courage of those who do.

According to most conventional religions, one's innermost essence does not cease to exist upon death. Most of us envision a utopia where believers will travel in the afterlife, while the rest will go to a place of damnation[2], or they believe in reincarnation, where we return to the world as another person or being. Atheists (about 7% of the world's population) don't believe in the concepts of heaven, hell, or rebirth; that when we die, we become worm food, plain and simple.

> In Canada there is nothing illegal about having extremist beliefs. Our Charter of Rights and Freedoms says that everyone enjoys the following fundamental freedoms:
> - Freedom of conscience and religion.
> - Freedom of thought, belief, opinion, and expression, including freedom of the press and other media communication
> - Freedom of peaceful assembly
> - Freedom of association
>
> And all these fundamental freedoms include extremist beliefs. Extremism only becomes a legal problem when it tries to achieve ideological goals using, supporting, or enabling violence. In cases such as these, the law is intolerant. And so it should be, as it is meant to keep our populace safe and free from the those who cross that line.

Over the course my time in Homicide, I have been exposed to many ideologies held by families suffering loss due to an unexpected death. From this experience, I have also seen my own spirituality evolve. It is true: the things I believe in today are wholeheartedly different from the things I believed

---

[2] With some variations such as Limbo, Purgatory, Fólkfangr, or the possibility of remaining on Earth to haunt the living.

when I was twenty. Through the accumulation of experience and the sharing and input of others, how could it not?

Examples of Beliefs

Saint Michael is believed by some to be the patron saint of police officers and the protector of our order. However, if an officer were to die in the line of duty wearing a Saint Michael's medallion or a tattoo of Saint Michael's image, would that change the view others may have that Saint Michael is, in fact, a protector? Faith allows one to continue to believe, even in the face of evidence to the contrary, so—likely not.	If you were to ask the most seasoned police officers, "Do evil people truly exist?" what would their answer be? In most cases, probably a yes, with a follow-up story about the most evil person they have ever met or the most wretched thing they have seen one person do to another.
If you have been present to watch someone die, when you see the physical changes that occur in the body immediately after death—could the hollowness of the corpse you now view signify to you that a soul really exists because that emptiness you now see reflects that it has left the body? Perhaps or perhaps not.	If you are a family member who has lost a loved one to a violent crime, do you find yourself denouncing the existence of a spiritual being like god—or drawing closer to one? From what I have seen you could do either.

Years ago, a career criminal was in custody yet again for series of drug crimes and trafficking offences. Throughout his life he had chosen to chase the money: easy money, money that comes from this easiest type of crime. By his mid-twenties he had actually become quite successful and was now recognized as a mid-level organized crime figure in our city.

He lived in a nice house and had a nice car, all furnished by his commitment to keep the illegal drug trade afloat in our community. But *this* new stint in jail would change the way he saw his relationship with the universe—and it was not because of some fancy rehabilitation exercise. It came from a near-death experience he had one afternoon in Cellblock B.

One evening in the local remand center, another inmate (who had successfully secreted a knife onto the unit) attacked him without warning. The drug dealer was badly injured and coded twice in the ambulance on the way to the hospital. During those times when his heart stopped beating, he had an experience that made him take a hard stop in the direction he was going in his life. He believed he had gone to hell.

In an interview I had with him after he had recovered, I asked (as I always do), "So, did you see the light?"

His answer surprised me. "No, I didn't," he replied.

"Well then, what did you experience?"

"There was no light at all. I was trapped in very large room like a gymnasium. There were no windows or doors. It was just a dark, vast, echoey, a terrifying space." He then made a declaration that it was time to change his ways: to do better and to get a job—a real job.

From what I know, once out of jail, he did exactly that. He turned his life around for about a year until the sins of his past caught up to him, and he was charged for a robbery he had done while still living the criminal lifestyle.

Today, I have no idea where his life is at, but I believe his near-death experience is always front of mind.

One of my own ideological epiphanies came about years ago. Although I didn't go to hell to find it, during that time I sure felt like I was living in one. After losing a special person in my life, I grappled with what the stability of my own future looked like—how could I ever find companionship like that again? Seeking counsel from my closest allies, I remember one dear friend sharing with me a thought I have hung onto and shared with others who had been going through the same.

She believed that when our body dies—or even experiences a sudden grief or loss—it ascends above our body, rising high up and exploding into a thousand little pieces. Each piece falls to the earth and is absorbed by other souls. The secret to finding love and happiness in our own lives is not seeking out our one true soulmate but instead focusing our search for one of our soul's shards, because those shards will feel as familiar to you as any soulmate ever could. And because of the number of shards, that connection is not limited to finding a single individual.

These words held meaning for me that day and provided me with hope and a sense of inner peace, believing that all would be okay. I took solace in them, and since, I no longer cling to the idea that there could only ever be one person for me. Perhaps, in part, this is a function of growing older; being able to say goodbye to those I have loved has come to be easier for me each time it has happened.

> **An expression of belief can bring comfort to others**

A second epiphany was served up by my son, who was ten at the time. Born with a bum heart, his first corrective surgery came at four months of age. He had a second at three. By ten it felt as if the appointments and anticipating the next surgical procedure were becoming old hat for both his mother and me. However, as time ticked by, some things changed as well, the biggest coming with his age. By ten, he was able to express his feelings, anxieties, and his own thoughts. He also understood much better the gravity of what was about to happen.

A few weeks out from his next date with the surgeon, I remember him coming to me one evening with a reflection he wished to share. "Dad," he started, "I just want you to know that if something ever happens to me, I will never leave you. You will always find me over your right shoulder. Do you understand?"

Why this was so important for him to state, I will never know for sure. The truth was, he made it through this surgery like the ones before—like a champ. But this moment revealed to me how important it is for us to listen to those who have the courage to share and express their own beliefs. When we do so, they can come to a place of inner peace with whatever the struggle may be.

When we have the courage to open ourselves to others, to really listen as another expresses their viewpoint, it can give them peace of mind

My third epiphany around belief came five years ago when my father lay dying of cancer. In the hours before his death, the family had assembled at my parents' home to be with him. His unconscious, shallow breaths filled the quiet space while streams of sun meant to usher in spring came through the large windows, warming the room. My mother spoke softly to him, and I will always remember what she said. "Oh, Art, you are going to get to see the first robin this year."

Her statement struck me. In all my years, I had never heard of such a competition between the two—who was going to see the first robin. But clearly, there had been one. From that moment on, every time I saw a robin in spring, I thought of it as an affirmation that perhaps my dad was closer to me than I could ever have thought. My mother's expressed belief left me an opportunity for remembrance every spring, making it a much more meaningful time of year.

> The expression of belief can enrich our lives, providing new meaning where there had been none before.

And my career has also provided me with a unique lens. In my time as a police officer, I have had the privilege of hearing from so many people who wished to share their own beliefs with me. Perhaps it is because, as death investigators, we often develop intimate relationships with families who look to us for answers. In these conversations, prompted by life's most precarious moments, they also struggle with, confront, and share with us their most personal reflections on belief.

About five years ago, I was sitting at my desk working through the reams of paperwork that my career entails (no one ever tells you about that when you join) when my phone rang. It was the father of a young woman who had been killed by an ex-boyfriend about six months earlier. He liked to call for a check-in from time to time. His devotion to his faith, which I had learned about during our chats, taught that after a person dies, their spirit is reincarnated.

"Dave?" he said excitedly.

"Yes, my friend? What's going on?"

"Dave, can you meet me for a coffee? I have some very exciting news to tell you."

Within an hour, I was on my way to see him at our little coffee shop. Once we were seated, he couldn't contain his news any longer and blurted out that his deceased daughter had come to him in a dream the night before. She had been born again and was now a baby wrapped in a blanket.

Where was she? He wasn't sure, but he was certain it was her. "Now that I know she is here—back on earth—all I need to do is live another twenty years."

"Why twenty years?" I asked.

"Well, within twenty years, she will have grown up to be a woman," he said. "A woman capable of travel. A woman who will have access to planes, trains, and cars." For this reason, he believed they would be able to cross paths again.

His belief led him to a new purpose: to have the courage to live and live well, live for years to come so that one day he could reconnect with the soul of the person he believed he was destined to see again. A person he so desperately missed.

Other families have shared with me a conviction that their loved one's passing had been fated. This concept—that everything is predetermined—may bring peace to some, but it can bring scoffs from others. Are we just rudderless ships at sea, at the mercy of the ebbs and flows of the ocean waves? Or are we in control of our own choices? Most murderers don't wake up one morning knowing they will kill; it is often an unforeseeable set of circumstances that leads to a person's untimely end. But are such circumstances set in stone by an immutable future or a combination of decisions that could go either way?

There are circumstances over which we have no control. Call it serendipity: being in the wrong place at the wrong time, for instance. Consider the story of three separate women who, one evening, were followed from a transit platform by a sexual predator before he selected the fourth, whom he went on to viciously rape and murder.

Others have shared with me their medium and psychic experiences. A decade ago, a young man had been found shot and killed on the south end of the city without apparent cause. This twenty-something kid had no history to suggest he would be a target for homicide. What he did have, though, was a shady brother-in-law, who, over the course of a year, had borrowed almost thirty thousand dollars from him—money the young victim now wanted repaid. In the investigation, the focus turned to the shady brother-in-law early, but without physical evidence to place him at the scene, the investigation ground to a halt. During this time, the heartbroken family met several times with a psychic who believed the killer was close to the victim, that the killing was over money, and that, after the murder, the killer drove to a bridge and a body of water.

This seemed right on at least two of three points. We believed the victim did know his killer and that the killing was over money, leading the investigator to wonder if this psychic had spoken to or knew the killer. Not so.

But. The psychic's information became more than interesting when the killer eventually spilled to a group of "new friends" (undercover cops) that, after committing the murder, driving back to the city, he threw the gun he'd used from a bridge into the river.

The issue here is not whether you believe such things are

possible or if you are skeptical. What is important is that individuals examining, confirming, and sharing their beliefs have found the courage to continue, and the strength to do so because of the peace their beliefs bring.

> Through belief, we construct meaning and purpose in our own lives.

Envisioning

I once heard that successful people create their future by envisioning it and then have the courage to reinvent themselves to live it. Both of these steps are daunting, but the person willing to do this will have great clarity about what they will agree to, reject, or need to mull further. They can say "no" when a decision they are making does not align with the future they are envisioning. They can orient their actions to their core beliefs; they do not lose sight of big dreams, and they follow their hearts to this end. They believe in the law of attraction: what you believe unreservedly, you create.

I think those who dream big, who wish upon a star or have faith in putting out to the universe what they want are more often the same people who get what they want and need. To do so requires a person to be aware of and honest with themself; to be vulnerable to and humble with disappointment; and maybe to release skepticism and embrace a bit of faith. They clearly see a desired outcome, and they work to make it happen.

As homicide investigators, members of our unit and I have, over the years, been blessed to be abundantly supplied with "lucky breaks." Cases we believed would be difficult to crack were resolved because of a stroke of "luck"—often made possible because *believing* that combing that murder scene one more time or reviewing evidence with a new eye would unveil our blinders and reveal a previously hidden pattern.

Beyond the explicable, I have sometimes put out to the universe my intention to find a killer; to ask the universe for help in finding that one piece of evidence which would ultimately lead me to determine who was responsible for the crime I was intent on solving.

In one case I had several years ago, a young man had been abducted in a bid to extort his family for money—which he was rumored to have in abundance.

It was a July day in 2017 when the victim was hired by an aspiring criminal group to create fake identification. As this was his racket, the request was not out of the ordinary. He made the replica driver's license. Being underground and shady, discretion was key to evading the law, so he and his soon-to-be abductors engaged in a series of texts to plan a meet away from watchful eyes.

At the meet, his clients seized the fake identification and abducted him, planning to extort him for thirty thousand dollars. But the plan went south. Over the next several hours, he was beaten and tortured until, eventually, his body gave out, and he succumbed to his injuries.

When the body was found, my team and I opened an active homicide investigation to find his killers. And I did what, superstitious me, I have always done early in an investigation.

I quietly spoke to the deceased, asking for help. It worked.

As we began to piece everything together, one of the key evidence recoveries was a printer used by the victim to make the false identification. The lucky break came when we discovered the ribbon in the printer retained an impression—a ghost—of the last identification made: an image of my suspect and her new alias name. Armed with this new obscure piece of evidence and other clues collected from CCTV video and forensic crime lab testing, it did not take long to locate her in Toronto—hiding in an apartment which, on a wing and a prayer, we had decided to check in the name of thoroughness.

> When you are inspired by some great purpose, all your thoughts break their bonds: Your mind transcends limitations, your consciousness expands in every direction, and you find yourself in a new, great, and wonderful world. Dormant forces, faculties, and talents become alive, and you discover yourself to be a greater person by far than you ever dreamed yourself to be.
>
> —Indian philosopher Patanjali

In another case, a phantom camera operator was the lucky break served up by the universe which I needed to understand the viciousness of a crime and each person's role in it.

New Year's cheer was just beginning to wear off as we entered the second week of 2018—but not for everyone. An impromptu house party was in the works at a residence across from a large retail space. Six guests had been invited, but there were eight people in the house when things began to sour—two late attendees had arrived uninvited, making some of the other guests uncomfortable. These boys had history, and everyone knew it. They carried themselves differently and walked like they would in a prison meal line, and the chips on their shoulders were evident from across the room. The host's decision was to leave them be. *Don't poke the bear.*

An hour passed, and the consumption of alcohol increased, the perfect formula for something twisting off. Of course, it did.

To this day, I am not clear what lit the match, but something led to the uninvited guests brandishing mace and knives and chasing two of the legitimate guests out into the snow, one suffering knife wounds.

Although the attack probably lasted less than twenty-five seconds, it was worth asking the universe for help. An exterior, motion-sensitive security camera installed to patrol the mall parking lot captured the action on the street out front of the residence. Set to sequence over the course of two minutes through multiple angles, this camera would also pan and zoom without operator control. We collected and viewed the camera footage, and the results were remarkable.

As if it was being controlled from the grave, the camera picked up and recorded the attack as it unfolded. The automatic camera zoomed in and panned out at perfect times to capture on video the entirety of the violent assault, better than if someone had been operating it themself. Although the video's night resolution was insufficient to identify both accused, it helped the the court see for themselves the level of participation of each accused in the murder. If this wasn't enough, the camera continued its two-minute cycle to record the stabbed victim staggering across the street to the mall entrance, where he collapsed—again zooming in as if it needed to capture his last breath for posterity.

The universe had again responded to my plea for help.

For some people, manifesting hopes and dreams looks more like prayer; this was the case for my next lucky break. Some might explain what happened as a coincidence, but for me ...

I'm still not so sure.

Several years ago, two sisters were found murdered in a car on the north end of the city. Through a series of investigative steps, our team was able to identify several suspects and possible vehicles of interest in the crime. I felt that one of those vehicles, a white pickup truck, might have been used in the murder. Therefore, it was imperative we locate it. But after several weeks of looking, it did not turn up.

Keeping families informed is a big part of the homicide business. So, after the initial onslaught of investigative leads had settled, it was time to meet the slain sisters' family to share some details of the investigation and tell them where I expected to go from here.

On the day of the meeting, I arrived a few minutes early and was surprised to see more than a dozen family members already in attendance. I readied myself for some tough questions.

Instead, I found myself listening to family speak fondly of the girls they had lost. I heard from their children, from aunts and uncles, brothers, sisters, and cousins too. It was a lovely, open dialog about the girls. There was no hate in their hearts—just a desire to see justice done. They asked what they could do to help.

I told them about the white truck, and my hope was that it could be found. I said, "Perhaps we could all just give a shout-out to the girls and ask them for their help in this regard."

The family was open to this idea. Some of them closed their eyes, as if in prayer. Others muttered something to their creator. I watched each take what I had said and express it in their own way. Following this somewhat ceremonial "shout out" we ended our meeting with hugs and firm, committed handshakes.

As I left the restaurant, I felt, all in all, things had gone well. With the necessary "touch base" out of the way, I could get back to organizing the massive jumble of case materials for the prosecution team.

I had been on the highway back into the city for about ten minutes when my phone rang. "Detective Sweet?"

"Yes, sir," I replied.

"Have you been looking for a white truck?" the officer on the other end of the phone inquired.

"Yes. For several weeks now."

"Well, we just found it parked on a street near a condo building. Would you like us to hold it?"

"Yes!" I replied, and when I learned exactly where it was found, I thought it even more interesting—only a few blocks from my mother's house. The truck had been under my nose the whole time.

The idea of proclaiming your intentions into the universe as a way of manifesting hopes and dreams defies logical explanation. If it brings someone peace, great. If it doesn't, no problem. You are not wrong to be skeptical.

People who do believe such things exist take the chance of being seen as ridiculous, which may require exercising a quiet spiritual courage to maintain such beliefs in the face of others' disbelief.

No matter what side of the fence you are on, belief in a force beyond ourselves or belief that our own thoughts direct our behaviors in subtle ways that influence our path, the lesson we can all take away from the attribute of connecting with the spiritual, is that uncommon people influence their futures by putting their intention to it. Here is one final example.

From the time I was just a wee lad, I had a dream to one day play in the National Hockey League (NHL). For young, naïve me, this dream was what I thought my purpose could be in this world; therefore, much of my youth was spent joyfully outside on the front street shooting pucks into a net with my best friend or at a local rink practicing and playing hockey with my community team.

I dreamed about what it would be like to be a pro hockey player, to skate out for warmup before a big game with a packed house of chanting and cheering fans, to stand on the blue line and hear my country's national anthem sung before a game—swaying back and forth on my skates and looking across the ice at my opponent who stood tall, rocking back and forth on his. I wondered what it would be like if some of my hockey heroes were there—Peplinski, Fleury, Murzyn, Paterson, McInnis, Sutter, Nelson, Vernon, and, of course, the man with the big mustache, Lanny McDonald. I thought about what it would be like to hear my name called by the great color commentator Peter Mar.

But—as is the case for most of us—our hearts often don't end up matching our talents. And so, at some point, that dream fades just as our belief in Santa does, relegating many of us to the beer leagues to live out the "what could have been" fantasy. This fate rang true for me.

Well, that is, until thirty years later, when I discovered that what I had put out into the universe all those years ago had come back to me like a boomerang.

Regrettably, it began with a tragic set of circumstances that stained our city from the day they unfolded.

In June 2014, a beautiful young family became the center of a case that gripped, shocked, and traumatized everyone connected with it. Following her five-year-old's sleepover at his grandparents' house, a loving mom arrived to pick up her son only to find that he and her parents were missing. Worse, there was evidence something violent had transpired.

In the investigation that followed, an unprecedented number

of police resources were poured into the search for the three missing family members. An even more impressive number of people from the community came together to support the family, who were living through anyone's worst nightmare. The case became national and then international news.

Though all of us wished for the best possible outcome, we knew it likely would not come. Days after the initial Missing Person's Report was filed, a suspect was identified and arrested. Days after that, crime lab findings went on to conclude all three members of the family had been murdered, even though their bodies were never found.

Suffering such an unfathomable loss can be enough to destroy anyone. I have seen this happen: parents grieving the loss of a child who descend into such a dark abyss they can find no way out but to leave the world they've known through drugs, alcohol, or even suicide.

In this instance, however, it went the other way.

Why? Perhaps it was how this particular family drew strength and fortitude from the support of so many people who loved them. Perhaps it was their own spirituality. One thing I know for sure, it was their incredible resilience which allowed an idea to grow in their minds: the establishment of a children's foundation, a legacy to their young son who, through his name, could leave a lasting impact on this city forever.

To bring their vision to light would of course require funds, support, and a lot of effort. Knowing this, they got to work. Their first major fund-raising event came seven months later: a charity hockey game at our city's NHL rink. The symbolism of the venue was powerful: an arena where their son could be remembered with a game in his honor, playing a sport he adored.

The day I received the call to play as a member of Nathan's

Heroes was humbling. The family wanted to see those who contributed to the case included in their very special night. The venue was the home of our city's hockey team. The opponents were members of the NHL alumni. All proceeds raised would go to the Nathan O'Brien's Children Foundation. Simply awesome.

I remember vividly the hours leading up to the big event. I spent the day at the office a mess of nerves, circling in my head through the worst possible outcomes that could leave me feeling embarrassed on the ice. I decided instead to make myself useful and leave the office early, get my skates sharpened, and arrive at the rink a couple hours ahead of the seven p.m. puck drop. Maybe that would give my mind a chance to settle.

Parking in the *players-only* lot was the first of many thrills to come that evening. The second came moments later as I entered the arena through the *players-only* door and walked down the long corridor—a corridor I knew well from watching hundreds of hours of televised games. Security officers, ushers, and all manner of employees along my route to the visitor's room were welcoming, kind, and as enthused as me to be part of such a special evening.

In the dressing room came even more thrills—reuniting with the family who meant so much to me and who were, ultimately, the reason I was there. Then there was the fruit tray and refreshment table and the realization that hanging in my own locker space were my socks and jersey for the game. Number 14, *Sweet*.

I took a moment to breathe, to really take it all in, to take time to acknowledge and understand the significance of the night. For Nathan, for his family, and for his legacy.

I also took the time to introduce myself to my new

teammates, who included a local sports journalist, a country music star, several MLAs, Nathan's father, his older brother, his old coach, and a young man who, in a city three hours away, had experienced the terrible loss of his own when his family had been found murdered only months earlier.

An hour before the puck drop, it was time to check out the building from ice level. Standing in the players' box, I looked out on the rink. I could hear the buzz from the concourse as the building began to fill with people, and the stands were already beginning to show signs of life. Because this was to be a family event, kids were encouraged to show up in their favorite superhero costumes—a salute to the young man we were there to support, who was known to wear a superhero costume on his off-hockey days. From my vantage, I could see a couple of Spider-Men, some Supermen, and a spattering of Captain Americas.

It was from this vantage that I also had the opportunity to see that blue line, the one I had imagined standing on as an eight-year-old kid—the same blue line I now hoped would not trip me up in front of an arena full of people during the opening memorial ceremony and singing of our national anthem.

I don't remember much about the experience of this getting-ready journey except feeling a little shaky in the legs. I'd never played in front of this many people. Still, when I returned to look around the dressing room, I believe I wasn't the only one feeling this same anxiety. Things did seem remarkably quiet. It was during this quiet time I learned that the rumors were true: Hockey Hall of Fame commentator Peter Mar would be announcing the night's play-by-play. My mind tripped right up on that one.

As game time drew closer, it was time to actually hit the ice for a quick warm-up. This was my first-ever experience on major league ice. Music played as we came onto the ice. Lights turned the ice brilliant, and the stands faded into shadow. Camera flashes were everywhere.

It was just as my six-year-old self dreamed it to be.

Better, really, as—parked behind my players' box—I could see my family. All of them—parents, brothers, sisters, nieces and nephews, and of course, my own children as well. The night was going to be perfect.

Snagged for a quick on-ice interview by one of the many journalists covering the event, I was now in full-on *groove* mode. Everything felt like it should. The ice felt great under my skates, and I could feel the love in the building. That is something I doubt even the most seasoned pros feel before a big game.

For our pregame talk, our coach was Nathan's mom. Warm, receptive, and full of grace, she wished us all luck then sent us out for the puck drop with Nathan's dad and brother leading our charge.

That night, I lived out a dream I had envisioned as a child. I stood on the blue line, listened to our country's great national anthem, and looked across to my opponents—

There they were. Peplinski, Fleury, Muryzn, Patterson. A bit older but no less impressive.

For one night, I got to live my dream of being an NHL superstar. But, even better, I was doing it while watching a loving, caring family live their dream of creating a legacy for their son, keeping him alive through his name, and providing charitable donations to multiple children's charities and programs across our city.

In the end, the team made up of NHL alumni graciously allowed us to lose by only a couple of goals. And I will always remember this event as one of the greatest nights of my life—

one that will play back in slow motion when the day comes that I die. Yes, because it was a childhood dream realized, but more so, *how* it was realized: in the service of a tragedy and a triumph greater than me.

> Some of the most courageous people in the world are dreamers.

Grace

Grace. The ability to face suffering with unwavering calm, kindness, and giving takes great courage of a type very few can muster.

One image of grace that comes to mind is the character of Melanie Wilkes, as portrayed by Olivia de Havilland in the movie *Gone With the Wind*. Melanie could never see Scarlett O'Hara's scheming, only admired her spirit and determination. Melanie's (religious) faith was unwavering. She worked hard without complaint and always put others first despite her own tribulations. Grace is the beauty of the soul, and it is inspiring. It is also rare.

The second image of grace which comes to my mind is the face of a mother who lost her daughter in our city a decade ago. But first, some background.

Back in 1988 Naima had just given birth to her second

daughter, Natasha, within a year of her first. Naima and her infant daughters lived in Somalia and, as a single mother, Naima was doing her best in a country that was beginning to come apart. With civil unrest all around she made the decision to emigrate to Canada, thankfully before all hell broke loose in 1989.

Settling in Toronto with her daughters, both still under a year old, life was difficult for Naima. However, her strength, perseverance, and desire to see her daughters live in a country of safety and opportunity saw her through those challenging first years. Juggling work and college, she counted her blessings that she had learned English before leaving her homeland.

As years went on, Naima had two more children: a son and another daughter, creating a tight-knit family led by a matriarch who did her best in the eyes of her children.

Natasha, her second oldest daughter, was described by her mother and siblings as an extroverted child who was easy and outgoing, a seeker of information, full of crazy off-the-wall facts. Natasha was also someone who could be relied upon to give good advice.

Naima told me a story about Natasha, which today seems like eerie foreshadowing. When Natasha was seventeen, she and some friends went to the Eaton Centre, a large mall in the heart of Toronto's downtown core. It so happened that members from two rival gangs bumped paths in the crowded mall that day and, in a brazen show of force, opened fire on one another, tragically striking and killing an innocent fifteen-year-old girl. Natasha, who was unhurt, later thanked her lucky stars that she and her friends had just moved past the store where the shooting had occurred. This incident was alarming and caught the attention of Torontonians and our nation. Naima thought, *how could someone be so reckless and careless to shoot a gun in a crowded mall?*—a sentiment shared by many.

Years went by. Near the end of summer in 2014, after completing university in Ontario, Natasha followed one of her best friends and moved to our city to pursue a public relations career.

It was late August, and young people across the city were spending their final weekends of vacation blowing off steam before school started again, and the clubs and bars were packed.

As night bled into the early morning hours, Natasha and her bestie were out front of a club saying final farewells to friends when a gangster from the other side of the tracks decided he was going to show off to his gangsta buddies in front of the large group of congregated young people, by *being the man*. He pulled a handgun from his waistband and carelessly fired three rounds into a crowd of people for no better reason than "he could."

And, just like that, Natasha's life ended on the sidewalk.

By all accounts, Natasha was a beautiful soul to all who knew her. In fact, in the years after her senseless murder, a friend built a school in Somalia in her name.

The first time I met Naima was only a few days after her daughter had been killed. Still in shock, she flew to our city from Toronto and came straight from the airport to our office. Until this time, I had met only a handful of people like her: a person who carried herself with unwavering calm and kindness despite the suffering she now faced. Over the coming days, weeks, and years, I am proud to say we have gone on to form a beautiful long-distance friendship that endures today.

What made Naima different from so many others who have had to walk in such shoes? To answer this question, you would have to meet her—then, like me, you would just know. But let me try to describe some of the things about her that demonstrate her grace, even though I fear that, in black and white, I will miss the mark.

In those early days of the investigation, I remember Naima saying to me, "What is done is done." And although finding out who was involved was important, she recognized that this would not change her world. Her daughter's death was something she would just have to find the courage to accept.

Naima drew strength from her faith, believing what happened was God's will. Naima believed Natasha knew her life was fated to end that night. Recalling an earlier phone call she had with Natasha hours before she was killed, Naima shared how Natasha took the time to offer *I love yous* to her and her siblings before heading out. The call to Naima was reminiscent of what some might see as a final goodbye.

Naima believed the bullet's path to her daughter—and only her daughter—was another sign Natasha was to be called to heaven that morning, a fact confirmed to her the day she helped wash and dress her daughter's body for burial and saw the precision of the bullet strike into Natasha's chest which ended her life instantly. Naima later told me, "Natasha died with a smile on her face. That was Natasha in life: always smiling."

The person responsible for this crime was a young man. Originally charged with second-degree murder, he was convicted in a plea deal of the lesser offense of manslaughter and received a nine-year sentence. Naima said to journalists covering the case, "I know in my heart it's going to hurt him for the rest of his life because he is going to have to live with what he did to my daughter. And that is enough punishment from God. I don't hate him. I will forgive him."

It breaks my heart that people are still dying in this way, year after year.

Naima said, "In my faith, you forgive. If you don't forgive, you will never move on. I do not want to carry anger toward him for the rest of my life."

This type of grace in dealing with the unfathomable paved the way for this rare courtroom moment. The accused stood before the family and apologized. "I'm here today to let the family know I am deeply sorry. I had no intention to cause harm." Such words might offer no solace, but in this case, his words were backed by action. The day this young man became eligible for parole, he did not apply. In fact, he chose to remain behind bars to do the full ride until he was eventually statutorily released.

Natasha is buried in a cemetery just west of the city, a tranquil setting with a view of the mountains. Naima always believed that because it was Natasha's choice to come here, this should be where Natasha stays. Grace.

> Through grace, forgiveness is given a chance to grow.

Mindfulness

Living in the moment. Centering yourself. Taking time to smell the roses. Quieting your mind so you can focus on and make real your hopes and dreams. Mindfulness is a skill, usually developed through meditation, of sustaining attention to one's own mind in the present moment. Mindfulness derives from sati, a significant element of Hindu and Buddhist traditions, and is based on Zen, Vipassanā, and Tibetan meditation techniques. It is also a virtue found in uncommon people.

When people live their lives for someone else—or something else—and are not being true to their own hearts, they may find their purpose for being elusive. This is an issue that faces many suffering from substance abuse disorders who live their life for that next high or that next bottle, blind to their true authentic purpose.

Anger arising from grief can do the same thing. It takes courage to let go of the "why?" *Why did that loss happen to me?* Focusing on the *why* puts one's sense of purpose onto something we cannot control. Mindfulness comes from letting go of regrets from the past or worries about the future and focusing on *the now*. And it takes courage and strength to give up clinging to anger and worry; choosing to live in the moment is a daily—hourly, moment-by-moment—decision.

When I first began contemplating the difficult decision to leave a career I had loved for twenty-five years, there were two incidents which made me realize that I was, in fact, truly done. It was time to move my life in a different direction.

The first incident that found me reflecting was quite grim. My team and I became involved in a missing person case after the missing person turned up dead in a home where an autistic child and an elderly woman lived. Believing a cat had died in the basement, the house's occupants did not investigate, and the body remained undiscovered for months, hidden under some bed sheets.

We suspected the elderly woman's granddaughter or one of her friends had some involvement in the death as, up to this point, they had frequented the elderly woman's home to party undisturbed and use drugs. We believed during one of these parties, the victim succumbed to an unreported overdose and was hidden until the day police, attending the address on a secondary complaint, found her.

I was assigned to attend the autopsy and confirm that the victim had indeed not been murdered. This was an unenviable and uncomfortable task that I had performed dozens of times before. But on this day, it was a task I remember dreading more than any other time.

Standing in the autopsy suite and watching as the blankets were carefully removed from the victim, I remember asking myself multiple times, *Why? Why am I still doing this, swatting the flies rising from the body, fighting with the bugs that now filled the medical examiner's theater?* This was the first time in my career I realized I was nearing the end of my rope—and my career.

It was this second incident, though, that was the icing on the cake. The team and I had been working ourselves to near exhaustion for days in an effort to find the body of a missing man whom we all believed had been murdered by an associate. The motive, we believed, was greed, as evidenced by the fact our suspect had begun racking up significant credit card debt and took over the victim's bank accounts soon after the victim disappeared. Believing this to be a significant clue, we made the decision to arrest and bring our suspect in for questioning.

During the questioning, as a matter of course, we offered several times to bring the man something to eat and drink, to which he always replied, *no*. Then, at one a.m., as the interview was winding down and we were all dreaming of bed, he finally demanded food—an "everything" bagel with cream cheese.

His request was benign. But for me, the go-fetch-the-food guy, his request made me see red. I got upset and snappy with my colleague and friend, who'd come into the boardroom to place the order.

If he had asked for cinnamon or raisin, plain, or even a cheese bagel, I don't think I would have snapped. But for a suspect who had taken the life of another for *greed* ... the request for an "everything" bagel made me angry beyond belief. Storming out of the office like a two-year-old in a full-on tantrum, I went to get the requested item.

Returning fifteen minutes later and still seething, I launched it from the bag and into the hands of my friend, who'd done absolutely nothing wrong. It was at this not-so-proud moment I became abundantly self-aware:

I needed to resign and leave law enforcement.

No more mindfulness or reflection was required. I settled on my course of action and have never looked back from that day since.

Leaving a career—by choice—is one thing, but when people face the sudden, involuntary loss of a loved one, the need to find out the reasons why it happened can become all-consuming. Unfortunately, when a family receives an answer to "why," it is often underwhelming. In the case of a homicide, the person providing the "why" (the offender's) self-preservation kicks in, and it becomes like receiving a bowl of vanilla ice cream when what you really wanted was rocky road crunch. Even in the case of other circumstances, the reasons why something happened can be vast and varied, but learning why may provide only an intellectual answer that does nothing to ease the pain.

A mélange of time, support, active grieving, and active building of a new life, cycled through again and again, is hard, hard work. It requires strength and courage to move into—at first, glimpses, then more sustained—peace.

Sometimes one discovers in oneself—a family member, a friend, or a colleague—a pattern of repeated crises. This can be expressed, for instance, in an individual who repeatedly falls in love with an abusive or addicted partner, has relationships blow up in explosive arguments, or loses jobs. It can take huge courage for an individual to make personal changes in their life to steady such patterns of instability. Whatever the psychological causes of such volatility, Dialectical Behavior Therapy (DBT), which is a key component of mindfulness, can be helpful.

DBT is named for the process of being able to accept two opposing ideas at the same time: to accept—without judgment—that a situation exists, while at the same time accepting the need for change.

One example of this might be the acceptance of strong feelings of anger at a partner who seems to be leaving, such as by staying in the moment (mindfulness) and acknowledging, "I feel furious. My fists, arms, and shoulders are bunching. I feel hot, and my breathing is coming fast. They have left the apartment, and I don't know if they are coming back. I said things I don't mean and now wish I hadn't, and I have an overwhelming fear that they won't come back." And, at the same time, acknowledging a need for change, thinking, "This situation exists and it is real. I can't change what has happened, and I can't change the other person or force them to come back, but I can change how I react. I can do self-help. I can call on others (friends or professionals) for help. I can keep the situation from getting worse by ..."

Mindfulness is key to accepting, without judgment, what *is* and, at the same time, what *could be*. DBT teaches techniques for regulating one's emotions, increasing tolerance to distress, and developing tools for more effective interpersonal relationships.

It takes great courage to recognize the need for self-change, courage to reach out for help, courage to embark on a course of change, and courage to stick with that plan in the face of slips and setbacks. Being mindfully aware of oneself, one's circumstances and actions, and to do so without judging oneself or others, is key to this courageous action.

> Being present in the moment is the essence of sustaining attention to the contents of one's own mind.

Chapter 7—Apaniiwa: Resilience

Most of our obstacles would melt away if, instead of cowering before them, we should make up our minds to walk boldly through them.
— Orison Swett Marden

A friend of mine once shared that the Blackfoot name for butterfly is Apaniiwa. For me the symbolism of the butterfly has always been significant—it represents transformation; transformation through adversity.

Colonialism, starvation, and the spread of disease, guns, and whisky dealt a smashing blow to the First Nations people of Canada. Residential schools were used to force the "wild" out of children, to force assimilation by separating them from their families, their language, their history, their songs and foods and stories, initiating a cascade of trauma to multiple generations of Indigenous people.

But despite this despair, something positive has endured: the strength and resiliency of people to overcome their continued challenges.

Through advocacy and reconstruction of their heritage, Indigenous people have drawn the world's attention to the many issues of the past they still face today. The voices of the women carry particularly strong messages when it comes to understanding what happened to children forced out of their arms to attend residential schools. When school children died—how? Neglect? Starvation? Beatings? Illness?—their custodians had so little regard for families that neither were parents informed, nor were bodies returned, nor even markers left on the graves.

Through all this tragedy, the community still holds a deep connection to the greater world around them. Like Apaniiwa, like the butterfly, First Nations people are journeying to transform their world, and part of this process includes bringing greater awareness to the plight of murdered and missing Indigenous women and the cultural biases that have left many of these cases unsolved. Persistence and advocacy—mostly from Indigenous women—have led the government to act. The final report of the federal government's National Inquiry into Missing and Murdered Indigenous Women and Girls listed 231 calls for justice, identifying that Indigenous women and girls are twelve times more likely to be murdered or to go missing than members of any other demographic group in Canada.

Through their strength and perseverance to face, head-on, the trauma of their own experiences, many Indigenous women continue to be the collectors of medicine to heal and bring comfort to the communities to which they belong. Like they did thousands of years ago, they work to bring their people home and keep their families protected. By doing so, these Indigenous women display many of the qualities we admire in courageously strong, perseverant people. They are resilient, they are patient, they have had the stamina to endure, and they've shown the ability to adapt through challenges and changes.

This is the courage I have called Apaniiwa: Strength and Perseverance.

Rebound

Resilience is the capacity to recover, to rebound from the upheavals of life. It is more than a person's survival story; it is a determined, perhaps even joyful, forging of new life beyond grief.

> Never be ashamed of a scar. It simply means you were stronger than whatever tried to hurt you.
>
> —Unknown

Several years ago, I had a conversation with a talented investigator I've had the pleasure of knowing for many years—a seasoned detective who's seen a lot over the course of his distinguished career. Running into each other at the end of another hectic day, we caught up in our back lot for a few minutes where, in passing, I mentioned my plans to write a second book, one focused on the greatness and courage of people.

We swapped stories about the incredible zest some have when it comes to life; uplifting stories about people who find themselves with the cards stacked completely against them yet they survive and even flourish. From his own vault of experiences, he shared two examples of inspiration which he felt demonstrated the resiliency of human spirit—and I couldn't have agreed more.

The first story began on the last day of a ten-day festival in our city that showcases the talents of rodeo cowboys, chuck wagon racers, artisans, ranchers, Indigenous people, musicians, and farmers. This annual celebration also brings plenty of tourists. For ten days our city transforms into one big party with beer gardens, outdoor patios, pancake breakfasts, and private events that brim with urban cowboys in their best denim and plaid. Inevitably, there's also sure to be a baby boom—nine months later.

Despite all the fun, though, events such as these can also bring out the dark side of people, especially when alcohol binges blur the lines between right and wrong.

The victim in this story had just left her final party to take in the cool night air that comes to our mountain city in the late evening. Her plan was to walk the few blocks back to her place—alone. Along her route, a surveillance camera mounted on a nearby home captured her tiny frame strolling down the sidewalk. A figure was visible in the distance, standing at the corner. As she appeared about to go past him, the camera captured a brief interaction between the two. Then, without warning, he began a violent and brazen sexual assault against her, right there on the sidewalk, in plain view of the camera and any potential passersby.

She fought and screamed. Several neighbors called police to report the attack. The culprit dragged the woman into a nearby front yard, where he continued his rape, beating her so badly about the head and face she lost consciousness.

The first officer responding to the scene arrived moments after the attacker fled. He found the victim behind some high bushes, naked from the waist down, unresponsive, and drowning in her own blood. Officers and emergency medical services worked feverishly to keep her alive on the way to the hospital.

Although comatose for more than a week, the woman lived. After waking from her coma, she couldn't feed herself, and she had no recollection of what had happened. Over the coming weeks and months, she faced the challenges that many suffering from a significant brain injury face: re-learning how to walk, talk, and gain the use of other motor functions.

But despite this incredible blow, she not only found her will to live, she also found her sobriety, making a clean start in another province after her release from hospital four months later.

Her persistence and resiliency left an impact on this investigator that he never forgot.

His second example involved a man originally from a small community in Pakistan. As a teacher, he believed in fundamental human rights and equality, which included a girl's right to be educated. But where he came from, not all believed this, and it was dangerous for people with his perspective to espouse such beliefs.

Regardless, he went forward with his dream to build an all-girls school in a region of his country controlled by the Islamic State of Iraq and Syria (ISIS), an organization that believes girls should not receive an education outside the home. Nevertheless, with hard work and persistence, within a year of his idea taking shape, he opened the doors to a school for girls in his home town.

Sadly, the authorities learned of the school and burned it to the ground. Then they came looking for him. Tipped off that he was now in the crosshairs of a terrorist organization, he made the difficult decision to flee his homeland to Europe, leaving behind a family of three small children, a family for whom he had been the sole breadwinner. He escaped.

From Europe he came to Canada, seeking asylum. He wholeheartedly embraced all the freedoms Canadians often take for granted, and for nine months he worked with immigration officials to have his family join him.

But the wheels of bureaucracy are slow, and in the interim, he planned how he would celebrate his very first Canada Day, intending to give thanks to everyone with whom he crossed paths for his opportunity to be Canadian.

July 1, 2019, started as he dreamed it would, with friends sharing in the activities offered along the river and plazas and parks of our downtown core. No alcohol, no drugs; just high on Canada, he and a group of immigrated doctors and engineers hit all the high points of the day. As day turned to night, one of the group members proposed they all go and play a game or two of pool before heading home. The group traveled together to a local billiard hall. Arriving close to closing, one of the group members decided he would go inside and talk to the staff to see if there was still time to get in one or two last games while the teacher and his other friends waited outside.

As patrons left the hall, the teacher and friends wished them "Happy Canada Day." Most enthusiastically replied with the same good wishes.

One couple responded differently. "Happy Canada Day," the young lady replied playfully.

Her boyfriend found her response to be flirtatious. "Stop talking to my girlfriend," he yelled at one of the men.

"We don't want trouble," the teacher said in broken English.

The offender began to walk away.

But not for long. He stopped. He returned, releasing a string of profanity at the doctor.

The teacher, in an effort to de-escalate the situation, asked the belligerent man to stop swearing and to stop threatening.

The teacher became the new target. The offender struck out.

The teacher had never been a fighter and had no way to defend himself except to cower. The others tried to pull the man off as he repeatedly stomped, kicked, and punched the teacher in the body and head until he was rendered unconscious. When paramedics arrived, they rushed him to the hospital, not expecting him to survive.

Weeks went by. He lay in an intensive care unit in a vegetative state. No amount of medical intervention could wake him from his traumatic brain injuries.

After a series of difficult conversations between the teacher's family back in Pakistan and doctors here, the decision was made to discontinue life support.

But the teacher did not die.

This outcome baffled doctors. They put him on a feeding tube, waiting for the Grim Reaper to arrive.

Months went by. Yet, instead of declining, he began…slowly…to wake. He began to communicate. His recovery was so miraculous he was eventually moved to a long-care brain trauma unit for rehabilitation. He had to relearn English and math and reacquaint himself with his family, erased as a result of his injury.

My colleague, like the doctors, was inspired by his recovery and he told me he believed it was the teacher's joyfulness and positivity that saved his life. The teacher would often be heard saying, "I am so happy to be alive and get this opportunity to breathe and talk again." His statements dumbfounded many, because in this case, the teacher had every excuse in the world to be angry, bitter, and full of hate.

Back home, his family had become destitute because of his hospitalization and inability to send funds home. The Canadian government refused to issue visas for them to travel to Canada to be by his side in case they disappeared after arriving.

And the person who was accused of the vicious assault?

After his arrest, the offender was released on bail within twenty-four hours. Prior to trial, he pled guilty to his crime but skipped town and went on the lam for eighteen months. Eventually caught, he went back to the same court and received a sentence of just four years, even though his own counsel had asked the judge to consider a sentence in the six- to eight-year range while the crown prosecutor had asked for ten.

The teacher, my colleague told me, was not even angry about this. In fact, he wished his attacker only forgiveness. After spending eighteen months in care, the teacher now lives with friends who help him with the day-to-day stuff. And his resilient spirit? It continues to live on.

Resilience.

As much as the challenges of life can get us down, there are those who find ways to pick themselves up after disappointment or tragedy.

It was an early spring day back in 2016 when a father, enraged with his wife and daughter, shot both in the face inside their family home while the other two children, huddling together in a corner, looked on. The catalyst of the event was an argument that spiraled out of control to the point where the father felt justified in killing both with a gun he had retrieved from a back bedroom.

The wife succumbed to her injuries in one of the children's bedrooms. The fifteen-year-old daughter lay motionless on the living room floor. Playing dead, she heard the last words her father would ever say to her. "You deserved to die," his self-justification because she had come to the aid of the mother whilst the couple had been arguing.

Following the shooting, the man snatched up the two remaining children, a three-year-old and a twelve-year-old, loaded them into a black truck, and sped away.

The surviving daughter managed to phone 911. "My dad has a gun," she mumbled through her broken mouth, "and my mom has also been shot."

Through her own pain and grief, her resiliency and desire to see her mother and siblings survive gave her the strength to provide dispatchers with a description of her father's truck so responders could be on the lookout for it as they sped toward the scene.

It did not take long to find the truck. An alert officer reported the vehicle's direction of travel to other police units in the area. As the line of police cars grew behind the suspect vehicle, the thoughts of the officers must have been drawn to the safe recovery of the two children believed to be inside the vehicle— hopefully, still alive.

As the truck continued down the road, speeds were uncharacteristically low, a sign perhaps that the offender was thinking hard about his next move. The truck meandered through residential streets followed by police vehicles with their lights and sirens blaring.

Then, the officer in the lead car made an unsettling observation. The killer's arm extended from the driver's side window.

Before he could react, he heard the unmistakable sound of a gunshot.

Then, the father slowed the truck to a crawl, pulled the truck to the curb, and stopped. With his arm still outstretched, gun still in hand, he exited the vehicle.

The officers drew their cars to a stop. "Police! Don't move!" they yelled. "Drop the gun!"

Each officer drew down on the suspect. No doubt, each thought, *this will most certainly become an officer-involved shooting.*

Then, the father did the unexpected. He tossed the gun onto the roadway. He submitted and was taken into custody.

Charged with the murder of his wife and the shooting of his daughter, the man pled guilty almost immediately. The two children inside the truck were rescued and reunited with their resilient older sister.

Strength.

If you have ever been a parent, then I am sure you have also experienced wanting *just one night of peaceful sleep*—the type of sleep that seems almost non-existent with a newborn in the home. The constant up-and-down to deal with a crying infant is enough to drive any new parent wild. Without the support of a spouse or partner, I could imagine this experience is amplified tenfold. The endless loop of *eat, sleep, poop, repeat,* which plays out like Groundhog Day, on top of sleep deprivation, could lead a parent to do the unthinkable: shake.

Despite all the best advice, all the literature, and all the parenting courses out there, inevitably, there will be a parent who will make the catastrophic choice to shake their infant. When this happens, the baby's brain jolts inside the skull, bruised. The jarring can be permanently damaging—to those who survive. Many don't.

Survivors of shaking can require lifelong medical care for conditions such as partial or total blindness, seizures, learning disabilities, intellectual disabilities, and behavior issues. This is a high price to pay for a caregiver's inability to put down a colicky baby and simply leave the room. In my area of work, shaken baby files would sometimes make it onto our radar while we waited to see if an infant rushed to the hospital would die. I know: grim, but true.

Several years ago, a colleague of mine who worked in our child abuse unit shared the story of a wee one who, by indications, was going to become our city's fourteenth homicide of the year.

It was a cold March when the stepfather of a charming four-year-old girl named Destiny frantically called her birth mother at work. "Honey, you need to come home quick. Something is wrong with Destiny."

Pedal to the metal, Destiny's mom broke land speed records on her way back to the family's two-bedroom apartment the family shared along with Destiny's three-month-old brother. The apartment was a scene of chaos and confusion.

Destiny lay on the floor, unconscious, with marks covering her body from head to torso.

Confronting her husband, the mother could not get a straight answer about what had happened. And, incredibly, over the course of *an hour*, the two deliberated what to do. All the while, Destiny lay on the floor, unconscious and barely breathing.

Finally, Destiny's mom convinced her husband that they should take her to Emergency. They drove her to the nearest medical facility where a physician immediately arranged for her to be transported to the Children's Hospital.

There, a team of doctors and medical staff performed brain surgery to relieve the swelling in Destiny's head. Surgeons had no other option but to remove pieces of Destiny's skull and brain—but by making this decision, doctors knew her life would be forever altered.

Destiny remained in the hospital from March to December. Investigators routinely checked in on her and the doctors who'd saved her life. They learned that Destiny's injuries could be equated to the trauma she would've endured if she'd been traveling in a small car that hit a semi-truck in excess of one hundred kilometers per hour—repeatedly.

Investigators also learned that, although Destiny's surgery went "well," her brain no longer functioned as it should. Surgeons believed it was only a matter of time before she would die. If, by some miracle, she didn't succumb to her injuries, she would be severely handicapped for the rest of her life.

But Destiny was resilient. Her four-year-old body was

determined to heal, to survive. As every day passed, signs of Destiny's fight were documented by staff. First, she began to react to stimuli in her environment—she regained her startle reflex.

Though doctors were grateful for this first sign of healing, their optimism was cautious. "Although these signs are positive, you must understand that Destiny will never walk, talk, see, or be able to do anything on her own again."

But. Eight months after this little girl came to the hospital, she took her first step during a music therapy session.

Today, Destiny is nine years old, and although she still has disabilities, she walks with a brace on only one of her ankles, can talk and feed herself again, goes to a regular school with supports in place, loves to sing, and by all accounts is as happy and healthy as a nine-year-old who was never expected to survive could be.

In the words of the investigator who has remained inspired by her, "Today Destiny is *killing* life!" Destiny is also now living with a new family along with her brother.

People who exemplify the virtue of rebound can teach us all a valuable takeaway:

It matters not how hard you get knocked down, but the heights you achieve when you bounce back up.

Patience

Patience truly is a virtue.

I would argue that many in our world have lost the virtue of patience and have replaced it with a desire for instant gratification. We need faster internet, faster phones, and faster computers because we require the answers to our greatest questions *now*, not later! We want to lose ten pounds before our next beach holiday. As parents, we lose patience watching our children struggle to tie their own shoes, and so we end up doing it for them or buying Velcro shoes—teaching them what, exactly? We buy the big house, the big truck, and the shiniest camper—on credit or with a mortgage—without considering if we can afford that lifestyle. The Canadian household-debt-to-disposable-income ratio has risen from 86% in 1990 to 182% in 2022. For these reasons, I believe patience is becoming more and more a quality found in the uncommon person.

And patience is necessary in police investigations.

Unless those lucky breaks all investigators hope for come within the first couple of days of a new case, families can end up waiting excruciatingly long periods of time before the identity of their loved one's killer reveals itself, if it ever does. This is a hard reality for everyone involved. This is one of the reasons why innovative investigators, advancements in science, and the talents of people like our genealogists are so welcome. The truth is, despite everyone's best efforts, in my community, approximately two in every ten cases my former unit received will remain unsolved.

Imagine going to bed at night, always wondering who the perpetrator was who took the life of your son, your daughter, your partner, or your best friend. As stated earlier, for those in this unenviable place, wondering *why* and the more pressing, *who* can become all-consuming.

There have been times when some families or friends, unable to be patient enough to wait for these answers, put on their own detectives' hats to try and learn the truth. This can cause more harm than good. I've seen rushes to judgment made by families or friends who identify an innocent person as the perpetrator, which in turn puts the innocent party's welfare and reputation at risk. I've seen names offered to investigators based on assumptions and street rumors that cause unnecessary distractions and loose ends for investigators to clean up while trying to stay focused on where the actual evidence is leading them to resolve the case. I've seen individuals fabricate or stretch evidence to fit their own theory of what has happened and who they think is involved.

All these outcomes cause investigators to spend valuable time focused on distractions away from fact-based and scientifically collected evidence. Several of our most notable cases over the years began with chasing the wrong individual based on a hunch or a rumor before verifiable evidence revealed the error, and the focus switched to the actual offender.

Though family members might find it hard to understand, in fact, the greatest pressure for any investigator to resolve cases quickly comes from the investigator themself and their own drive to solve the mystery. It doesn't come from a supervisor or the upper brass or even from the victim's friends or the media. This type of pressure builds with every hour that passes in which a case remains unsolved, and I believe every investigator I've worked with feels it. That is, in part, why we work long hours.

When families *can* put trust in the process and practice

patience, they gift investigators some relief from that internal pressure, and that often leads to better outcomes.

I remember early in my homicide career, I served a wonderful family who, over the years, has really become more to me than "another victim's family." Today we are friends, brought together the day their son was callously murdered. I remember from the very beginning the support and trust they provided me by sitting back and patiently waiting as I delved into one of the most complex cases of my career. In total, they had to wait ten months.

As I was nearing the end of the investigation and anticipating that arrests were imminent, I was sitting with them one night over coffee. "We know you are doing your best," they told me. "We know you're working hard every day. We'll wait until you've finished your investigation. In the meantime, is there anything we can do to help? Just let us know."

Their words to me were so relieving. They lessened a little of the internal weight I was feeling and freed my mind from my own internalized pressure so I could remain focused on collecting those last few nuggets of evidence that would ultimately lead to the identification, arrest, and conviction of the two people who took their beloved family member's life.

Outside of families who have lost someone to murder, there are others who must not only face the loss of a family member but also live with the fact that a medical examiner or coroner was unable to determine the exact manner of their loved one's death.

In other words, despite everyone's best efforts, the investigation could not definitively determine the manner of death, leaving them to wonder if it was suicide, an accident, a natural death, or even a homicide. And if it was a homicide, who was responsible for their death?

Seems unreal, right? But the truth is, we aren't always able to know for sure. This becomes the reality some families must face.

When we recover bones or human remains (depending on the extent of what is recovered), it's often true that without a full skeleton, a medical examiner or coroner will have difficulty concluding the manner of death beyond "undetermined." There simply is not enough evidence to prove whether a victim was murdered or not. A person could have been choked to death, stabbed, or even shot, but if the collected remains do not have evidence of this—and many don't because human remains are often scattered great distances by scavengers—then the medical examiner cannot conclude any finding from the evidence they can't see. This leaves families not knowing how their loved one died. Fundamentally, they become the poster children for the virtue of patience: knowing the answer to their greatest question may never come.

Many years ago, Susan gave birth to a full-term, stillborn daughter. Cause of death? She will never know. She was checked for the condition of gestational diabetes after the fact, but gestational diabetes, if it is a factor in an unborn child, usually clears up in the mother after the child is born, so the test was inconclusive. However, at the time, Susan was married to a medical resident who, through his study of medicine, was aware that a high percentage of stillbirths have an undetermined cause. Although this was not an answer to her question, it helped her, knowing not to spend fruitless emotional energy searching for a cause.

Almost a decade ago, I had a case in which, after spending the weekend in another province, a distraught husband came home to find the love of his life dead in the basement of their home.

The scene's first responding officers were horrified by what they saw. The victim lay motionless and cold on the floor of the basement, partially clothed. Her blood appeared to have been smeared, even "painted" onto almost every hard surface, from the floor to the walls.

At autopsy, her cause of death was determined to be from exsanguination (blood loss) and hypothermia. The medical examiner was able to determine that the loss of blood came from a wound on her forehead, which she presumably received when her head struck, or was struck by, a ceramic piggy bank at the top of the flight of stairs leading to the basement.

At the time of her death (which we initially believed was a homicide), we learned that she had been talking to her husband on the phone when he heard the dog yelp, and the phone then disconnected. In the investigation that ensued, members of our crime scenes unit poured over the entire scene, looking for any evidence that might identify her perpetrator—but none was found. Even the piggy bank was fingerprinted, with no prints found and no sign that the thin layer of dust on the piggy bank had even been disturbed.

When samples of blood and other biological materials were sent away for testing, they returned with even more puzzling results.

There was no evidence to suggest that any other person was involved in her death—in fact, the opposite, the evidence was beginning to point in the direction of an accidental fall down the stairs. This conclusion was supported further by a team of behavioral profilers and biomechanics experts. The issue, however, was evidence that didn't make sense. To *everyone*.

For example, the victim lived with two animals: a dog and a cat. But there were no animal tracks found in the blood. So, neither the cat nor the dog entered the basement to check on her. There was also no evidence in the blood that any footwear impressions were left behind either. Further, there *was* evidence from her own barefoot impressions that, at some point, she was still walking around in the basement and had walked to the foot of the stairs but, in the end, did not ascend. Why?

These facts have always remained troubling. Perhaps the animals did not go down the stairs, and she did not venture up because there was a threat still in the house. On the stairs? And maybe that threat remained in the home while she died.

In the end, this case remains "open" until some piece of new evidence is brought forward to explain how this all transpired. For me, personally, I must put trust in the experts and the evidence at hand and I believe that the victim likely died from a fall down the stairs. However, absolute certainty will likely never come, and in the meantime, the family will be left with no choice but patience.

In another investigation I was involved in, not all questions sought by a family could be properly answered through a thorough investigative process.

In this case, a young man in the prime of his life went out one night to meet a young woman after "liking" each other on a dating profile. Their date eventually led the two back to the young woman's home, where, according to her, the pair indulged in some opioids and had sex. In the morning, when she awoke, he was dead on her couch. Sadly, in this day and age, this is not that unlikely an occurrence. But the next part of the story, I would argue, is.

The victim in this case was 6'6" and well over 230 pounds, while the woman was 5'5" and 125 pounds. She reported she was strong enough to wrap him up in a blanket, move him out of her residence, and place him in the trunk of her car with help from her grandmother, who lived nearby and required oxygen to survive. From there, the woman transported the victim out into the mountains, about an hour's drive from the city, where she removed him from the trunk, discarded his body into a pond, and returned home to continue with her day.

The first indication police had that anything was amiss came when the young man's mother called investigators several days later to report him missing. Months went by as missing persons investigators combed through the evidence to determine what could have happened to the victim. Ultimately, they came to learn through phone records and records maintained by the dating app that on the night of his death, the victim had been contacted by the female suspect from a "fake" account she had set up earlier that day and then took down the day after.

Hmm.

Investigators also learned that, on the same day she set up the "fake" account, the female suspect had been in contact with a male who also happened to know the victim and had a vendetta against him over a drug deal that may or may not have happened. With this new information, suspicion grew that the missing man could very easily have been a victim of foul play. Acting on this belief, a warrant was executed at the female suspect's residence and on her vehicle. Several small drops of the victim's blood were found in both her residence and the trunk of her car—inconsistent with the suspect's report of death by opioid poisoning. Suspicions grew further. The suspect was brought in for questioning the following week.

However, as members of the missing persons team and I began to prepare for the arrest, one thing remained a mystery. The location of the victim's remains.

As luck would have it, the answer came on the weekend before the planned arrests. A photographer out for a stroll through the foothills noticed an unusual amount of bird activity in the middle of a mountain pond. As he steadied his camera and zoomed in, the unmistakable outline of a human body floating face down became clear. Our victim had been found. Police arrived at the scene to recover the remains and have them sent to the medical examiner's office for autopsy.

"Undetermined," the doctor said after his examination and all the tests were in. There was too much predation from animals and too much decomposition after being in the water for months to understand conclusively how this man died. And with that, a charge of homicide became impossible.

In the end, despite an extensive investigation that included undercover operations and wiretaps, no further details were learned that would shake the female suspect's story. She met the victim on a dating app, they used drugs, he died on her couch, and she and her eighty-year-old grandmother transported his body to the mountains. She was eventually convicted of an indignity to human remains offense and was sentenced to a short stint in jail. But for the family, I imagine believing there was something more and having half the story never told must eat away at them every day. Their quiet patience to know the full account of what happened to their son remains today.

Outside of families awaiting justice, police interviewers and hostage negotiators must also practice patience.

Whether in an interview room or out in the field on a negotiation with a suicidal gunman, officers entrusted with the responsibility to negotiate in tense situations must be prepared to put in the time to build the kind of rapport that an interviewee or an individual in crisis will need in order to open up and do what is asked of them: tell the truth, surrender a weapon, or let a hostage go.

It's true, apart from some very rare examples, most suspects do not "give it up" the minute an investigator enters the interview room. Instead, the interviewer must work patiently to create the type of atmosphere that will lead to obtaining a truthful statement. This can take hours. From my own experience, most major crime interviews I've been involved with can last six to eight hours—and with breaks for sleep, food, and washroom, up to twenty-four.

There are many ways to build rapport, and every investigator I have seen does it a bit differently, but we all follow a similar path.

First, we create a positive presence in the room by remaining respectful toward the individual we are interviewing despite the allegation against them. A lesson from my first book was "You catch more flies with honey," and this is absolutely true. But trust me, it is not always easy being the one to bring the honey. Imagine interviewing a sexual predator who has been arrested for kidnapping a five-year-old, and when the interview starts, you have no idea where the child is or if they are alive or dead. Or, an offender accused of raping and murdering a woman he followed off a train platform. Or a mother who broke bones, tortured, and burned their own child.

None of these real-life scenarios is easy. Experienced interviewers must put mind over matter as they work to empathize with the killer's plight of being accused of such horrible crimes. The stark reality is that if they don't, the interview will likely go nowhere.

Ask yourself: if you were a bad guy, would you talk in detail about the most heinous and intimate parts of your savagery to a stranger with whom you have no connection? I would say never. It is up to the interviewer to create an atmosphere where this type of free-flowing conversation can occur. And, believe it or not, such techniques work more often than you may think.

The patience piece to the rapport puzzle will always come down to fighting the natural reaction of wanting to jump in and start with, "Why did you do it, you scumbag?"

A disconnecting, off-putting, and rushed statement of judgment—or at least that is how it would be viewed by the interviewee—will not result in bringing a criminal to justice. Instead, it is a balancing act to know when it is time to strike with the tough questions and copious amounts of time spent getting them to talk a little about themselves while the interviewer shares a little about themselves, too. *Where did you go to school? Did you grow up here? What have your previous experiences with the police been like? What kind of hobbies are you into? What is your family like? Are you hungry?* are all questions designed to build a connection with a subject you hope will begin to warm to you.

In my view being likable to an interview subject is a key to building an initial connection and rapport. Robert Cialdini is right when he said people are more apt to like someone we share common ground with, who pays us compliments and who agrees with us. To knock these important line items off in an interview room takes time but taking this time is worth it if it gets you closer to understanding the whole truth—including the ugly.

In the world of crisis negotiations, there's an old slogan: "Time, talk, and tear gas." Perhaps crass sounding, the simple message is the instruction manual for police operations teams dealing with very dangerous situations involving barricaded gunmen, hostages, and people in crisis. The first two words, time and talk, account for the virtue of patience, which must be possessed by those sent to resolve these types of incidents so that these events do not turn into *shit shows* right out of the gate.

The third, "tear gas," represents an alternative that is always there if, for some reason, the time and talk break down and there exists no alternative but some form of tactical intervention to resolve an emergent crisis and protect life. Thankfully, in our jurisdiction, the talents of our negotiator teams usually result in "talk" as the final outcome nine out of ten times.

A friend of mine spent a good portion of his career developing his expertise in both crisis negotiation and interviewing. He has honed his skills so much that he is one of our service's resident experts and mentors in both disciplines. He teaches other officers here and across the country on both subjects regularly. He is a salt-of-the-earth guy who talks a bit funny (being from the East Coast). He's also one of the most patient people I know and gifted at developing rapport with some of the most unlikeable characters out there.

Outside of work, he finds enjoyment sitting in an animal blind for hours in near-freezing temperatures, waiting for the sign of a deer or moose to cross his rifle's sights, a perfect hobby for someone who possesses his type of patience. At the office, his skills jump out in the interview room or negotiator's van as he takes the time to build a connection with someone he has just met. Over the years, we've talked about some of the craziest things he's had a hand in resolving, and I am always mystified about how, 99 times out of 100, these crisis situations work out with successful resolutions. This is a testament to the time-and-talk mantra and his skills and passion for interviewing and negotiating.

One incident he shared with me occurred a decade ago when he became involved as the team leader in charge of a negotiation with a male who was suffering from a full-blown mental health crisis. It began one morning when a man in his early thirties in psychosis entered a bustling downtown shopping mall, proceeded to the third floor, then climbed with only socks on his feet to the top of an inch of glass that acted as a railing over the floors below. Shoppers in bewilderment and alarm watched, fearing the man would fall or jump to certain death from the edge of his precarious perch.

Police were called immediately.

As the team leader, my colleague assigned two experienced officers to conduct the negotiations. It would be their job to build a relationship of trust, to take the time to listen, acknowledge, and understand what was going on in the man's life that led him to a point where he now stood: on the edge of a glass partition no wider than what you would see in a hockey rink.

Negotiators listened to the man as he described how he believed demons were chasing him. They empathized with his fear when he said demons occupied the mall's second floor. They acknowledged the man's concerns for almost eight hours until, finally, he moved from the glass edge onto the solid tile footing of the floor.

For my colleague, running a negotiation for as long as this one lasted required putting complete and total trust in his negotiators whose boots were on the ground. But as you can imagine, this could make a less patient officer uncomfortable, perhaps leading him to attempt to rush the man to bring him down to safety sooner rather than waiting hours for the negotiators to perform their craft. Such a sentiment would be one my colleague would have to acknowledge and then move past, in order to reach a successful resolution.

Have you ever been in a room full of silent people? Inevitably, at some point, the silence will be broken. A room can become so uncomfortable with only the sound of humming lights that someone will take it upon themself to say something to break the quiet. Now imagine you are one of the support officers who has been tasked with standing in the mall with your hands in your pocket while the negotiators move through the slow time-talk continuum. You are told, "Just be patient and wait to see how negotiations go."

But this can be a lot to ask of people who come into policing who want to help. Like the person who speaks up to break a silence, officers, in this case, began formulating their own plans about what they could be doing. Well-intentioned, they took it upon themselves to pad the floor and the railings below the psychotic man in the event he did jump or fall, with the faint hope that this padding could do anything to protect someone plunging three stories.

However, such actions had to be quashed before they worked against what negotiators were trying to do. Their actions would have spoken louder than the negotiators' words. The message this person in crisis might read was that they were getting ready for his jump. I would hedge a bet and say such actions would be interpreted no differently than if the medical examiner or coroner van rolled up and parked outside.

However, this is not the end of the story.

After spending only twelve hours in the hospital, the subject was released. He left the hospital and marched onto an overpass railing above a major thoroughfare and again threatened to jump.

After the debriefings had finished and the tired negotiators' heads finally hit their pillows, their phones rang again, and they were called back to this new event with the same male. Negotiators hoped all the positive work they had done with this gentleman only hours earlier would still work.

They were not wrong. After only a few minutes on the scene, the officers and the subject greeted one another like old friends. With a warm cup of coffee in hand, the negotiators were able to bring him down in short order, and the incident was resolved before it even really began.

This time, on his second return to the hospital, he was held for several weeks and treated for his illness—a relief for all who had come to know him.

The courage of strong, perseverant, and patient people can teach us valuable lessons.

> Patience is not passive. On the contrary, it is concentrated strength.
> —Bruce Lee

Stamina

I believe, if we want to achieve extraordinary things in our lives, we may need to tolerate a certain amount of discomfort to do so. The ability to endure through extended periods of difficulty in environments that make us uncomfortable represents our next virtue of strong and perseverant people: stamina.

Often, the things we most cherish are directly related to what we had to give up or the pain we went through to get them. Across the board, every police officer you will ever meet will have stories about how they also had to "embrace the suck" while keeping the community safe and free of threat. From vomiting drunks in the back of their cruisers, balancing baby schedules while working night shifts, sitting in the house of a decomposing person, being spit on, punched, or kicked by some pompous prick, or being cross-examined on the stand for hours, are all part of the process that prepares each of us for the next phase of our career.

Most of the members I know who work in Homicide would agree that staying in a career such as ours requires physical and mental stamina. In this case, stamina is developed through years of acclimation to the dirty, the bad, the ugly: the "suck." No different from how a long-distance runner trains to build endurance before a marathon, investigators with the heavy responsibility of investigating homicides, child deaths, suspicious deaths, and suicides do not develop their stamina overnight. It takes years to become accustomed to the unpleasant sights and smells of a death investigation. Entering the Homicide Unit's sixty-hour work week and witnessing bloodied, broken, beaten bodies too early in a young officer's career often results in a quick exit. Conversely, if a person joins the unit with experience and time under their belt, they may find themself to really come to love the work and the pace.

But it's not just about how we are exposed to experience prior to arriving in Homicide, which aids in our survival stamina. Thriving here also requires members to come up with strategies to mitigate, forget, or move on from the things they see, hear, and experience. This helps prevent the ugliness from coming back, over and over again, in the form of PTSD. Compartmentalization is one technique people who exhibit stamina can use: moving the sights, sounds, and smells of an unpleasant experience out of mind and replacing them with more useful thoughts. For instance, I never look at a young victim and think, *Oh my god, that child is the same age as mine,* or examine a crime scene and get hung up on all the blood covering the floors, walls, and ceilings. Instead, I look at the child and the scene and think about the treasure trove of forensic clues around me, which will aid me in identifying "who did this." What I am not focused on is the unpleasant sight; full attention is put on solving the crime.

Other techniques can include focusing on your body, perhaps your breath, or relaxing a particular muscle group. If your mind is too stressed by anxiety to focus, distraction—a book, a movie, exercising, seeking out friends—can allow time to pass and anxiety to dissipate.

For years now, I've admired a good friend partly because he's always kind, gentle, supportive, even-keeled, heartfelt, and warm. But I also admire him because of his ability to stick to the laborious, "head and heart heavy" work he's done for the last fifteen years of his career. I first met my colleague in the early 2000s when I joined our city's Drug Unit. It was during our undercover time together that he became one of my most trusted colleagues. In 2008, his extensive body of investigative experience earned him a promotion to detective and, shortly after, an assignment to the newly formed Integrated Child Exploitation Unit (ICE), where he's remained ever since.

To me, he's the perfect description of the superhero Ironman. He's confident, innovative and creative. And like his superhero doppelgänger, he's passionate and committed to an ideal—sometimes sacrificing his own personal feelings and wellbeing for the betterment of people—specifically, the fight to locate and save sexually exploited children.

As an ICE investigator, he has seen more than his fair share of awful. ICE investigators are responsible for identifying, locating, and saving kids around the globe, from newborns to children up to the age of seventeen, who have been subjected to the manufacturing of child sexual abuse material (pictures and videos of children being sexually abused). In his career, he has saved over fifty kids from the clutches of pedophiles and has assisted in countless other investigations that have gone on to save thousands and thousands more from falling *into* the hands of perpetrators. In addition, he has helped shut down consumer access to such materials and to shut down distributors.

Using a variety of handles and aliases, he sits down every day at a computer screen and goes undercover surfing the internet. Specifically, he searches platforms used to distribute the most vile and graphic images to pedophiles and predators around the world, looking for pictures that may assist in identifying and locating the young victims. Birthmarks, scars, or clothing common to a particular region of the world; dialects of language spoken on a video; or even the inadvertent utterance of a name—all are clues that can assist him, and hundreds of other ICE investigators globally, intent on putting a stop to this type of grotesque content. And their mission is an international one. Hundreds of police officers like him, from at least seventy countries, work together to resolve these files. The people behind the big tech must also be applauded for their laborious efforts to remove this type of content from their platforms as well.

Similar to us in Homicide, to become proficient and effective in their roles, my colleague and his peers have had to go through a process of learning how to reconcile the deluge of *bad* and *ugly* so they can continue to maintain the mental stamina and endurance needed to capture the abusers and the users of child sexual abuse material.

And also similar to us in Homicide, they hear the same things from people, sometimes in the form of a statement or a question: "There is no way I could do what YOU do. How do you do it? How do you deal with it?"

My colleague says these questions make the job he does more about him and less about the greater mission at hand—saving the victims of child sexual abuse and preventing their further exploitation. He says that if he made his career about himself and his own feelings, then his ability to do this work would be severely diminished. And in his case, the big picture behind every image or video is a child enduring the worst violations a person can endure.

Thinking in this way, the viewing of the actual material becomes irrelevant because the pursuit to save the child comes first. There is no room in his day for a "poor me" moment. The sobering truth for him is that, when he hears a dad talk about his family's Friday night movie with his kids—popcorn, maybe a pizza, and a G-rated movie on the Disney channel—there are other children out there right now for whom, when a dad offers a movie night in, it takes on a completely different meaning.

Thoughts like this are where his fire and drive come from and where his courage to endure uncomfortable and unpleasant things is rooted.

Identification of victims and perpetrators is only one aspect of this investigator's role. Other facets of the investigations include interviewing perpetrators, distributors, and consumers of child sexual abuse material.

Of the approximately eighty-five offenders arrested each year in our city, each is treated with respect, as a suspect is presumed innocent until proven guilty. In the interview suite, they are given an opportunity for their side of the story to be heard. Unlike what you might see in the movies, they are not hit with phone books or bars of soap wrapped up in socks. The lighting in the interview room is not one bulb hanging from the ceiling. The truth is that so much work goes into these cases that an investigator *must* have the self-discipline to not ruin a case with a lapse in judgment. Anything less than complete professionalism is a slap in the face to the greater efforts of the investigation. The victim and all those who have worked so hard to seek justice for them depend on the investigator to conduct the interview skillfully, as an accusation of bias can have the case thrown out and the perpetrator continue his exploitation.

At work, his thoughts are with the sexually abused; outside of work, his ability to compartmentalize his exposure to sexual violence is essential. He must practice self-care to keep his mind healthy, keep his energy levels up, and maintain his stamina.

For example, when he is viewing a video with sound, he listens through the audio only once, focusing on the dialect, listening for a name or any clue to aid his search for the victim's location. After that, he does not listen again unless necessary. He also disciplines himself to avoid viewing his screen before going home by doing most of the heavy lifting at the beginning of the shift. This allows other daily tasks to be his last thoughts as he leaves at the end of the day.

Finally, he has found outlets away from the office that he enjoys. He has developed a love of cooking and an appreciation for music, which soothes him and allows his mind to keep a tune inside his head. And his friends are not all police officers; instead, he enjoys the company of an eclectic group who never ask him what's going on at the office—because they really never want to know.

Is the self-care 100% effective? No. There are moments

when he is jogged back to memories that sit deep inside the back of his head—certain noises being one trigger. And there are things that can be uncomfortable, things he will never understand, like a perpetrator's wife's undeterred support for her husband despite the grim accusations he faces after police come knocking on their door with a warrant for their computer in hand.

But despite his scars, people like this investigator teach us a valuable lesson about the courage to endure unpleasant and uncomfortable things in the service of the greater good. He is an outstanding example of the virtue of mental stamina.

Recently, I read a post from him over social media that captures his reasons for continuing this important work (excerpted):

"We will go anywhere in the world to rescue children. Some of our investigations have worked for years. There are no boundaries—time or geography—to our work. To all the children out there waiting for help, we want you to know that we won't stop looking for you. Please hold on. We are coming."

Often the things we most cherish are related to "the suck" we endured to get them.

Adaptability

The ability to pivot—to bend but not break, to change focus, or to flip processes and adapt to a crisis, change, or uncertainty—is a key virtue of a courageously strong, perseverant person.

Undercover police officers are admired for their ability to remain adaptable. Thrust into unpredictable situations, they must be able to melt into their environments like chameleons. They must be able to think on their feet and react to unplanned changes with ease, all the while *not* throwing up red flags that could compromise themselves or the operation they are part of. As a group they continue to be some of the most adaptable and creative people I have ever known.

During my own three years working undercover, I got to see my teammates' talents day after day and night after night. I also saw how we, as a larger group, worked behind the scenes of any drug buy or undercover scenario to provide support to our operators so they could move freely in the environment they were working in. Having it any other way would put the operator at the pointy end of the stick. We didn't want them in a situation where they could be challenged about why they couldn't walk around the corner or go down a side street or alley to make a drug purchase from a trafficker.

Of course, working in an unscripted world could lead to safety challenges that we always had to be aware of. I remember more than once having a pit in my stomach when a team member's tail lamps disappeared from view or when things started to go off the rails.

One such incident occurred on a warm summer night

downtown. The officer involved was a veteran in the drug unit. Known for his big personality, he was popular with his teammates, and the bad guys loved him. They loved him so much that, more than once, he had opportunities to be introduced to larger drug suppliers.

After months of investigation, the operator had negotiated a deal for a kilogram of cocaine, which at that time cost about $45,000.00. The undercover officer was to meet the drug supplier, and once the money and drugs exchanged hands, members of the Tac team (SWAT) would swoop in to make the arrest.

On takedown day, everyone was nervous. The target was a well-known drug supplier in the city known to carry firearms and no doubt he would have one with him on this day. The meet was set and after our operator arrived at the agreed-upon location he entered the target vehicle with a hot coffee, seating himself in the front passenger side.

Everything began as planned. The officer and the target were jovial with one another as they began their exchange. But an unmarked police vehicle positioning itself nearby caught the attention of the target, seated in the driver's seat of his decked-out Mercedes. From the rearview mirror, he spotted the approach and muttered under his breath, "Oh, fuck."

He reached for a gun tucked under the driver's seat of the vehicle.

The officer had to deal with the situation. Thinking fast, he spilled his coffee. The suspect's eyes shifted—for only a moment—from his mirrors.

A flurry of flash-bang grenades shattered windows.

The target—and, for that matter, the operative—was disoriented long enough for each to be taken safely from the vehicle before a shot could be fired or the car gone with our member still inside.

The courage to adjust, take a risk, and act off-script saved the situation.

But adaptability is not just reserved for the covert world of policing.

It was springtime, and one of our uniformed officers had been assigned a citizen ride-a-long instead of a regular partner for the day. The pair drove casually along the officer's normal patrol route, which took them down the streets of his district neighborhoods. They turned a corner to glimpse a woman waving frantically. The constable pulled over.

"Help me, help me!" the woman screamed, rushing to the passenger window. "Help! My friend's being beaten! He's going to kill her!"

"Get in," the officer said. "Where do we go?"

She climbed in the back and they pulled away, updating dispatch.

"Turn there! It's the second house on the left," she blurted.

At the residence, the lone officer told the woman and his citizen ride-a-long to stay in the car. He hurried cautiously to the front door, which was ajar. From within, he heard blood-curdling screams.

He updated dispatch and entered. The screams led him to a basement bedroom where he checked the door. Locked. "Police!"

Silence descended.

No time. The officer forced entry.

A large man knelt over a half-naked woman on the bed, his hands around her neck. Her face was a deep purple.

"Police! Don't Move!"

But the man ignored him.

The officer leaped on the offender and pulled him off.

The offender—huge—possessed adrenaline-fueled strength and was impervious to pain. The officer, though trained in person-to-person combat, could not physically restrain him. He deployed his Taser.

The tool had no effect. The offender turned and grabbed the weapon. He fired it back as the woman crumpled into a corner.

Electricity jolted the constable's body. He fought the shock, thinking, *if I don't survive, neither will the woman I've come to save.* He yelled out to her, "Run! Get away!"

The victim scrambled from the room.

The officer struggled to stave off the offender's wild grapples.

Then—backup arrived.

It took four officers to subdue the man. Once in handcuffs, the offender became almost tranquil…he'd also stopped breathing.

Stopped breathing.

The officers now had to pivot—and turn their skills to saving the life of the person who had tried to take theirs.

Pushing the bed out of the way, they laid him on the floor and began CPR.

After four minutes, he began to breathe again.

The officers sat back in relief. Everyone would survive this day.

Adaptability. The officer, in a matter of minutes, transitioned his role from teacher to sentry to lifesaver to victim, and back to lifesaver, with no hint of what would come next. Each role required a different set of skills. His mettle was tested that day for sure.

Adaptable people use the resources they have and turn setbacks into opportunities. On a less dramatic scale, people who reframe their negative experiences into positive ones, also pivot, change, and adapt.

In my first book, I described reframing as a paradigm shift, turning the coin over to see the other side. That analogy remains the same here. Reframing allows us to find the silver linings in tragic circumstances.

About five years ago, in awe, I watched a death investigator from the medical examiner's office work with a family who'd lost their baby suddenly. At the time of the baby's passing, there were no concerns that the death was anything but natural; however, by virtue of our policies, a member of our homicide team was required to attend to all deaths of children under the age of two, on the off the chance the initial scene assessment turned out to be wrong.

I arrived at the home just after two a.m. on a cold, dark night. As I approached the house, I remembered an owl sitting on a fence post about eight feet away from me. As I neared, it flew off silently despite its massive wingspan.

Two young officers met me at the front door, jotted my name and badge number down in their notebooks, and they parted for me to enter. The baby lay motionless in a bassinet in the living room. Mom and Dad stood over their infant son, grief-stricken.

The death investigator pulled me aside. From what she could see, she had no concerns. No obvious signs suggested either parent had a hand in their baby's death. She took a few pictures to document the scene.

It was an unfathomable situation for any parent to have to face.

The body removal team arrived, and as they entered the home, the reality that the parents were going to be without their son became all too much. "You can't take him! Why does he need to be examined?" they pleaded to the death investigator.

Oh God, how can this be reframed? Where is the positive spin?

The medical investigator spoke quietly, her soothing and experienced voice calming. "Your son needs to be properly examined by a doctor so that we can understand why he died."

The parents stilled, listening.

"His body may provide those answers, and those answers may become a gift to you and your other children, present or future."

The parents' gaze fixed on her, trying to process.

"For instance, if your son died because of a medical condition he was born with, knowing that could empower you to be proactive with your other children."

The mom looked at the dad, questions in her eyes.

"This is the gift the examination of his body could provide."

And there ... a seemingly *unreframable* situation, reframed. The death investigator was able to find a perspective which made sense to the parents. And it did. They accepted the explanation of why an autopsy was important. Then, they were able to say goodbye to their son for a final time.

This case demonstrates that we can pivot and reframe almost any situation, but doing so requires skill and practice. Uncommon people use reframing to adapt, moving through crisis and adversity to hope and change.

For eight years, Dr. Cassandra Arnold worked with Médecins Sans Frontières (Doctors Without Borders), an organization where members must often adapt to the rules and laws of countries they have not visited before, where they deliver care. She, like her colleagues, delivered medicine in remote and/or resource-limited settings, a type of medicine outside of a clinician's usual scope of practice. Because it was often impossible to follow accepted clinical guidelines in areas with little or no infrastructure, or in politically contested or active war zones, doctors and other health professionals frequently had to pivot and use sometimes unorthodox methods when providing essential medical care. Dr. Arnold's story about working with Medecins Sans Frontieres (MSF) is a story of service, perspective, reframing, and courage and it's a story filled with examples that display the virtue of adaptability.

Dr. Arnold joined MSF because she was looking for adventure. Of course, she also wanted to serve people as a doctor in the global community—but for her, it was a two-way street, and when things went sideways, she remained steady and at peace, knowing the journey she was on was one she'd started for herself. There was no need to get upset if people didn't appreciate her help. She knew her skills as a doctor would be of benefit to the people she cared for, and if some weren't grateful, the experience was still personally fulfilling for her because she'd gained the adventure she was seeking.

This perspective is one I appreciate for it is honest and because when I think back to why many of us choose policing as a career, it was also for the adventure.

One thing she did not do was script herself to be perfect. She did not start her adventure with an unrealistic expectation she was going to be able to save every starving or sick kid she encountered. Instead, she accepted she would always do her best and allow her love for medicine, for people, and for service be her guideposts.

Dr. Arnold's first deployment was in Niger, a country north of Nigeria that was experiencing a meningitis epidemic. She was to join a large contingent of health care practitioners for a massive vaccination campaign, but before she could go, she was required to travel to Geneva and complete specific training and the required paperwork, including a "proof-of-life questionnaire."

She was told, "You will be going close to the border of Darfur and Sudan, where there are a lot of kidnappings. The Proof of Life questions are things we can ask if you're kidnapped. They must be information other people can't know. They can't look online and find out that thing about you. And only if you're alive and can provide the answers you left with us we'll know you're not being impersonated. So you have to think about this very carefully. You have to be able to remember the questions and answers when you are massively stressed because you've been kidnapped. You might be ill, you might be beaten, you might be hungry, but you have to be able to remember them."

Gulp. Adventure begins.

Dr. Arnold served most of her years with MSF in Africa and was exposed to much that gave her a new perspective. One of her first such experiences occurred in a community east of Chad. A bus had been attacked by the militia, and a seven-year-old girl had been shot. A bullet shattered her bones just above the wrist, and her hand had to be amputated.

When Dr. Arnold came to see her young patient the next morning, the nursing staff said the girl was on Tylenol and doing well. Dr. Arnold's brain tripped up on this fact for a moment, believing, at the very least, the child would need a morphine drip for pain relief. Entering the ward, she saw the young patient with her mother, sitting up in bed with a bandage around her stump.

"Wow. Is that not hurting?" Dr. Arnold asked.

"So what if it is?" Mom replied. "Life is full of pain, and the sooner she understands this, the better she'll be."

Surprised, Dr. Arnold studied the young child for any sense of distress and saw none. She wondered if this was partly because her mother was not giving the girl those signals. This scene was a pivot compared to anything she had seen before in the emergency rooms in her home in Australia.

Another time, a woman arrived at the hospital's ICU with her starving nine-month-old child. The mother and child had been identified by a roaming team of healthcare practitioners whose daily mission was to go into the different markets looking for people who required care and bring them to the hospital. Although it appeared this child might be too far gone to survive, of course, they must try.

About four days passed, and the nine-month-old was still very unstable. Although his mother had remained at his bedside for the entire time, she told Dr. Arnold that tomorrow, she would have to go home.

"But your child is sick, and you're his mother," Doctor Arnold told her. "Why do you plan to go home tomorrow?"

"Because last week your team came to the market and scooped me up and said, 'Your child is really sick.' They said I must go to the hospital, and I did because I wanted my child to live. But my husband doesn't know where I am, and I have no way of contacting him. I've got five more children at home. He can't work and care for them. If I don't go back today, he'll have to take another wife. I don't want this child to die, but I have no choice."

Dr. Arnold reflected. "And that is a situation that is just unbelievably heartbreaking. The bravery of people who face those kinds of choices, you know? It's true. Most of us will never know what others on this same planet must do each day to survive."

New perspectives. Conditions, including rules and societal norms, can be very different, and Dr. Arnold had to be adaptable.

Another instance of differing societal norms occurred when the medical team Dr. Arnold was a part of had to stand by as a woman bled to death in childbirth, hemorrhaging from a medical condition known as placenta previa.

In this case, the location where MSF was operating had no blood banks. If blood was needed, medical staff had to find a donor at that moment. The woman's husband shared a compatible blood type, but when asked if he would give his blood to save his wife and baby, he refused. "If she dies, I'll get another wife."

But this was not the only issue the medical team faced. Emergency surgery could save the baby, but it would mean certain death for the mother. "We couldn't operate because when she died, the community would view the death as the surgeon's fault and kill him or force him to flee. Not only would this endanger the surgeon, but it'd mean the hospital no longer had a surgeon for all the other patients. But if the woman bled to death and the child died, that would be seen as God's decision."

And so the team watched helplessly as the woman sat in a corner with her father beside her, holding her hand. Both she and the baby died because of limitations imposed on the medical group, both medically and societally. Dr. Arnold remembers the experience to be "just brutal."

Dr. Arnold had to be adaptable. But watching such an event from a Western sensibility required incredible courage.

Despite the sadness of these stories, there were also happy ones. Stories where the outcomes, despite limitations, could be celebrated. And stories where the outcome would not have been possible if there had been no opportunity to pivot, to go outside of what a textbook could teach.

Dr. Arnold remembered a case where an eighteen-year-old

man came to the hospital with Tetanus (also known as Lockjaw), an ailment nonexistent in the Western world due to vaccination. The young man had been working in the fields and cut the tip of his finger off with a machete, which allowed the Tetanus bacterium to infect him. When he arrived at the hospital, he was rigid and spasming. His brother looked after him, not leaving his side for three days, keeping him hydrated and taking care of his basic needs. Dr. Arnold believed that if it had not been for this care, this young man would have died.

Due to its rarity, Dr. Arnold had never seen a case of Tetanus so she checked the treatment guidelines which said Valium can be used to stop the spasms. She directed the nurse to start with a low dose. The patient continued to spasm. Dr. Arnold ordered more Valium. Still spasming.

Well, I guess we should give him more.
Dammit, still spasming.
"Okay, we should give him *more*."

She relates: "At this point, the national staff nurses took me aside and said, "Dr. Cassandra, none of the other doctors have ever given anything like this amount. Are you sure?" She thought, *No! I'm so far from sure. I'm completely out on a limb. I've never—but if I don't do it, he's going to die. So I might as well try.*"

So she took a breath, straightened her spine, looked like she knew what she was doing, and said in a voice of conviction, "Yes, I'm absolutely sure. Let's do it." And ...

He lived.

He walked out of that hospital a week later, wobbly and skinny but alive.

Adaptability.

From her remarkable adventures, Dr. Arnold came back to the Western world with perspectives different from those who did not make the journey with her.

Dr. Arnold remembered one specific case when she returned home, in which a young patient arrived in the hospital with diarrhea. After her examination of the child, Dr. Arnold sent her home, knowing the little girl would be fine. But by doing so, she raised the ire of her boss, who questioned her decision. "Why are you sending this child home? She's dehydrated! This child needs a drip. She needs to be in hospital!"

Dr. Arnold could not help but roll her eyes, thinking, *You've never actually seen a dehydrated child, have you?*

For her, returning to a medical system where X-rays and MRIs were the norm required her to once again—pivot.

Uncommon people pivot to embrace change.

Chapter 8—Lion-Hearted: Physical Courage

Bravery is not the lack of fear. It is acting in spite of it.
— Mark Twain

The week for me started a little different from most. In my first few years as a young patrol officer, I made a commitment to myself to stay up on my tactical and physical skills well after recruit classes ended. For this reason, I was keen to jump at any training that could expand my knowledge and keep me current on the latest skills and tactics, particularly around the use of force. So, instead of answering calls for service that fall, I enrolled in a week-long conference that attracted law enforcement officers and training experts from across North America to my city.

Day 1 of the training was superb as we wrestled on mats and listened to a variety of subject matter experts speak about the perils of policing in the 21st century and the need for preparedness for whatever the world might one day throw at us. Feeling invigorated from the day, I went home looking forward to the week to come.

As I got up the next day, my mind focused on Day 2 of the conference. I had no idea that the breaking news I would hear over the car radio a few minutes later would change our world forever. Reports that a plane had crashed into one of the two towers of the World Trade Center interrupted the song I was listening to—ironically, "Mad World" by Gary Jules.

I remember thinking this news didn't sound good, but it was a world away, and I had no way of knowing how serious this situation was to become. Arriving at the conference venue, I went to the hotel restaurant where the out-of-town delegates were finishing up breakfast. A small contingent of NYPD officers were among the attendees, and as I approached their table, my naïveté was clear in the flippant way I broke the news to them. This is something I will always regret.

"Fellas," I asked, "have you heard the news about the plane hitting the World Trade Center this morning?"

Color rushed from one officer's cheeks. Clearly, they had not.

One officer told us the towers were in his policing borough and his shift—his buddies and colleagues—was scheduled to work that morning.

I called home while they tracked down a television to understand better what had happened. We found a large television in the hotel atrium tuned to CNN, and I listened to my wife's shrill, "No, no, no!" on the phone as we all watched in horror when a second plane hit the other tower, folding into the building like a hot knife in butter.

This was real. It was really happening.

September 11, 2001, changed the Western world in the blink of an eye and brought to light the reality that terrorists, from what seemed to be a world away, had the ability to strike at will on our own continent.

This day also cast light on something else. Unselfish acts of bravery: the type of courage people think of first played out before us on the screen as first responders and volunteers of every stripe dove in to do what they could.

Valor in the face of extreme risk—bodily harm and death: this was the type of courage shown repeatedly across news networks around the globe as office workers, paramedics, fire fighters, K-9 teams, iron workers, national guard, police, and other emergency workers choked back smoke and fought off flames to enter these two buildings to help the injured.

Simultaneously, in the skies above America, passengers on Flight 93 took it upon themselves to fight off terrorists who had taken their plane hostage, causing it to plummet to the ground and killing all on board. A fourth plane crashed into the Pentagon.

No doubt what makes valor so impressive is witnessing a person fighting fear, but seeing them work through it and *still* act decisively.

For some, the ability to act in the face of shock is unexplained, almost instinctual. For others, it starts with training and mental rehearsal. Preparedness is a virtue found in valor.

Preparedness

In chapter two, we introduced you to Michael Rosenbaum and an old tactical team colleague of mine who both spoke of the importance of training and how training assists us in moving through our fear responses. As pointed out by the former tactical member, competence leads to confidence.

An example of this comes from an officer I know very well.

On December 23, 2000, my classmates and I had just celebrated our two-year anniversary of policing. At the time, all of us were still reasonably young, free of wrinkles, stress lines, and gray hair. Each of us was also beginning to navigate our own paths within our organization after being unharnessed from our officer coaches only months earlier—our training and the skills received through recruit classes were still fresh, still front and center in our minds.

With only two days before Christmas, the downtown core bustled with people: last-minute shoppers, carolers, and impatient business folks marking time for the last few hours in the office before the Christmas holiday season began.

Although this time of year can be exciting for most, it can be deeply stressful for others. For people who perhaps do not have dreams of turkey dinner with family because they are estranged. For people who do not have the financial means to afford even a basic gift for their child. For people who are homeless, who are just trying to find shelter and survive the brush of arctic air that sweeps our city this time of year. Or, in this instance, for the parolee who had just been released from prison after serving a long sentence with nowhere to go and no future plans—except one.

With only a few minutes before closing, the parolee, armed with a large chef's knife concealed in his jacket, entered a packed mall. Moving past throngs of holiday shoppers oblivious to the danger this man posed, he arrived at the mall's pharmacy counter. Seeking out a lethal injection of drugs, the parolee brandished the knife, making his intention, his threats, and his demands very real. Today was the day he'd chosen to die.

The pharmacist pressed the counter alarm, alerting the police.

"Units in the 1 District area be aware of a 10-30 (robbery) hold-up alarm at the mall pharmacy," the dispatcher broadcasted, giving the address.

Silence.

Although those words are meant to cause a chain reaction of multiple units responding to the scene, in this instance, all were tied up on other emergency calls.

All but one. Unit 1132, operated by my classmate, who was riding solo that day. Close to the scene after clearing from his last task, he booked himself onto the call.

Inside the pharmacy, the parolee had become aggressive and confrontational, escalating his threats of violence. He brought up the pharmacy employees—three women and one man—behind the counter, where he controlled them at knifepoint. By this time, he surely must've known the police were on their way. For the captives, those minutes must've felt like an eternity.

My colleague, barreling toward the scene, was an officer we all admired for his steadiness under pressure. He'd excelled at the academy in skill-based training; training meant to prepare all of us for the type of call he was now responding to in real time: a call where he would be forced to make immediate life or death decisions.

He entered the pharmacy and moved toward the back counter, toward the offender and the victims.

"Police. Don't Move." My classmate drew his service firearm.

"Fuck you." The parolee grabbed the pharmacist from behind, placing him in a loose choke hold, the knife pressed against his neck.

"Drop the knife," my classmate said.

"Fuck you," the parolee said.

Sighting in his service firearm, the officer rehearsed the five evaluative conditions his training had taught him:

Target Identification. Is the person you are about to shoot identifiable to you? Yes. He's the guy holding the pharmacist hostage with the knife.

Weapon. Is there a weapon? Yes. The offender has a knife.

Delivery System. Does the offender have the means and ability to use the weapon? Yes. The knife is at the pharmacist's neck.

Intent. Do you believe the offender intends to cause grievous bodily injury or death to you or a third party? Yes. The offender is extremely aggressive, and by his actions, he is threatening to take the life of the pharmacist.

Target Isolation. Is the person you are about to shoot isolated from other people? What is beside, behind, or in front of the target? Yes, but this is sketchier. There is definitely no one behind the offender, and the backdrop is a wall and shelving. However, the victim is being held in front of the offender, making only the offender's face and forehead visible.

Previous recent training and mental rehearsal of this scenario provided the officer with the confidence he would need to make a precision shot. He squeezed the trigger.

The bullet struck the only visible part of the offender from eight feet away.

The pharmacist's life was saved. The parolee was killed.

In the days and weeks to come, my classmates' actions were supported by the many witnesses and victims who survived this ordeal. No one questioned the decision he made, the timing of that decision, or the reasons he made it. The answers were as clear to them as it was to him. He'd had to decide: to take one life to save another.

Not everyone will have the opportunity to be trained as a police officer or be put into the life and death scenarios our officers serving the community must face. This doesn't mean, though, that they haven't practiced some level of preparedness prior to whatever crisis they may someday face.

For the uncommon people whom we look up to for their valor, this type of courage comes from somewhere. Perhaps it comes from their own maintenance of physical fitness, which gives them the physical ability to perform the action we see as brave. Perhaps it comes from their own social or moral codes or altruistic views, which call them into action like the individuals we introduced you to in chapters three and four. Perhaps it comes from a first-aid course they took, which gives them the confidence to know they have the requisite knowledge to save a life. Or perhaps it comes from laps and laps of mental rehearsal of "if, then what" thinking. The point is, although it may seem as though people acting with valor are responding spontaneously, this is not, in fact, the case. Physical bravery rests on physical or mental preparedness.

If you have ever flown, you know the flight attendant goes through a safety manual at the beginning of each flight, preparing all passengers for potential emergencies. Even if you are a person who puts these demonstrations on *ignore* because you've seen them a hundred times before, the process still gets you thinking, and that thinking puts all passengers on a path of preparedness and retraining. Again, a mentally prepared and trained individual will always perform more optimally than the untrained, unprepared person.

As a young officer, I frequently practiced mental rehearsal with my partners while driving around in our police car. "What would you do if we turn this corner and see a man running from a bank with a gun?" they would grill me. "Or worse, masking up to go into a bank with a gun?" "What would you do if the next license plate you ran came back stolen?" "What would you do if, at our next call, an offender was hiding in the bushes and ambushed us?" Thinking through these types of scenarios helped provide me with the confidence to know I was prepared for whatever crisis might await us in the next call-out.

Because of its usefulness—in fact, necessity—I continued this practice when I transferred to the Drug Unit. Here, before every undercover engagement, the team discussed an Immediate Action Plan (IAP) laying out the parameters of the operation. IAPs would also outline what role members of the team would take if the undercover operator found him or herself in a precarious situation, such as being robbed or assaulted by the target of the investigation. These types of reversals happened more often than one might believe, and when they did, the announcement of the IAP over the radio helped each of us respond optimally. We needed to know we had a plan to safely mitigate the dangers to which the world of drugs exposed us because of the unpredictability and violence inherent in this lifestyle.

Mental rehearsal is something we should all do with our families to prepare for emergencies. Of course, we don't want to turn our homes into the boogeyman's lair, but discussions with our families about what to do in case of a fire, for instance, could save the lives of the ones we love. How would each of us exit the house, especially if one of the doorways or corridors was blocked? Where would we meet afterward? Parents have died returning to a burning house to rescue a child who was no longer within because the child wasn't immediately visible. And to make this plan even more concrete, walk through your planned evacuation routes with your family. This is the training that could make each family member more confident if such a scenario ever occurred.

What about other scenarios? What would you do if someone approached you on the sidewalk and tried to abduct you? If there was a sudden natural disaster? Or, if you were being robbed, would you give up your purse or wallet, or would you fight? (Hint: hopefully, you would give those things up—they aren't worth your life.)

Training and mental rehearsal are two parts of the formula. Taking care of the "little i's" is the third.

Going back to the advice of my tactically trained colleague, taking care of the "little i's" is a proactive step to prevent someone from having to risk life or limb to save you in the first place. Take care of the little i's before they become big I's.

He explained that a climbing guide he'd met was a great coach and mentor. During the time they climbed together, he learned some valuable outdoor wilderness skills. A lower case "i" meant a *small incident*—one that would need to be dotted before it became an upper case one. The upper case "I" represented a *large incident*. A small incident plus a small incident plus a small incident could easily turn into a large incident if those little i's are ignored.

"You see," my colleague lamented, "you can typically get away with one or two small mistakes before things begin to snowball and roll downhill." This type of scenario often exists with victims of violent crimes. It exists for police officers—and it exists for anyone not paying attention to dotting those little i's.

He gave an illustrative example. "Two friends decided they wanted to go out climbing on Saturday, but to do so, each of them needed to get up early the next day. However, one of the two friends opted to go out for a couple of pints on the Friday night before the big climb. Because he went out for those beers, he also chose to not pack his bag the night before.

"The next morning, the friend slept through his alarm and woke up late. As he rushed to pack his bag, he forgot his headlamp. No biggie: why would he need a headlamp while climbing outdoors?

"Finally ready to go, the pair left the city at 8:15 instead of 7:30. As a result, they arrived at the trailhead later than anticipated. The walk to the base of the climb was brisk to catch up for lost time, and because of this, the friend who'd stayed out too late began to sweat. The other friend, inattentive due to focusing on how late they were, fell behind in his duty to check his watch for the barometric pressure.

"Now, at the base of the climb, the pair began to ascend, but because they were in a hurry, neither noticed the weather changing around them. The ascent to the top went well enough, but after reaching the top—later than anticipated—the friends realized it was getting dark and the temperature was dropping. Because each had worked up a sweat before their climb, they were cold and wet.

"Because only one in the pair had a headlamp, when they rappelled down from the summit, the friend who forgot his headlamp (the one responsible for retrieving the ropes) could not untangle the ropes, now invisible in the dark.

"The series of little i's had caught up to them, and they were now in one Big Incident—which would require rescue if they were to survive."

Training, mental rehearsal, and taking care of the *little i's*. These are things everyone *can* do, but do we? The truth is:

Preparedness breeds confidence; confidence breeds decisiveness in moments of truth.

Decisiveness

Decisiveness is an action taken in response to a situation. It has three key features: it is an action taken immediately; it is an action that directly addresses (and possibly resolves) the issue that prompted it; it is an action followed through without reversal. It's easy to see why decisiveness is based on the confidence that arises in a person with training, mental preparation, and who has addressed the *little i's*.

How many times have you been frustrated by someone's inability to decide on a course of action? Sometimes, we beg them to make a choice, even if it's wrong. Nobody enjoys watching someone toil over the "should we or shouldn't we" while the house burns down around them. In fact, most of us appreciate people who are brave enough to make the call, even if it turns out later that it wasn't the right one: they had the guts to make it in the first place. It is one of the most visible virtues courageous people show, and often seen in our most beloved leaders.

On a cold January night in our downtown's core, two husky doormen stood vigil at the front doors of a local nightclub. At midnight, a car pulled up to the front entrance. Both doormen assumed it was someone stopping for a moment to pick up friends, saving them a cab fare or a walk home in the frigid air. A passenger got out of the front seat.

Gun in hand, he walked up to the front doors, shoved the doormen aside, and opened the door.

WTF?

He fired multiple rounds into the crowded bar.

Shocked, both unarmed bouncers tackled the gunman and, after a brief struggle, pushed him against the hood of the car and disarmed him.

A back seat passenger, realizing the valor of these two doormen threatened their plans for a clean get away, leaped from the vehicle to join in the fray. Fortunately, police in the area heard the gunshots and responded immediately, assisting the doormen by arresting the two culprits and the driver. Thankfully, no one inside the bar was seriously injured. The actions of these two heroes, captured on surveillance cameras posted outside the bar, demonstrated bravery and decisiveness that evening.

Why? Undoubtedly, they'd had training; almost certainly, they'd mentally rehearsed for potential violence, and more than likely, they'd taken care of the *little i's*, leaving them with confidence in their own abilities, as well as those of each other. But clearly, their actions were decisive as well. Had they not been, the outcomes could have been far, far worse.

Their actions were not unlike those of an officer I heard about a decade ago. This story began when a thirty-year-old man who'd made a series of mistakes became the target of some seriously bad men over a drug debt. Overwhelmed by three bandits, he was tied up and forced into a van at gunpoint. The kidnappers demanded one hundred thousand dollars for his release.

Desperate to survive, the victim attempted to comply by telephoning criminal associates of his who might raise such funds. However, unbeknownst to his extorters, some of his calls were also surreptitiously made to the police. His quick thinking was the first step to possibly living through this very serious situation.

The communication officer who took those initial 911 calls was able to figure out what was going on and play along, dispatching plainclothes police officers to the money drop location. Speed and decisive action were required if the victim had any chance of being rescued alive.

The team leader in charge of the rescue mission volunteered to drive the ghost car they would use to block in the suspects' vehicle, preventing escape. With bated breath, the undercover tactical officers moved into position, concealing themselves in the trees, bushes, and garbage receptacles within sight of the rendezvous.

The kidnappers showed up for the money drop.

Would the kidnappers harbor suspicion or perceive a threat? Run or attack? The officers had no time to choreograph their movements in advance, so each was going to have to be ready to improvise within the parameters of the plan if things went awry.

Go time.

The sergeant, dressed in jeans and a T-shirt and looking like any other bad guy, rolled up in front of the suspects' vehicle.

This was the cue. The rest of the team leaped into action, hurtling flash-bang grenades at the offenders' vehicle to stun and overwhelm the suspects, giving the officers the time they needed to get in close and save the victim.

The plan worked. The victim was saved, and three bad guys went to jail. How lucky was the abducted man? In the subsequent search of the car, investigators found a loaded gun and a jerry can of gasoline. I would say, in the end—he was *very* lucky.

And yet, analysis shows the outcome had very little to do with luck and much more to do with preparation and decisiveness on the part of the officers and decisiveness on the part of the victim—as well as his creativity in calling 911.

> Doing something—anything—is often better than doing nothing at all.

Selflessness

Selflessness, putting one's neck out to save another, epitomizes what many of us believe is courageous.

Selflessness was evident when the passengers on board Flight 93 attempted to commandeer the plane back from the terrorists on 9/11. It was on full display when the two doormen jumped on the gunman firing shots through the club's door, and it was shown by the sergeant who put himself in front of possibly armed kidnappers when he positioned his vehicle in the escape path of the suspects in the last story, putting his own safety secondary to that of the victim. Selflessness is shown in the next examples as well.

On November 29, 2019, during a conference, an assailant entered Fishmonger's Hall in London, England, with two knives taped to his hands. There, he threatened to detonate a bomb, then began a stabbing rampage.

But several conference attendees fought back. One brave man armed himself with an ornamental spear taken from one of the walls inside the hall. A second fought with a decorative narwhale tusk. Their actions in defending the conference participants drove the offender into the street.

The assailant fled onto the nearby London Bridge, where surveillance cameras captured more selfless acts. A man using a fire extinguisher helped subdue the assailant before he was eventually tackled and disarmed. In the end, despite the many who placed themselves in harm's way in defense of others, the stabber killed two people inside the hall and seriously injured two others. However, without these selfless acts by civilians thrust into this dynamic situation, there was no doubt the outcome would have been deadlier.

These acts of altruism are not just done by adults.

A young American boy, Bridger Walker (six years old), saved his younger sister from a vicious dog attack while both were playing outside their home. Placing himself between her and the large dog, he was bitten multiple times and received more than ninety stitches to his face. After the attack, the boy told his aunt, who asked why he'd stepped in front of the dog, "I thought if someone was going to die. I thought it should be me." This boy was lucky to be alive, as dog attacks can be deadly: an eighty-three-year-old woman in our city was killed by two dogs while she tended her garden several years ago.

In November 2008, two police officers arrived at a domestic complaint called in by a neighbor. Observing through a window, the officers saw a woman covered in blood lying motionless on the kitchen floor.

Time was of the essence. They had to enter the home without waiting for additional resources, despite not knowing where the offender was or in what kind of mental state he might be. They forced their way through the front door, splintering the jamb in the process. The noise of their entry did not stir her. Inside, the two constables moved through the house quickly to ensure the threat was no longer on scene, then approached the motionless victim.

Using a towel, one of the officers applied pressure to the victim's lacerated throat. Chilled, he realized an artery in the victim's neck had been badly nicked by a knife blade. To get enough pressure on the wound to stop further blood loss, the officer pushed his fingers several centimeters into the cut.

But a healing laceration on the officer's hand put him at risk for contamination by disease. The victim survived her attack thanks to this officer's selflessness. Fortunately, the officer, too, survived.

In another incident, three first-responding officers, alerted by a passerby that a man was in the river—in November—braved the icy waters, forming a human chain and wading out to attempt a rescue. The first attempt failed when the current swept the man past the human chain. But the officers kept at it until another officer arrived on the scene and risked his own life to swim out to the man, who had now slipped out of sight beneath the water's surface.

The officers worked frantically to find him in the depths and, by some miracle, did. Pulling his unconscious body to shore, they tended to him with first aid until paramedics arrived. Miraculously, the man made a full recovery, but without the selfless acts of those officers, he never would have survived.

Another story of selflessness occurred one April not too long ago.

It was early in the morning when a man woke to screams coming from his neighbor's home. He rushed next door to offer whatever help he could. Smoke leaked from his neighbor's front door.

"There are children still inside the basement!" an upstairs tenant yelled out.

The man, snatching a blanket from the porch to protect himself from smoke, entered. He made his way through thick smoke and flames to the basement. Despite poor visibility, he was able to see two young children standing in the hallway. He led them upstairs to safety, then returned to the basement to search for other victims.

He was met by a man fully engulfed in flames coming down the hall. Using the blanket—his only protection from the fire—he covered the man to extinguish the flames, then led him also to safety.

Thanks to his selfless acts, everyone survived the fire.

Professionals train their minds and bodies so they might be prepared to one day be that person who is decisive and who does not run from a threat when confronted. But it takes that moment of selflessness to cross the threshold from preparation to action. Preparation—training, mental preparation, and attending to the *small i's*—leads to self-awareness of their own ability; situational awareness allows them to navigate their way through the three fear responses, and gives them the ability to be decisive.

However, selflessness is the ingredient that allows them to use this training when the situation demands it.

> There is no other time in your life where your courage will shine brighter than those times when you practice selflessness.

Discipline

Isn't it true there are times you just want you reach out and pop someone right in the nose?

But you don't. Something holds you back. Perhaps violence doesn't align with your values. Perhaps you're concerned it will negatively impact the greater good or the process you are negotiating. Whatever it is, having the restraint to not act on those impulses is a virtue of uncommon people: discipline.

Several years ago, I was involved in a case where the offender, whom I had known as a troubled youth while I was still early in my career, decided he would commit the most horrific of crimes. Breaking a court order to have no contact with the target of his rage, on a sunny July morning, he returned to his childhood home to murder his mother, as well as a young disabled girl in her care.

> **Islamic beliefs present self-control as a key factor in courage.**

Beyond the savagery of his crime, he did something more. Before departing, he positioned the victims in provocative poses. Why? To shock the senses of whoever found them deceased? To degrade them even further in death? To defy society by showing he had no repentance for any of his actions? To place exclamation points on what his depravity was capable of, or prove to the world he was what he'd always been told he was? We will never know.

A common task in the early stages of any investigation is to speak with family members as we pour through evidence to identify persons of interest or a suspect. So, on this particular day, there I sat with the victim's son across from me in an interview room. He appeared to be a mild-mannered and quiet individual with his wits about him. He answered questions about his mother and spoke openly about their past differences. I remember thinking, *could a son ever do this to his mom*?

But...something didn't feel right. I saw several red flags in this initial interview. However, without evidence to expressly implicate him in the crime, he was released.

Over the following week, the case built with reams of evidence accumulating. As it did, it became clear that, yes, a son could do this to his mother. The evidence to prove it emerged. He was arrested and charged with both murders, and the case was sent to the crown prosecutor's office, where it was eventually set for trial.

In the weeks leading up to the trial, I heard rumblings that the offender had made the unusual decision to represent himself in the proceedings. It was his right to do so, and the case proceeded to trial by jury two years after he was arrested.

The trial became a circus, an absolute vile circus of vulgarity and disruption.

On many mornings, the accused had to be moved to another courtroom, and his mic was muted because of his constant interruption of witnesses on the stand. What became apparent was the affecting of a mental illness that he'd tried to fake to the court. The man we saw on trial was a stark contrast to the person I remembered speaking to in the first hours of the investigation. His meekness was replaced with erratic, over-the-top gestures. He held signs up to the CCTV cameras asking people in the courtroom to call the FBI. When he had the opportunity to question witnesses, his questions focused on the worst details of the crime—the posing of the victims, the way they looked in death, or personal questions unrelated to the court proceeding.

Because of these antics, I suspect everyone—and I mean *everyone*—was getting close to wanting to just wind up and punch this guy in the face.

But no one did. Why?

Despite the actions of the accused, everyone knew their ability to control themselves mattered. It mattered for the successful prosecution of the case, it mattered for the justice of the trial, it mattered for the family and friends of both victims.

Imagine the consequences if one of the officers on the stand, one of the family members or friends of the victim, or even the judge or a member of the jury hit the accused. Would this action have changed the offender, brought him to his senses, or stopped his attempts to feign a mental illness? Would it have brought the mother and girl back to life? Would it have prevented future copycat crimes?

Or—would the offender's grotesque actions still be what was on trial?

No. The headlines would have switched to the undisciplined actions of the individual losing control. None of these consequences would in any way lead to a positive outcome.

Discipline is a virtue of the brave. The ability to use self-control is a key factor in physical bravery.

I once found myself in a difficult spot in an investigation that had caught national attention[3]. In this case, a young woman had been found murdered in her home, and her five-year-old daughter was missing. Surveillance video collected from the area of the home, along with accounts of witnesses, led us to believe the little girl had been taken from the home alive.

---

[3] Described in chapter five

Investigators worked tirelessly to identify a suspect—which they did—and he was arrested posthaste. But the child was nowhere to be found. Now, the more pressing concern remained: where was the young girl? What was happening to her? Was she still alive? Or was she in distress and dying?

I was assigned to interview the offender. The lead detective instructed me to "go as far as you can without crossing the line." A tall order, for sure. Even taller as I entered the interview room to find the suspect—sleeping.

From the moment I walked in, his aloofness and indifference to the gravity of the situation was apparent. It did not take long before I knew that showering him with praise was not going to find the youngster any time soon.

I began to ratchet up the temperature, hoping to get the job done. Through this process, I thought, *How far is too far in a situation like this?*

I also clearly remember thinking as I offered him water that it should be from a bucket, not a cup, just in case I needed the bucket later for drowning him.

Harsh? Perhaps, but a child's life was on the line. The suspect had a history of sex trafficking women; was it possible he'd found a person who wished to "own" a five-year-old? These thoughts raced through my mind as I walked the minefield of keeping the interview "legit"—after all, we didn't want to lose the case at trial—while battling thoughts of "bringing in the booster cables."

In the end, it didn't matter; I was pulled out of the room after about thirty minutes and informed that cellular phone data showed that, several hours after the kidnapping, the suspect's phone left the city, traveled into a rural area, then immediately returned to the city.

This information was all any of us needed to know. The

child was dead.

Now, all that was required was the recovery of her body, which was done within a few hours because of good police work, not because the location was provided by the offender.

The ability to use self-control is not an easy gift to possess. I myself cannot preach and say that discipline is one of my virtues. However, for the officers whose stories come next, discipline is exemplified in several different ways.

Discipline in the face of threat to themselves

On an early December morning, police were called to a home with which they had become well acquainted over the months. Husband and wife had not been getting along for some time, and the police had become the middlemen in their violent quarrels. The court had imposed a condition on the husband to "no go the residence," but that was just a paper restraint and these, unfortunately, are often ignored.

On this night, the husband was up to his usual mischief and not obeying the court order.

Police responded.

The officers had been in the home for some time and had convinced the man he needed to leave. Agreeable (not that he had a choice), he asked if he could first use the phone to call a friend and his lawyer, which the officers allowed. But as he strode off to the kitchen, his demeanor did not match the request.

Passing the phone, he grabbed a six-inch blade from the counter knife block.

Repeatedly, he stabbed himself in the stomach. Blood foamed from his mouth, and he yelled at the officers to shoot him. A violent confrontation—even shooting the man—seemed inevitable if the offender turned the knife on the officers.

But he did not have time.

The officers were disciplined and worked as a team. One drew his service firearm while the other drew his Taser. Putting trust in his teammate who held the gun to cover him if the Taser failed to subdue the offender, the constable with the Taser fired.

Electricity coursed through the man's body. He stiffened and collapsed to the floor. The officers restrained him and went on to save him despite the threat he'd posed to them only moments earlier.

Discipline in the face of threat to others

In December 2009, uniformed officers responded to a mental health and assault complaint in which the offender had allegedly stabbed someone. When police officers arrived, they were met by a female standing outside the residence, covered in blood. She had been stabbed several times.

She said her brother was going to kill their mother. Rushing into the residence, officers could hear the sounds of a struggle. They dashed down the front hallway to where a man was choking an elderly female. The woman appeared weakened from the assault.

The officers told him to remove his hands from around the victim's neck—several times—but the offender was undeterred. The officers were potentially facing a deadly force situation.

There was one other option. The Taser.

It worked. The offender released the victim, and the officers were able to restrain him. Both he and the stabbed woman were transported to hospital for treatment.

Discipline is needed to overcome one's first impulse—an impulse to leap in without restraint.

Discipline to move past the past.

In June 2010, a canine officer on patrol observed a sport utility vehicle driving erratically at high speeds—a car which, officers learned later, had been stolen. The officer attempted a traffic stop, but the vehicle took off at an even higher rate of speed. Following protocol, he did not give chase as experience has shown a car chase can pose more harm to the public than benefit.

However, a few minutes later, the same canine officer came upon a crash a few blocks away. This same vehicle had struck a tree, careened into a house, and was engulfed in flames. He called dispatch, and within minutes, officers responded. They worked feverishly to extinguish the fire and free the occupants from the burning wreckage.

Twisted metal entombed the driver, making his rescue impossible, and he died on scene, but the passenger was pulled from the carnage. Was the man thankful for his rescue? No. He struggled, kicking one of his rescuers and breaking his wrist.

Discipline. No officers struck back. There was no vindictiveness or failure to respond because of past acts. Instead, they continued to work to save this man's life. They assisted medics in securing the man to a spine board for transport to the hospital, where, in the end, he also died from his injuries.

What makes the actions of the bravely disciplined so

uncommon is the fact that they remain reserved in the face of extreme situations. They do not get carried away and go from hero to villain.

> Self-control comes from the mastery of your thoughts.

Chapter 9—Ghandi: Emotional Courage

Opinion is really the lowest form of human knowledge. It requires no accountability, no understanding. The highest form of knowledge is empathy, for it requires us to suspend our egos and live in another's world.
— Bill Bullard

One could argue that, because fear is an emotion, each form of courage, from the physical to the spiritual, is rooted in emotional courage. Combatting fear requires us to face that emotion.

But beyond the courage it takes to face a bear or a fire, to face an angry group or friend, to face the deepest mysteries of our heart and universe, or to face what might be a never-ending grind, there is a distinction with emotional courage. This is the courage to open ourselves up to face emotions: our own and those of people closest to us. To do this, we need empathy, vulnerability, and love.

Empathy

Empathy requires us to feel deeply for others. Empathy may lead to action: getting in the trenches to help others fight their fight, or it may simply allow a person to comfort another by sharing a moment of significance.

I once read a story on social media about a four-year-old boy whose next-door neighbor's elderly wife died suddenly at home. Perched in the window of his home, the little boy watched as medics and firemen packed up to leave after an unsuccessful effort to resuscitate the elderly woman. The boy noticed that the woman's husband had removed himself from the gravity of the moment; he'd slipped away to his backyard to catch his breath and grieve on the back stoop. The little boy came to the old gentleman's yard and climbed onto his lap. Later, when his mother asked what he had said to the neighbor, the little boy replied, "Nothing. I was just there to help him cry."

This, to me, is empathy personified.

Empathy can be defined distinctly from sympathy as an emotional response rather than a social one. Sympathy avoids emotion and makes connections more transactional. In its lowest form sympathy is pity—and who likes to be pitied? "You poor man, I'm sorry for your loss."

Understanding the difference between empathy and sympathy became perhaps one of my greatest *Ah-ha!* moments as a homicide investigator who'd grappled with this each time I had to inform a family that a son or daughter, mother or father, had been found murdered or deceased. Recognizing that sympathy is social response from an outside perspective and empathy is an emotional response putting you into the other's skin is one that served me well over my homicide career. As I began to practice empathy instead of sympathy, my ability to connect with and help families struggling with unfathomable losses or with bad guys who had committed a heinous crime increased tenfold.

I also believe practicing empathy can be a relationship saver. Without this understanding and practice, we may default to sympathetic reactions because they feel safer to us. The social, outside perspective is useful in settings where emotion is not appropriate or in situations where we must protect ourselves, but at home, emotional distance from your closest people may, over time, build walls of resentment.

Nevertheless, there are times when sympathy can be an appropriate response, such as when we wish to keep a social distance from someone. For example, in work environments, clear social boundaries are usually established, particularly boundaries between levels of hierarchy, such as bosses and workers. It may be more appropriate to acknowledge your boss at work who has just lost his father with a sympathetic response such as a condolence card or an expression that you are "sorry for their loss." In some environments, becoming too emotionally involved may be dangerous for the caregiver—and it may also be unwise for the person who wishes to help—such as a sober sponsor responding to an alcoholic in need.

What are some flags that show we are using sympathy instead of empathy?

Perhaps your wife calls because she's frustrated at home with a colicky baby. The sympathetic and disconnecting response would be, "I'm sorry you're dealing with our colicky baby. I'll be home later this afternoon." An empathetic response could sound more like, "It must feel so frustrating when our baby can't settle despite your very best efforts. I've felt that frustration, too. I'll be home later this afternoon, and I'll be there to support you and give you a much-needed and earned break."

You learn that your friend's mother has died suddenly. The sympathetic reaction might be, "I'm sorry for your loss," or "my condolences." An empathetic course could sound more like, "There are likely no words that can express what you must be going through right now—I know how close you were to your mother. I haven't lost a parent, so I don't know what you're feeling, but I can imagine it's one of the most difficult things to face in life. What can I do right now to support you?"

You are a police officer tasked with notifying a family of the death of a young man who's just been killed at a house party. The sympathetic expression after the notification might sound like, "I am sorry for your loss," as the investigator walks out the door. This isn't a bad response *if* it is the investigator's intention to maintain a social distance. However, a police officer willing to express an empathic response to this situation could end up being a godsend, not only to the devastated and grieving family but to the investigation as well. By being empathetic to the family's tragedy, the officer may find the closer bond leads to valuable information from family members that helps lead to the identification of their son's killer.

Why? I believe a family that senses a true connection with the investigator may relax in their presence and actually remember details that they otherwise might not—and be less fearful of sharing what they might think is silly or inconsequential. Such information might include the names of any individuals the victim was connected to or having trouble with, or information about the lifestyle he was leading—some of which might be embarrassing for the family to admit to a stranger.

Through my own experiences as an investigator, I came to learn people would become more willing to share information with me if my exchange with them was empathetic and not sympathetic. A sentiment such as, "I'm certain this news has come as a complete shock to you. I cannot begin to imagine how you must be feeling. If it's okay, I'm going to stay for a few more minutes while this terrible news begins to settle in. By doing so, I'll be here to answer any of your questions. Is that all right?" leaves control and permission in the hands of the family while demonstrating through action the support the investigator is willing to provide.

> **Forms of Intelligence**
>
> Intelligence Quotient (IQ)
> Emotional Quotient (EQ)
> Social Quotient (SQ)
> Adversity Quotient (AQ)
>
> IQ measures a person's memory and ability to use information and logic to answer questions or make predictions.
>
> EQ measures an individual's ability to maintain peace with others, being mindful and considerate of a person's time, remaining humble, fulfilling responsibility, being honest, and respecting boundaries.
>
> SQ measures our ability to build a network of relationships and maintain those relationships over time.
>
> AQ measures an individual's ability to deal with obstacles and overcome adversity in life.
>
> People with higher emotional and social intelligence often have more success in life and are more gifted in leadership roles than those with a high intelligence quotient. Makes sense, right?

We have all heard we shouldn't criticize another until we have walked a mile in their shoes. Wise words. They smacked me in the face more than once when I entered the world of undercover work.

Here, I became part of a three-year social experiment where I was my own guinea pig. Through this journey, I learned what it must feel like to be a person the rest of society wishes to cast away. Of course, in my case, I only felt the struggles I watched others endure while trying to survive on the street for brief bursts of time over a forty-hour work week. The rest of the time, I had an escape—paperwork to complete back at the office, a family to return to, a home to sleep in, and a supportive team and organization I could turn to if things ever felt too dark.

My reality was not the reality faced by those who had no escapes. I gained a sense of how cruel a world it is for those on the fringes. In the end, this experience made me a better cop and a person who could empathize in unique ways with the downtrodden, and for that, I am grateful.

The next officer's understanding of what others had been through also came from his own personal experiences.

In early 2009, a military veteran who had served with the Canadian Armed Forces for years was now working in our city as a police officer. Assigned to the mountain bike unit, he and his team patrolled the downtown core. Bicycles afforded this unit increased maneuverability as they patrolled alleyways, congested downtown streets, and the city's river pathway systems. They also allowed members of the team the opportunity to not only interact with commuters who came into the core every day for work but also with the growing homeless population who used alleyways behind the high office towers and high-priced condos as their makeshift homes. This officer learned, through listening to each person's unique story, that each had come to their situation by vastly different paths. The commonality was that their stories were often very sad.

One subsection of the homeless population touched this

officer deeply. Some of the homeless included military veterans like himself: people who'd once served our country but who now found themselves without a home. Empathizing with their situation, knowing the struggles many had gone through and the sacrifices they'd made, he was determined to help get these courageous men and women off the streets and back into their homes.

Working with Veteran Affairs Canada, he learned about several services available to those once called to serve Canada, services that could assist them in accessing affordable housing, pensions, and benefits. One individual at a time, he began to help, providing them with whatever was needed: a telephone so they could make a call, transport to a library so they could access a computer, a few hours of his time to help fill out forms and plow through the morass of bureaucracy which had created a barrier between the veteran and the services he or she had earned. In the end, his empathetic concern helped place countless homeless veterans into programs to move them from the blankets of the alleys to warm, affordable homes. Remarkable.

Many North American police agencies know that experiential learning builds understanding and awareness; and that understanding and awareness form the building blocks of empathy. *Treat people the way you would wish to be treated* is one of the mantras heard within police academies across the Western world.

When it comes to training, police officers' instructors go to great lengths to teach what it might be like to live in another's shoes. When their curriculum is to learn about what a victim of crime may go through, trainees are introduced to a victim who will share their story, both the good and bad. When it's time to understand what people who come from diverse backgrounds go through when immigrating to a new country, officers are introduced to people with those diverse backgrounds and experiences. I remember that, in my recruit class, I spent time in an English-as-a-second-language classroom, meeting people who had recently immigrated to Canada. Some had never—up to this point—had reason to trust a cop. Powerful.

Officers bear a heavy responsibility when they are required to administer force. To make this learning impactful, officers are required to experience what they might one day have to deliver while performing their duties as officers. Experiencing things like a Taser, pepper spray, tear gas, and physical restraint tactics does several things. First, it allows a recruit to understand how uncomfortable it really is and what the body goes through when exposed to a noxious substance like pepper spray or the shocking experience of a Taser.

Daniel Goleman, author, psychologist, and expert on emotional intelligence, believes there are three kinds of empathy and it is essential for leaders and teachers to know and use all three: cognitive empathy, emotional empathy, and empathetic concern.

Cognitive empathy is the ability to see the world through another person's eyes. This is a critical skill in the workplace. It enables strong relationships and effective communication to motivate, inform and support the people we work with.

Emotional empathy allows us to tune into the feelings of another person and read their facial, vocal, and a stream of other nonverbal signs which illustrate how they feel.

Empathic concern is expressing care and concern about another person. This means showing people they will be supported and that they can trust the leader. This encourages people to take risks, try new approaches, and be open to others for collaboration and team learning.

With this knowledge, it is the organization's hope that recruits appreciate the impact of such actions on members of the public and apply an increased layer of restraint and an understanding of when the use of these tools is reasonable or not reasonable. Second, such experiences provide each officer with a visceral understanding of the subject's needs after restraint and control—what this person is going through physically and emotionally after the fact, and what medical and psychological support they will need to bring the effects back under control sooner, rather than later.

George R.R. Martin, in *Game of Thrones*, encapsulates a similar concept dramatically: "The man who passes the sentence should swing the sword. If you would take a man's life, you owe it to him to look into his eyes and hear his final words. And if you cannot bear to do that, then perhaps the man does not deserve to die."

Not every expression of empathy must come from a human. Victim Assistance Dogs feel a person's pain and react to provide physical and emotional comfort. They may be used in courtrooms to calm a victim or witness or taken to a home to help a family suffering loss. Once I was working on a tragic case involving a young victim, and my supervisor requested a dog come visit the unit. But—the whole time it was there, the dog followed me around or rested next to my foot. Despite my efforts to shoo it away, it wouldn't go. It obviously knew what I knew—I was hurting inside. Thinking back on it today, it still seems so remarkable that a dog would be willing to take on all that heaviness for us, but they do.

Because practicing empathy exposes an individual to vulnerability, it takes courage as well as skill and practice.

> We can make a huge impact on a person's life by walking alongside them, not in front, and not behind.

Vulnerability

Over the years, I have seen master investigators in the interview room a hundred times. I have also seen investigators flounder through an interview. In almost all such situations, the common denominator is connection. Whether the interviewee feels safe and comfortable with the investigator interviewing them and whether the interviewer can promote a sense of care for that individual through empathetic expression will ultimately dictate how the interview will go.

One of my favorite interviewers to watch is an investigator gifted with the ability to connect to her subject by sharing some of her own experiences. She builds common ground. This connection cannot be faked. She has lived the experience she shares. When Susan and I asked her about this for the book, she told us she recognizes the risk she's taking when she opens herself up to share an experience, but she does so because she feels a strong obligation to her task.

> But there is no need to be ashamed of tears, for tears bear witness that a man has the greatest courage, the courage to suffer.
>
> —Victor E. Frankl

Before coming to Homicide, she worked as an investigator

in the child abuse unit, a difficult position and one I always forbade myself from entering. Here, she honed her interview expertise and discovered that sometimes opening herself up and making herself vulnerable was necessary if there was a possibility the offender would be released from custody. By taking this chance, she hoped to help children she believed were still at risk.

Still, each time, her internal voice warned, "Oh God, am I going to do this? Hopefully I'll be okay."

She pointed out the differences between the Homicide and Child Abuse Units. In Child Abuse, the victims were still alive, and for that reason, the risk remained if an abuser was not stopped. In Homicide, the victim had already died, and therefore, the burden was centered on the importance of finding justice and holding someone to account. And, in the world of homicide, a deceased child could not tell their story to the investigator. For those gifted officers who have the fortitude to work in the Child Abuse Unit, I can only imagine how heart-wrenching it is to hear about ordeals of abuse and trauma from the mouth of a little one. The way they must fight to explain what has happened to them, no doubt, can break even the most stoic cop's heart.

The first time I watched this exceptional officer open herself to be vulnerable occurred close to a decade ago. We had been called to a woman's home to investigate the murder of her six-year-old daughter. The woman lived with a man she had met recently, and no other adults or children lived in the home. The list of suspects was two. The woman, and her new live-in boyfriend.

Sitting down with Mom, the investigator's job was "simple." Get Mom, who we suspected was the non-offending parent, to waver in her commitment to the relationship with her new beau so she would explain what was going on when the young victim had been killed.

Readers might think this would be easy. If you were the non-offending parent, you would not rally behind the new boyfriend but behind your child. Right?

However, in cases like these, the dynamic within the couple being investigated can be confusing. In a surprising number of situations, after a tragedy where a child has been murdered, and one of the two adults is responsible, couples draw *closer* together: the absolute opposite reaction you'd expect.

This was exactly what happened in the early days of this case, too.

But the police investigator had points of commonality with the mom.

"I know how confusing and awful this must feel," she said to the mom. "I'm a single mom, too. I know how difficult it is to raise a child on your own—what it's like to juggle priorities and how difficult it is to find happiness with a new partner. But your daughter needs you to use your voice right now."

With those words, the investigator planted a seed of hope, a connection.

The power of that moment, forging a relationship, was shared by all of us watching the interview from the briefing room. It was reinforced as, over the next several hours, with more stories of the commonality of motherhood our investigator shared, we watched the bonds of the relationship between Mom and beau begin to disintegrate. This was a critical first step in eventually securing a conviction against the man who took her young daughter's life.

The next time I saw this investigator's vulnerabilities occurred a few years later. In this case, a husband had already confessed to our investigator that he had killed his wife, but he stopped short of telling us where he had put her remains.

Our investigator opened herself up to share her personal experience of losing her father tragically and suddenly at a young age and then not being able to believe it had happened. She explained how many times after his passing, she'd search through the crowd, not quite understanding where he was. She told him, "If you don't give this to your family, they will forever be searching and hoping."

In the end, it didn't work. The husband did not confess. It took the dedication of searchers to find the wife's remains, buried in a flower bed at the back of the home they once shared.

Why would he not provide this final detail to the interviewer? We will never know, but likely, in his mind, he'd confessed to the killing once, and that was sufficient; to repeat the confession might have been too emotionally self-damning to live with.

The point was that the investigator cared so much about the emotional closure for the wife's loved ones, she had the courage to put herself at emotional risk to help them.

To be vulnerable requires us to relate to someone on a human level. It also requires authenticity. As my colleague would point out, "They're not dumb (the offender). They know when you're speaking from the heart and when you're giving them the standard cop speak most would expect to find in the interview room.

"If you can build that connection and elicit the truth, even if the truth is hard to talk about, then the risk of being vulnerable is worth it," she said. "Let's face it, the cases already make you feel vulnerable; the flood gate is already open because of how these events traumatize us. For this reason, it feels like being vulnerable is just part of the full experience."

It was summertime 2005, and the officer in this next story,

a good-natured friend of mine and transplant from the East Coast, was working as a uniformed patrol officer, responsible for call responses and proactive policing measures and, occasionally, assisting in field training recruits graduating from the academy.

On that day, my friend had just been assigned a recruit fresh out of class. "A big kid, a strong kid, second day on the job," my friend recalled.

The first complaint didn't take long to come in. A mental health call at a hospital situated in their patrol district. The partners buckled up and veered their police car to the site.

A young man had been brought to the hospital by family members concerned for his wellbeing. Concerned about potential suicide, hospital staff apprehended him under our province's mental health act, and he was being watched, under guard, by security officials until he could be seen by a doctor. But the young man managed to flee.

He sprinted across the parking lot to the east side of the building, where a large berm separated the hospital grounds from a major thoroughfare. On the berm, the young man produced a large hunting knife and waited for the police to come.

My friend and his still-green recruit were the first to arrive. They positioned their police vehicle a safe distance back from the crisis point and got out of their cruiser. The young man approached, then stopped just within hearing distance. He said, "One of us is not going home today."

Both officers drew their guns with no desire to use them. My friend began what would become a lengthy negotiation.

Reflecting on that day years later, my friend said, "You know, we all draw a line in the sand—or at least we think we do—setting out how far we will let a situation go before we make the difficult decision to shoot someone."

Profound words, borne of a deep conflict: on one side, to keep himself and his partner safe, and on the other, to keep a line open to the suffering young man. In police training, we are taught the twenty-one-foot rule: that an armed person with a knife can, conceivably, close a twenty-one-foot gap faster than the average police officer can unholster their weapon and fire two rounds, center mass.

"On this day, my line changed several times."

Why? Compassion, empathy, and a willingness to be vulnerable, possibly a trust—founded or not—in the young man and the relationship my friend, through his skill and experience, was forging. And potentially, a fatal error if my friend judged the situation incorrectly.

"Each time it changed, I knew it was inching closer to me. But I held on. I believed I could save this man from himself before he could hurt or kill me."

If the twenty-one-foot rule had been rigidly applied, my friend would have shot this kid a hundred times over the twenty-five-minute negotiation. There were several points where my friend knew he would not be able to stand firm. Instead, he backed up to avoid being face-to-face—confrontational—with the young man. Also, on several occasions, he felt his finger move to the trigger of his pistol—ready to squeeze.

He didn't.

Despite the danger, he felt he was connecting with the young man.

My friend made himself vulnerable, not only in the physical sense of allowing the distance between the two to shorten, but emotionally as well, by allowing himself to share his own life. He told the young man, "This morning, my kids knew I left the house to help people. They've always seen me as their superhero. How am I going to go home and tell my kids that I couldn't help you?"

The young man listened.

"Please. Don't take this from them. I don't want to go home and face my children and explain to them that I had to kill you. It will change them. It will change me forever. Your actions, my actions—they have consequences for everyone who touches our lives."

This theme resonated where all else failed—the young man dropped the knife and returned to the hospital to be given the help he needed.

Sweating bullets time was over.

Following the call's successful resolution, my friend's sergeant requested all officers involved to return to the office for a debriefing, to clear the air, decompress, and discuss the good things and bad things that happened during the call.

My friend analyzed his experience of the negotiation, the reasoning behind the decisions he made, and some of his own personal thoughts and reflections. When he saw the young man's vigilance de-escalate, he felt the need to protect his own safety begin to dissipate, and he was drawn into listening to the young man's problems. But this reduction in guardedness was premature, and he had to ramp back up again when the young man showed signs of escalation. It was during these transitions when things always seemed most dangerous for both him and the young man he was there to help. Good food for thought.

Once this necessary exchange of ideas and insights was done, the team was sent home for the remainder of the day with the expectation that everyone would return to work the next day, rested and ready to go. But the story doesn't end there.

After a night of tossing and turning, my friend returned to

the office to start his shift but didn't see his recruit in the locker room with the rest of the team—running late? He went to the briefing room where every shift starts and saw the new recruit, still in his civilian clothes, sitting quietly with the sergeant.

The sergeant called the briefing to start and gave the room to the recruit.

"Man, what you did yesterday was phenomenal, like so phenomenal," he said to my friend. "I went home last night, and I played out that scenario a thousand times in my head. Each time, I shot him."

The room was silent with empathy.

"But it's clear that the kid didn't need to be shot."

Each of us felt his words deeply.

"My judgment will never be as good as yours."

None of us agreed with this statement, but a person's decision has to be his own.

"Therefore, I must resign." Removing his badge from his pocket he slid it across the table and quit right there on the spot. A hard decision, to walk away from a significant commitment in his life. One only he could know in his heart.

People who are courageous enough to open their scars are some of the bravest people I know. People willing to face their own inner fears, let them out, or allow themselves to bleed a little for the greater good or the good of someone else, teach us an important lesson about the virtue of vulnerability. My friend showed this in the field, both physically and emotionally. The recruit showed this in our meeting.

It's a hard act to follow.

> When safe to do so, opening yourself furthers your closeness with others.

Love

The courage to love. The courage to allow yourself to be loved.

For some, loving comes easily and naturally, but for others—those who have experienced the deep pain that comes from the loss of love, for instance—it takes phenomenal courage to love again, to care enough to allow another to become so much a part of who they are that their loss means a loss of a part of their *self*. And there are so many kinds of love. Beyond romantic or familial love, there is the love for anything we feel a close connection to—other living creatures, objects of significance, places with strong emotional attachment.

> The problem is, we look for someone to grow old with, while the secret is to find someone to stay a child with.
>
> —Charles Burkowski

Love is the virtue behind so many brave deeds.

Love of our planet brings people from all races and backgrounds together to find solutions to our world's climate crisis. It allows others to rise in nonviolent protest in the defense of peace. The love of country strengthens brave women and men to defend their borders or go to war to protect their people. Love of community provides firefighters with the resolve they need to enter burning buildings to save lives or gives police officers the courage to run toward gunfire when need dictates. Love of people attracts individuals to the plethora of social agencies geared toward helping others. The love of a partner provides an opportunity to support another and learn from them—maybe even start a family. The love of self means we are more likely to take care of ourselves and be authentic to the real version of us. The love of our family can also drive and dictate many of our actions, as it did for one incredible young man I first met back in 2012.

Originally from Sudan, his father was a commanding officer in a revolutionary movement. As a young boy, life as he knew it was good. He had his father, his mother, and eight siblings, and he remembers days he and his older brother would venture into the savannah to play in the wild grasses and brush. Vigilant and aware of the dangers posed by wildlife, he felt safe under the watch of his older brother.

Recalling those early years, he once told me it was expected that a certain number of people would be killed by animals and this was, in fact, the fate of one of his younger siblings whose life was taken by a crocodile. He also remembered how scarce food was. He and his family did not have the luxury of eating every day, but this was life as he knew it, and in his mind, life was good.

Then, one day, it changed forever.

Sounds of gunfire were the first sign of trouble in the village the day a militia group attacked, killing indiscriminately. He, as an eight-year-old, and his brother, as a fifteen-year-old, ran for their lives. But his brother failed to keep up. Stopping to take a break, his brother looked down to see he had been shot and was bleeding. They stayed together until an aid worker from the Red Cross came across them and flew them to a hospital in Kenya.

They were a world away from the fighting but also from their family. The next few years would be incredibly difficult.

From a hospital in Kenya, the brothers were taken to a refugee camp housing over 200,000 people. Life in the camp was dangerous and frightening. Often robbed of their food rations, over the years both boys witnessed rapes and assaults daily. And they would learn that their parents had been killed in the fighting. But through this chaos, their love and bond grew stronger.

When they were fourteen and nineteen, the brothers were selected to be resettled in Canada.

Canada was like heaven. Food was always available and although the winters took getting used to, the freedom to just *live* trumped any cold day. They attended school and each helped the other learn English, while the older brother went off to work in the evenings to help keep food on the table.

The pair had been in Canada for almost two years when they were shocked to learn through the community that their mother was, in fact, alive—a dream both had hoped and prayed for over the years, but one they had been told would never come true.

Then, one week after this monumental surprise, life changed again for the two brothers.

It was a cold January in 2012 when the older sibling set off to attend a house party where, among friends, he'd have the chance to just enjoy the evening. But among the attendees that night were two men the older brother did not know who, for whatever reason, took exception to him and decided to fight with him.

The attack was brutal. The men kicked, punched, and struck

the elder sibling with a frying pan until he was unconscious. They left him for dead in a yard across the street. A few hours later, a passerby came across his body and called an ambulance. He died later in hospital from the injuries he received.

For the second time in his young life, the younger brother, now seventeen, had to deal with devastating grief: the loss of the person who had been his mother, father, brother, and friend to him.

Few people would have the strength to recover from this, but at seventeen, this challenge was devastating. For a time, there was a dark patch for the younger boy. He quit school and the soccer program he loved. But as he moved through his anger and sorrow, he emerged, finally, a better version of himself. Finding the courage to love himself again, when he was ready, he returned to school, returned to work, and returned to the game he loved—soccer.

Over the years since I worked on the investigation of his brother's death, we have stayed in touch, and I have been amazed at his strength and his continued efforts to focus his love on his family back home. As long as I have known him, whatever earnings he could spare at the end

> Grief is the price we pay for love.
>
> —Queen Elizabeth II

of the month would go to his mother and his other siblings, whom he has always longed to see again.

I was also aware of how much it bothered him that his brother, who was laid to rest in our city, had nothing more than a numbered grave marker to denote where his body was. The sibling he loved deserved a proper headstone. The day he came to me asking for help, I felt honored that he would put his trust in me and ask. Putting my thinking cap on, I reached out to a local journalist whom I knew might help. Together, they set up a crowdfunding site, and she agreed to do a story on him and his incredible life. The love shown by the community was tenfold what he expected. He had a proper headstone made, and I remember the day I went to the cemetery to help walk him through the final process.

He was thousands of dollars over what he needed for the headstone. I remember the conflict he had with this. There was no way to return the excess money. So what did he do? In his typical selfless way, the money was sent back home to Sudan to help his mother and his siblings have a better life. He did not use it for trivial indulgences. Love is about sacrifice.

Recently, I had the opportunity to see this young man again and share a plate of food with him and his mother, who, after years of effort and work on her son's part, was finally able to come to Canada. This work was his love made visible.

I asked her, "If you could bring three things you love about Canada back to Sudan, what would you bring?" Her answer: Peace, water, and shoes.

Love can also be about the simple pleasures that we all take for granted.

In a relationship with a spouse or lover, the virtue of love runs parallel with the virtue of vulnerability because when we open our hearts to love, we also expose ourselves to the potential for deep hurt if things don't work out. Yet most of us do choose to take that gamble because the rewards of intimacy are vital in so many ways.

I cannot imagine anything braver than what an abuse survivor must go through when deciding to open themself up to a new relationship. Think back to chapter one, where we introduced you to the young lady who was sex trafficked for two years. She was moved from hotel to hotel and forced into having sex with strangers. How—after she found the courage to escape that hell—could she find the fortitude to ever trust another man again? *And then*, to open her heart up to be loved?

Yet she did. She married and is now living her best life away from a past that daily reinforced how awful men can be.

Now, think of her new partner. Think of the courage required for him to help her face the demons that no doubt surfaced as their relationship grew closer. To support her and love her regardless as they moved toward marriage.

Love is not meant to control us. It doesn't beat us up.

In my world of homicide, I saw love appear in different ways and at different times. Those I served often told me how love had transcended the thin veil of life and death to deliver a message from their loved one or offer an answer to the question of what had happened.

For instance in a missing persons case, when a parent reported their son or daughter had vanished, the question I always posed was: *What do you think? What do you feel has happened, and where do you think your son or daughter is?*

If they said they felt their child was dead, I believed them because never once in the fifteen years of investigating cases like these did I ever find out that the parent was wrong—sadly. Deep down inside, as a parent, they knew.

But love does not only transcend the grave. What I have seen or heard many times—in every courtroom and in every victim impact statement ever read by a grieving family member—is the devotion of families to the deceased and the important place the person held in their families.

And, importantly, this is no different for every offender's family, who also brave their faces in court to support their loved one.

With the advent of body-worn cameras also comes an opportunity to see the rawness of what happens when love is lost or when it has gone completely haywire. What it looks like when a family goes to their daughter's home to check on her, only to find her dead from a shotgun blast to her chest and her killer overdosing in a back bedroom with the gun still in hand. Body-worn cameras provide a blunt perspective on the realities of policing today.

On New Year's Eve 2020, Sergeant Andrew Harnett stopped a vehicle for a minor traffic violation. After obtaining license information from the underage driver and identification from the adult with him, Sergeant Harnett went back to his police vehicle to check both subjects on police databases—a routine inquiry. The adult passenger was wanted on warrants, so he requested a backup unit to assist. After writing the driver a ticket and coming up with an arrest plan for the adult passenger, Sergeant Harnett and his backup unit approached the vehicle to issue the violation ticket and remove the passenger from the vehicle.

During this second exchange, the young driver pinned the gas and took off, catching Sergeant Harnett up against the vehicle's "B" pillar, the structural element behind the front door where the driver's seatbelt is attached. Sergeant Harnett did everything he could to hang on as the vehicle traveled at more than ninety kilometers an hour, hurling down the residential street for several blocks. Approximately a kilometer from where this tragedy began, Sergeant Harnett lost his grip and was flung onto the roadway and into oncoming traffic. A second later, he was struck by a vehicle going the other way.

As backup units arrived, all with body-worn cameras rolling, something else was captured outside of the haste and life-saving measures for Sergeant Harnett.

These are images that will stay with me forever. They help me come closer to understanding what love can be.

The driver of the vehicle that struck Sergeant Harnett was a black man. There, off to the side of the road, he stood by himself—grieving deeply. Grieving for the loss of the white cop who'd just been killed.

Seeing him there, alone, two members on scene made their way to him, not to find out what had happened, not to get his license or his particulars, but to console him. To offer him their love, their support, and assurance that none of this was his fault.

Captured on video at a time when the divide between police and the public was at an all-time high and "defund police" movements filled the media, the collective embrace among a black man grieving the death of a white cop consoled by two other white cops, all showing in their own ways what being human is supposed to look like—demonstrated how empathy, vulnerability, and love can transcend race and hate.

In the investigation that followed, both the adult and young man were located and arrested, and eventually convicted of their crimes. At the sentencing hearing, Sergeant Harnett's mother read from the impact statement her final words to her son the night before his life was so tragically taken: "*I love you forever. Be safe.*"

The courage to love—and the courage to allow yourself to be loved—is the joy of being human.
—Mary Anne Radmacher

Chapter 10–Strata: Developing Courage

"The truth is that courage resides within you; you must simply decide to embrace it.
— Jennifer McClanahan-Flint

Everyday courage is the seed from which all great things grow. The community in which you live—someone had to have the courage to develop the land. The job you have—someone had to have the vision to start the business you work for. The food you eat—a farmer or rancher had to endure drought and poor crops one year to provide a bountiful harvest for you the next. The music you listen to or the books you read—someone had to have the courage to put themselves out there and be judged for their talents.

Everyday courage is about facing the daily challenges of life with tenacity and determination to ensure we are performing and supporting excellence in ourselves and others. That we are making the tough calls when we need to and standing up for *right,* to make sure our communities and our families are safe.

The great thing about everyday courage is that it is something we can all strive to be better at, and you don't need to be wearing a uniform or a cape to do it. I believe everyday courage is synonymous with everyday courtesy, and it is within all of us to be able to do so.

So, what can we start doing today to join the ranks of the uncommon people featured in this book?

Ethical Courage

Remain True to Your Authentic Self

Champion those who have no voice. Be aware of those around you: the vulnerable, the bullied, the overlooked.

Take initiative to do things others don't do. Be brave enough to take action on what you observe, to make that proposal, to put your hand up in a meeting, and to lead by example.

Have the integrity to walk the talk. Align yourself with what is best for all: health, happiness, purpose, belonging, and generosity. Filter every decision through the lens of integrity and act courageously on each.

Examine your sense of purpose: crystalize your values, ideologies, and boundaries. Make decisions and take actions based on what you believe. Give thought to the meaning of your life. Then live by it.

Social Courage

Let Your Voice be Your Power

Challenge yourself to stand up to the group when you know you are right. When you see something that is not right—when an individual or group is on a hurtful path—say something. Disagree—respectfully—when you see a better way. Challenge the status quo.

At the same time, when you listen to others and see they have a point, have the humility to take the hit, admit mistakes, and apologize. We respect people who are willing to own up to their actions and mistakes. One of the most powerful sentences in the English language begins with the words "I'm sorry."

Work in synergy with others: Being willing to place your trust in others opens us up to the possibility of disappointment and hurt, but it also opens us up to new resources, thoughts, and opportunities to learn. The most successful police investigations, like the most successful life endeavors, begin and end with a team.

Take leadership when your skills and vision warrant, and follow others with different skill sets. Our viewpoints, beliefs, and values can be different from one another's and that's okay.

Intellectual Courage

Embrace Expertise

Find your passion and master it. There is joy in delving deeply into your passion. Learn to experience the fulfillment of mastery, then share your expertise generously with others.

Seek growth by having the courage to recognize your limitations and be open to new insights. Just because something—even your own practice—has always been done one way does not mean it's the best way. Both individuals and systems (your workplace, for instance) can benefit by trying new strategies, especially if those strategies are supported by evidence.

Use your ingenuity to see things in new ways. Creativity comes from new perspectives. Think hard about puzzles that throw up barriers to your goals, then allow your mind to rest. Often, it is in the stress-free environment of a long walk in the woods, a hot shower, or sleepy mornings with no agenda that solutions to the problems we face pop into our minds. Have the courage to examine them, share them, and act on them.

Spiritual Courage

Believe in Something Even if It is Nothing at All

Examine your beliefs. Remind yourself that you are in control of your own doubts, thoughts, and feelings. You are in charge of all the positive and negative self-talk you tell yourself. You are also in charge of how long you wish to remain angry or sad, happy or ecstatic. Although external factors influence how we may be feeling, we can work toward managing the duration of these feelings by radically accepting and facing what is and simultaneously acknowledging the need—and resources—for change.

Envision what you want in your life and predict your future by creating it. How you see your future drives how it will actually look. Know your dreams in detail and the steps to achieving them. Then, have the courage to do what it takes to achieve that future.

And when the universe dictates that loss and disappointment befall you, have grace. Find peace in harmony between yourself and others. Recognize that generosity is one of our basic human needs. Help others without fanfare or thanks, while still maintaining your own personal boundaries for health.

Practice mindfulness and embrace solitude to center yourself. Work to be comfortable with being alone. Spirituality is often found in this space, free of distraction and the influences of others. Quiet breeds contemplation and a greater awareness and appreciation of our world and universe.

Resilience

Do or Die, Sink or Swim.

This will put you on the right side of the path for an epic bounce back. Your scars are reminders of what you were strong enough to survive. They display your resiliency and should be something to be admired and not despaired. They were well-earned.

But have patience with yourself and others, too. Find a balance between acting on the world and allowing the world to respond. The obvious face of courage is the bravery to take action, but sometimes, the harder route—and more effective—is to allow others space to make their own choices. It took the parents of the sex worker described in chapter one a great deal of courage to have the patience to stand by for their daughter until they could be there for her when she left her daunting situation.

Have stamina and hang in. The road to your goals may be long. It takes courage to be patient, but even more so, it takes courage to be patient in the face of the grind of unrelenting difficulty. Find joy in the small things to help you push through.

Be adaptable and bend; don't break. As our circumstances change, our response must change.

Physical Courage

Take Actions that Scare You

Preparedness is key. Train. Train your body and rehearse in your mind. Training allows us to effectively respond to the things which try to hurt us. It assists us in selecting the appropriate response in a given situation. It breeds competence, and competence breeds confidence. When competence and confidence unite we have a greater chance of a successful outcome over a person who has not been trained. Take care of the little i's.

Be decisive. When you see or hear something you know is not right, take action. Don't ignore the child who walks by with the black eye—inquire. Become part of the solution.

Be selfless and empower others to take hold of their fears and move past them. Lift and inspire others to new levels. Manage fear in yourself and others by thinking positively. Provide a perspective that breaks the loop fear can create: submission that encourages bullying.

Have discipline to set appropriate boundaries for yourself and others. Set a standard for how you wish to be treated and stay within that standard. Don't allow others to set your boundaries for you. Remember: it's okay to say no when you feel uncomfortable about doing something that doesn't feel right.

Emotional Courage

Open Your Heart to All the Feels

Be empathetic and actively cast your mind into the circumstances of another. Understanding the background, context, environment, fears, and challenges of another person can break down barriers.

When it is safe to do so, allow yourself to be vulnerable. Forgive often. Allow the past to remain in the past and move forward. Holding on to anger serves nobody's interests, including your own. Anger is like an acid that does more damage to its container than to its cause. Getting stuck in the anger stage of grief can take away from the opportunities happiness can provide.

Love yourself and others. This is the emotion that gives us strength. Love—of self, others, our home—can give us the courage to stand up for things that matter, give us the courage to be vulnerable, and give us the courage to cross the boundaries fear creates.

And Finally

Practice courage every day.

Uncommon of people work on consideration of others, and lead by example. They are everyday heroes. They go through life undaunted and know they don't need a uniform or special appointment to do so.

Susan and I hope the stories we have shared about some of the most incredible people we have met on our journey to write *Undaunted* came through to you in a meaningful way. We also hope you are inspired, even possibly empowered, by some of the greatness found in others.

Some who recounted stories to us found that sharing came easily; for others, it was incredibly hard. We were touched by how many people had the courage to do so in hopes their experiences would make a positive impact on you. We could not be more grateful.

Personally, hearing these stories helped me in a myriad of ways—and Susan would agree. Some stories reflected my own service as a police officer, others so far removed. Each, though, gave me an opportunity to think about and be proud of the men and women who serve our communities in so many different ways. From everyday heroes who found themselves called upon to respond to an unanticipated situation, to family members who shared with the world their grief and loss so others might benefit through a foundation or legacy, to the doctors, nurses, and first responders who each and every day answered their calling—we applaud all of you and cannot thank you enough for your participation.

I can't explain why some of us are called into service. I know for me, it felt like a dull roar in the pit of my stomach which truly has never gone away. Even now as a retired police officer, it still hasn't. I am so thankful for the experience of my career, for the organization that supported me through all the ups and downs, and, most of all, I am thankful to all those I met along the journey. You made the trip worth it.

> *Blessed are the peacemakers,*
> *because they will be called children of God.*
> — Matthew 5:9

Courage doesn't always roar. Sometimes, courage is the little voice at the end of the day that says, "I'll try again tomorrow."

Appendicies

Solutions to Logic Challenges

Challenge 1

Most of us start the puzzle assuming our pencil lines must be confined within the space created by the nine dots. But to solve this problem, you must expand your mind beyond the implied boundaries of the box. The solution, when revealed, is both creative and logical.

Answer:

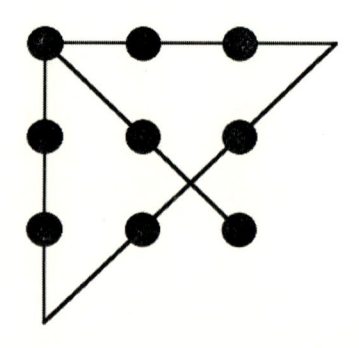

Challenge 2

Answer: The batteries. The suspect may have wiped down the flashlight's exterior, but his fingerprints were found on the batteries.

Challenge 3

Answer: When we first looked at this scene, we all viewed it from what it looked like at its conclusion. Reversing it to see how it looked in the beginning helped us to be comfortable with our assessment that this was, in fact, a suicide.

Step 1 – The deceased laid out a rope across the bed with two slipped knot ends, which would eventually be used to bind his wrists.

Step 2 – The deceased affixed the noose to the grommet in the wall behind the headboard.

Step 3 – The deceased tied a rope to the foot of the bed and, when he was ready, tied that rope to his feet while sitting upright in the bed.

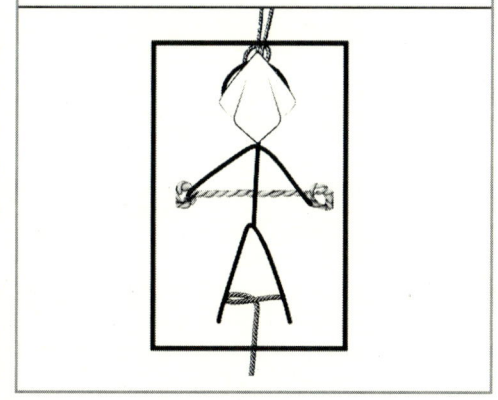

Step 4 – The deceased laid down on top of the rope with the two slip-knot ends, which would be used to bind his wrists.

Step 5 – The deceased positioned the noose attached to the grommet in the wall around his neck and then covered his face with the tea towel.

Step 6 – To prevent himself from removing the noose around his neck, the deceased slid his hands into the two-slip knot ends.

Step 7 – The deceased sat up. The pressure on the noose and the slip knots around his wrists tightened and gave the appearance that his hands had been tied behind the back. Sadly, the result was a purposeful death.

Why do people go to these lengths in instances like these? Unknown. Perhaps to create a puzzle for others, perhaps because of shame felt in being driven to suicide, or perhaps to protect loved ones. In cases like these, first responders always lean toward treating the death as suspicious.

Challenge 4

Answer: Arson. Of all the crimes in the criminal code, arson speaks best to the health of the community over any other. Why:

Arson is a crime that can be used to defraud. Therefore, increases in arson rates could represent an increase in the financial strain and desperation of people living within a community.

Arson is a crime that is sometimes committed by the mentally ill. An increase in arsons could represent an increase in mental health concerns for people living within a community.

Arson is a crime that is used to cover up other crimes, such as destroying evidence. For example, in the case of a murder, the assailant may burn a vehicle that was involved in the crime. Because arson is a crime used to cover up for other crimes, an increasing rate of arson could mean violent crime is also increasing in a community.

Our Take Aways

Fear is often a perception—not a reality.

Manage danger – unshackle yourself from fear.

There are many large and small steps on the journey to healing, and for some, healing may not involve overcoming the event so much as learning how to live with it.

Unlearning what scares us liberates us.

Fear is a natural and common response to danger, prompting us to freeze, fight, or flee. There are circumstances under which each of these is adaptive and some under which they are derailing.

Uncommon people are mindful that each person's reaction to danger is not always what they would wish it to be, and they learn from their missteps moving forward.

Training prepares us to face fear with greater confidence and understanding.

It's in all of us to be brave.

How we stand up for others reflects how we see purpose in ourselves.

Being part of a vibrant village requires us to speak up and take action.

Aligning actions, words, and beliefs reveals integrity.

Live a life that matters.

Finding the strength to respectfully disagree unveils unquestioned assumptions.

Finding the strength to apologize, to forgive, or to forgive yourself is a rare gift.

Teamwork recognizes the whole will always be greater than the sum of its individual parts. It takes courage to trust the strength of the team.

Social courage is courageous leadership.

Honest self-understanding can give the confidence to be exceptional.

People who seek growth recognize their limitations and open themselves to new insights.

Complex problems or dilemmas can be solved by thinking one of three ways: inside the box, outside the box, or from an entirely different box on the other side of the room.

Ingenuity is a trump card.

Through belief, we construct meaning and purpose in our own lives.

Some of the most courageous people in our world are dreamers.

Through grace, forgiveness is given a chance to grow.

Being present in the moment is the essence of sustaining attention to the contents of one's own mind.

UNDAUNTED

It matters not how hard you get knocked down but the heights you achieve when you bounce back up.

Patience is not passive. On the contrary, it is concentrated strength.

Often the things we most cherish are directly related to "the suck" we endured to get them.

Uncommon people pivot to embrace change.

Preparedness breeds confidence; confidence breeds decisiveness in moments of truth.

Doing something—anything—is often better than doing nothing at all.

There is no other time in your life where your courage will shine brighter than those times when you practice selflessness.

Self-control comes from the mastery of your thoughts.

We can make a huge impact on a person's life by walking alongside them; not in front, and not behind them.

When safe to do so, opening yourself furthers your closeness with others.

The courage to love—the courage to allow yourself to be loved—is the joy of being human.

Courage doesn't always roar. Sometimes, courage is the little voice at the end of the day that says, "I'll try again tomorrow."

DAVE SWEET with SUSAN FOREST

30 Virtues of Uncommon People

Acknowledgments

Susan and I would like to acknowledge that Undaunted was written on the traditional territories of the peoples of Treaty 7 region in Southern Alberta. This includes the Siksika, the Piikani, and the Kainai (collectively known as the Blackfoot Confederacy); the Îethka Nakoda Wicastabi First Nations comprised of the Chiniki, Bearspaw, and Wesley; and the Tsuut'ina First Nation. The city of Calgary is also the homeland to the historic Northwest Metis and to the Metis Nation of Alberta, Region 3. We would like to acknowledge all Indigenous urban Calgarians, First Nations, Inuit and Métis people who have made Calgary their home. We recognize it is their gift of storytelling which helped inspire the writing of this book.

Susan and I would also like to acknowledge all the amazing people whose stories have been told within these pages. Special thanks to those who took time to sit down and speak with us. Cst. Tad Milmine, Dr. Cassandra Arnold, Dale Portman, "K", J.F, A.D, M.S, K.K, T.M, B.W, J.G, R.S, E.H, A.H, S.W, T.P, M.C, K.C, N.I, J.A, A.S, D.J, C.W, G.B and C.T. We recognize it takes an incredible amount of courage to open yourself up and be raw, so one day someone else may learn from you and be inspired by your bravery. Thank you.

Special thanks to Stark Publishing, a publisher that supports writers and goes out of its way to ensure their success is above and beyond what any author could expect—we appreciate you.

Last, we would like to recognize while writing Undaunted, Susan and I relied on other creative works and subject matter experts to inform some of the stories within these pages (acknowledged within the text). In addition, we would like to specifically, acknowledge the Calgary Police Service's Youthlink documentary series *Black Friday* and *Policewoman*. We would also like to thank the Youthlink Interpretative Centre whose mission, in part, is to preserve the history and the stories of a very proud organization. Doing so, you allow your larger community to learn about the sacrifices and bravery of many amazing people featured publicly in your beautiful space. We gained much inspiration from within your walls. Thank you.

Dave Sweet

Dave is a retired veteran homicide detective from a large western Canadian police service. He now works as an investigative consultant for the Unconventional Classroom and provides a variety of workshops and corporate training opportunities to an array of clients. His first book *Skeletons In My Closet – 101 Lessons from a Homicide Detective* was published in 2023. *Undaunted* is his second book in what he hopes will be a three-book series.

You can connect with Dave at
http://unconventionalclassroom.ca

Susan Forest

Susan Forest is the author of dual Aurora Award-winners *Bursts of Fire* and *Flights of Marigold* as well as over 25 internationally-published short stories (Analog Science Fiction, Asimov's Science Fiction and Fact, Beneath Ceaseless Skies, among others). She edits an award-winning anthology series for Laksa Media Groups, and most recently was co-editor of *Life Beyond Us*, with the European Astrobiology Institute, as well as several biographies and memoirs. In 2021, she was Editor Guest of Honor at Keycon. *Gathering of Ghosts* (2023), confronts issues of addictions in an epic fantasy world of intrigue and betrayal.

A Call for Action

For anyone suffering from addiction, abuse or in crisis, or if you are a friend or family member of someone in this circumstance, please know there is help. Your local municipality or township will have services you can access to support you. From distress lines to shelters, please reach out if you are someone in need of this support. It will be the best gift you could ever give yourself and those that love you; or

If you have been touched by any of the stories contained within *Undaunted* and wish to learn more, or do more, for the organizations featured please find the following information useful. We all have a part to play in building safe and vibrant communities and these organizations are doing just that.

The Nathan O'Brien Children's Foundation

The Nathan O'Brien Children's Foundation was established to provide a helping hand to disadvantaged children. Our privately funded foundation supports children's charities through grants in honor of Nathan Kenneth O'Brien.

This foundation is committed to honouring the memory of Nathan O'Brien and his legacy of compassion and kindness by helping improve the lives of children giving them the opportunity to live, hope and pursue their dreams.

For Nathan's parents it is important that Nathan's spirit lives on and continues to inspire good deeds in the world. The Nathan O'Brien Children's Foundation is honored to work with other dedicated charities to be part of a community that wants to make a positive difference in the world. Together they honour Nathan while benefiting Calgary's children's charities.

Past foundation projects have included, building an indoor playground, annual sporting events, and food drives.

https://www.nathanobrienfoundation.com

Gems and Hopes Cradle

Gems is aware of the increasing need for action in the domestic abuse sector as the number of victims continues to climb. Gems is focused on scaling their current initiatives, remaining open to the community's needs, and remaining nimble enough to continue to pivot through times of transition.

Gems is committed to continuing to work with the community to save and enhance the lives of survivors of all ages and backgrounds. Together they believe we will always be stronger and create the change we want to see in the world.

Hope's Cradle is a collaborative initiative to support mothers in need and save infants from unsafe abandonment. When a baby is placed in *Hope's Cradle* it will be considered a surrender. Provided the baby is healthy, there will be no repercussions for the person who chose this safe option. Gems is honoured to make this resource available to women unable to provide safe places for their children to grow as well as ensure that child has their most basic right, to live.

https://www.gemsforgems.com

Bullying Ends Here

Bullying Ends Here is a series of educational presentations for youth & adults aimed at educating others on what bullying looks like and how to prevent it.

Their presentations have been presented around the world to educators, students and staff receiving overwhelming feedback with requests to return. Credited with saving dozens of lives and being shared with over 1 million people worldwide, Bullying Ends Here have proven results to not only change lives, but save them.

https://www.bullyingendshere.ca

The Unconventional Classroom

Undaunted is the second of a series of books co-authored by Dave Sweet and based upon his decades of experience in law enforcement and his resulting reflections, learnings and philosophies.

Look for the other titles in
The Unconventional Classroom series.

Skeletons in my Closet
101 Life Lessons from a Homicide Detective
(with Sarah Kades)

Undaunted
Dark Tales of Courage Witnessed Through the Eyes of a Homicide Detective
(with Susan Forest)

Whispers
What Happens When We Die
(with Mark Leslie)
Coming in 2025